Karl Marx

KARL MARX

the passionate logician

BY JOEL CARMICHAEL

CHARLES SCRIBNER'S SONS   NEW YORK

CONTENTS

Preface   vii

I   Childhood and Youth   1

II   Intellectual Beginnings: Hegel: the Young
       Hegelians   18

III   Journalism: A Conversion to Socialism: Paris   45

IV   Marx Becomes a Full-fledged Socialist   89

V   The Road to Exile: Belgium: 1848   110

VI   The Watershed: Exile and Decline   165

VII   A Return to Practice: a Consummation of
       Theory   197

VIII   Epilogue: Last Days   242

Suggested Reading   251

Sources of Quotations   252

Highlights in the Life of Karl Marx   253

Index   255

PREFACE

Karl Marx must be one of the most influential men who ever lived. Indeed, if one disregards the somewhat accidental relationship of other celebrated individuals to the events associated with their names—Alexander the Great, Jesus, Muhammad, Buddha—and recalls that Marx's influence was exercised primarily through his own writing and his personal activity, we are bound to ascribe a unique distinction to his role.

Not only has Marx's thought had the most far-reaching effect on mankind through its application by his followers, but through its influence on scholarship in general it has been of unusual consequence in many fields, notably history and the social sciences. In addition, the "Marxist" tendency became pre-eminent in the world socialist movement: one of its branches—Russian Bolshevism—took power in a great state and helped move another great state—China—onto a socialist course. This is not to mention the numerous parties, movements, and organizations elsewhere that have been molded in one way or another by Marxist attitudes.

Doubtless almost half of mankind today is under the direct effect of various interpretations of Marx's ideas.

Yet in this book I have attempted no more than a sketch of an individual. Biographers have often regarded Marx's life as a mere pendant of his remarkably potent ideas—I have thought it illuminating to do the opposite.

I have dealt with Marx's ideas only insofar as they were related to his life and merely hinted at the subsequent, or more external, manifestations of his personal influence —a field that is, in any case, practically boundless.

I have tried to give an account of an individual engaged in a strange kind of struggle, in its own way highly personal, whose consequences could scarcely have been foreseen. One of those consequences has been the petrification of Marx's person; he comes to us like a fly in amber. I have tried to extricate him from the mountain of myth he is buried in and describe him as a living person. I hope this approach will be helpful for an understanding of his ideas, too.

karl marx

CHAPTER I

Childhood and Youth

Karl Marx was born in 1818, a few years after his birthplace was made part of Prussia in the general settlement following the defeat of Napoleon.

His birthplace, Trier—at the time a country town numbering some 12,000—was in its own way appropriate to his adult cosmopolitanism. It was at once the oldest of German cities and the farthest extremity of German culture at the point where it merges, almost imperceptibly, with the culture of France. Built by the Romans as their German capital, it lies in the heart of a splendid wine region that rivals the Rhine valley. It was the Romans who had brought architecture into this part of Europe, as well as writing, law, and the wine-grape. Vineyards were the principal business of Trier.

The town was old enough to recall the Romans and the very origins of Western Christianity, as well as the beginnings of France and Germany.

In the nineteenth century, too, Trier was characterized by a special fusion of cultures. Shortly after the turn of the century, the French Revolution had swept through the city, bringing with it the end of what had been the sovereign Archbishopric of Trier, an ancient stronghold of Catholicism. The town was absorbed into the French republic for a while, finally to become part of Napoleon's Empire, in which, though it lost its status as a capital, it was given civic freedom. But with the collapse of the

French Empire and the remaking of the European map by
the victors of Waterloo, the fate of Trier took a turn that
welded it to the most powerful of the German states. By
1815 it was incorporated into Prussia; from then on its
German affiliation was reinforced, though its Catholic
character was largely unaffected.

Among other imports introduced by the Romans to
Trier at the beginning of its history were the Jews, settled
in Western Germany ever since the fourth century A.D.
And it was into a middle-class Jewish family that Karl
Marx, whose name was to become a synonym for social up-
heaval, was born on May 5, 1818.

The Jewishness of his family was somewhat ambiguous.
Though his father had been baptized a year and a half before Marx's birth, so that the head of the family was regularly inscribed in a Christian church, Marx's mother, on
the other hand, whom his father had married the year before his conversion, had refused to be converted at all, out
of consideration for her father, who was still alive. The
family remained split on this point for some years. Religious unity was achieved in a somewhat piecemeal way.
Marx's mother held out, in fact, for many years—it was
not until all seven children were baptized at the same time,
when Karl was six, in a ceremony at which she was not
present, that she overcame her aversion. She was baptized
a year later.

The complications bound to be ascribed to this stag-
gered sequence of baptisms were intensified by the origins
of both mother and father. On both sides of the family the
men had been rabbis for many centuries.

Marx's father, Hirschel, was the third son of Rabbi Meier
Levi, who was the Rabbi of Trier and was succeeded in
this office by Hirschel's oldest brother Samuel, Marx's
uncle. Meier Levi's wife, Marx's grandmother, was herself

the daughter of Moses Lvov, who had also been Rabbi of Trier, following his father. Long before coming to Trier, too, the forebears of Marx's father had been rabbis elsewhere. Indeed, for centuries the rabbinate had been the sole profession of the males in the family, which included many celebrated names—Joseph ben Gershon Cohen, Rabbi of Cracow at the end of the sixteenth century, and the still more celebrated Meir Katzenellenbogen, whose reputation among Jews had spread far beyond his synagogue in Padua, Italy, where he had died in 1565. The famous University of Padua had acknowledged him as one of the most important minds of the age; his portrait, strangely for the time, hung in its great hall.

Marx's mother, though herself far from cultivated, had an equally lengthy rabbinical lineage. Thus on both sides of his family Marx could look back upon an unbroken rabbinical background. Perhaps it was this heritage that made his father's conversion particularly notable in the midst of the general movement among Western European Jews to take advantage of the post-Napoleonic upheaval by slipping out of the synagogue into the church.

In spite of Napoleon's defeat and the monarchic-feudal reaction that followed his attempt to reshape Europe, the Jews had been greatly benefited by his activities. Part of Napoleon's design had been the destruction of the ancient social structure based on rank and privilege, with their accompanying restrictions rooted in racial, political, and religious differences. His own Code, meant to replace traditional institutions, was founded on the universal principles of equality and reason. Thus the basic effect of Napoleon's career, which survived his defeat, was the breaking down of the many barriers that for centuries had reinforced the Jewish Ghetto. For the first time the Jewish community, small in numbers but extending over an immense area, could escape from its immemorial segregation.

It was, to be sure, not more than a partial escape. Napoleon himself withdrew some of the privileges that were implied in his Code; his defeat, followed by the restoration of any number of German princes, meant that the exodus of the Jews from the Ghetto was often broken off in midflight. Those who had been quick to snatch at the opportunity of freedom and equality found themselves stranded in mid-passage. They either had to make their way back to the Ghetto, where their families were still often living, or else change their status altogether and identify themselves wholeheartedly with their neighbors. Concretely this meant joining the Church and becoming German patriots.

Such was the case of Hirschel Levi, Marx's father. Though brought up by his rabbinical father in the tightly inbred community constituted by the Ghetto, Hirschel had been touched by the Enlightenment of the eighteenth century. Even before Napoleon, Marx's father had been moved by the spirit of the French rationalists, whose ideas were to change the world via the French Revolution.

As a young man, Hirschel Levi was converted to the then vanguard religion of reason and humanism. He developed a somewhat simpleminded faith in pure humanitarianism, plus a kindhearted and rather non-denominational God. He cut himself off from his family completely, changing his name from Levi to Marx, his own father's first name. Trained as a lawyer, he was making his way into the society outside the Jewish milieu when the reaction following Napoleon's defeat, expressed in some anti-Jewish legislation among other things, abruptly threatened his status in Trier.

Since he was even less attached to the synagogue than he was to the established church of Prussia, and since his own opinions were of the fashionable deistic variety so common among the enlightened at the time, there was no particular psychological obstacle to his identifying himself with the relatively undogmatic Lutheranism of the Prussian Church. In any case, only a year after the anti-Jewish laws of 1816, Marx's father was formally accepted into the church. He took the name Heinrich Marx.

It seems not unlikely that Marx's lifelong detestation of formal religion, his unmistakable hostility to Judaism, and his curiously exaggerated aversion to individual Jews were somehow bound up with the slightly equivocal position of Jews like his father. Such converts often become fanatics on behalf of their new religion or, contrariwise, turn against all religion. In the last century the two celebrated parallels to Karl Marx were the German-Jewish poet Heinrich Heine and the British statesman Disraeli, who, chafing against the attitude of reserve they doubtless rightly assumed to lie behind the surface acceptance of their neighbors, could never hold a stable view of their own origins, but were instead scornful and defensive in turn. In any case, to quote Marx himself, "the tradition of all the dead generations weighs like a mountain on the minds of the living."

It is true that Marx's father, not unusually sensitive and for that matter not remarkably intelligent, seems to have felt no qualms concerning the general standards he had imbibed from the great leaders of the Enlightenment; he fused all his theoretical principles into a passionate advocacy of Prussian virtues. He became a Prussian patriot and a monarchist to boot, justifying the mixture by revering a somewhat idealized image of Frederick the Great.

Thus it was quite natural for Heinrich Marx to bring up his family as liberal Lutherans devoted to the status quo, which included whoever the ruler of Prussia might

be. This was made all the easier by his personal temperament, which apparently was rather retiring, even timorous.
The one occasion on which he is known to have expressed
himself in a nonconformist way was a public dinner where
he advocated moderate reforms inspired by the benevo-
lence of a wise ruler. When the Prussian police reacted,
Heinrich Marx simply withdrew everything he had said;
he successfully persuaded everyone of his complete harm-
lessness.

The elder Marx's profession involved him with all sorts
of people—lawyers, like physicians, were not businessmen,
and were supposed to practice their profession at home.
As a prosperous lawyer, Heinrich Marx saw a steady stream
of wine-merchants, wine-growers, landlords, and businessmen in his comfortable three-story house. His marriage to
Henrietta Pressburger, a Dutch Jewess, seems to have been
happy despite her reluctance to follow her husband into
the Lutheran Church. Witnesses are agreed that it was an
affectionate and happy marriage; religious harmony was
achieved when Henrietta also became a Lutheran.

Karl's character made a strong impression on his father
from the very beginning. Heinrich was aware that his son
was gifted, in contrast with all his other children. It is said
that as a child Marx was stubborn and masterful. He admired his father, but was always, it seems, distant toward
his mother. Her failure to learn proper German irritated
him; her vocabulary was small, and she spoke with a heavy
Dutch accent. Her letters to him never contained more
than elementary maternal admonitions, with a recom-
mendation that he "obey his dear father" in any major
difficulties.

Marx's school years were uneventful. The strenuous cur-
riculum of his school—eight hours of class work and ex-
aminations followed by hours and hours of homework—

absorbed his energies. Immense amounts of information were force-fed to the children by means of very strict discipline; the process enabled Marx to display unusual gifts, which naturally pleased his father. At the same time his father very quickly became aware of what he called his son's "demon." This "demon," which came surging forth in Karl's conversation, was not quite so manifest in his actual written work or in the classroom; Karl was hardworking, attentive, and well-behaved.

But though remarkably bright and lively, he had no intimate friends among his fellow-pupils, which was strange in view of his vitality and evident superiority. He apparently never saw a single one of his schoolmates later on— he neither wrote to them nor mentioned them. His conversational brilliance did not, perhaps, reflect any inner warmth, at least toward human beings. He did not feel a need for personal relations with people his own age.

He preferred, as his father was aware, the society of adults, more specifically the society of the two adults in his immediate vicinity—his own father and the Royal Prussian Privy Councillor Ludwig von Westphalen, who was eminent both as an office-holder in the provincial world of Trier and as an aristocrat through his father, who had commanded an army in the coalition between Frederick the Great and King George of England, and even more through his mother, a descendant of the Duke of Argyll who had ruled Scotland two hundred years before. Von Westphalen was socially irreplaceable for the Marx family and, because of his liberal views and intellectual interests, of immense value for the developing boy.

Marx seems to have been insatiable in his quest for information. Nicknamed "the Moor" early in life because of his swarthy complexion and black eyes—Marx's father shared Shakespeare's view that Moors are particularly warthy—the "Moor" made a speciality of "squeezing people dry," as his father put it.

There could not be the slightest doubt from the very beginning that the "Moor" had a special intellectual gift. It was of a kind that made an overwhelming impression on those he spoke with. His father, to be sure, was a little baffled by the curiously abstract, legalistic, casuistic, and highly analytical nature of his son's intellectual gift, which reminded him, it seems, of the sort of analytical abilities associated with the students of the immense Jewish legal compilation and commentary on the Hebrew Scriptures, the Talmud. For many centuries Jewish scholars, clinging to their religion in an indifferent or hostile world, had spun from the Talmud an endless series of examples in which they applied the basic precepts of the Scriptures to varying circumstances. This called for the exercise of a highly subtle form of logic, sometimes disputatiously arrived at, and in any case dependent on the extraction of logical implications from given premises. Called by those it irritates "logic-chopping," it was perhaps an inevitable method of elaborating into norms of behavior the broad legal principles laid down or implied in the Scriptures.

Karl Marx expressed himself instinctively in this abstract, analytical manner. To his father, who thought he had left his Jewish and rabbinical milieu buried once and for all in a discarded past, it was apparently a source of astonishment. Even though the collective character of Jews could scarcely be summed up by biological factors, there seemed an uncanny echo of talmudic controversy in the manner in which his son's mind worked with such effortless brilliance.

Perhaps the word "abstract" summed up Karl's approach to the world. The father was impressed, somewhat uncomfortably, by the ease with which his son's agile, argumentative, intense brain would evolve vast rhetorical structures from simple beginnings. The elder Marx's own views were both practical and idealistic, in the sense in which a belief in progress, characteristic of the enlightened people of the age, could be regarded as a combination of both qualities. The conquest of nature, symbolized at that time by the invention of the steam engine, the railway, and the use of piped gas for illumination, had captured his imagination. He attempted to interest his gifted son in the application of such things to a new and better world.

Marx's father firmly held a humanitarian view of human nature as being inherently kind and rational. Reasonableness and goodness could be achieved, in the nature of things, if only artificial and irrelevant obstacles were removed from man's path. All social powers, whether based on racial, social, political, or religious differences, were on their way out—they were no more than the artificial products of outmoded forms of government by priests and rulers. Ultimately all men would be equal, he believed, not only politically and legally but even in their personal relationships. For Heinrich Marx, the essential meaning of the world was progress motored by reason; the conquest of nature, exemplified by the swiftly multiplying flood of inventions, was simply a stunning example of the possibilities of a world rejuvenated and reshaped. It seemed natural to him to hope that his gifted son might play a role in the triumphal march of mankind toward a new horizon.

Yet Karl, perhaps strangely, did not have the smallest interest in either practical inventions or their theoretical background in the natural sciences. In the exact sciences as well as in mathematics he remained curiously mediocre. All his passionate energies were poured out into a con-

centration on language—rhetoric, literature, and in his
early youth, poetry.

It was not that he was, even as an adolescent, indifferent
to his worldly surroundings. On the contrary, he took both
dancing and riding lessons; he was even something of a
dandy. But his ambitions were those characteristic of many
intellectuals—he longed for distinction in the world of
thought. Reading was essential for anyone absorbed in
getting an education, just as reading aloud and discussing
books were the most serious diversions of the educated
people of the time. Books ranked even above music as an
occupation in leisure time. The little circle provided Karl
by Ludwig von Westphalen, which was both aristocratic
and intellectual, very naturally concentrated on reading
and discussing the classics.

The young Marx thus came into sustained and intimate
contact with Homer, whom von Westphalen could recite
by the hour in Greek; Shakespeare, who was to be an
abiding passion of Marx throughout his life; and, of course,
the famous French writers and dramatists, Voltaire and
Racine, who were his father's special favorites. Young
Marx plunged into the sea of literature. He could and did
quote copiously from a vast variety of writers, poets,
philosophers, critics, and even theologians. It seems to
have made his conversation altogether exceptional and
produced a powerful impression on everyone near him—
on his elder sister Sophie and perhaps more especially on
her great friend, von Westphalen's daughter Jenny. Both
girls, though a little older—Jenny was four years older—
were stunned by the young Marx's gift for talking, as well
as by his rapidly growing erudition.

All this was quite appropriate, even from a practical
point of view, because it was a natural training for a writer.

Significantly, Karl decided to become a poet while still at secondary school. The conquest of society by the pen was not a mere delusion. Torrents of poetry were gushing forth at this time in Germany; in the early nineteenth century the country was flooded by it, to the fascination of a growing public. Marx's predecessor, Heinrich Heine, somewhat older than he and also of Jewish origin, had become one of the most famous men in the country by means of his remarkably insinuating, melodious verses. Heine was literally a household word, recited and sung in every educated home in Germany. A career based on poetry was not only glamorous but practical. It was fashionable for the educated young everywhere to cherish secret thoughts of poetic eminence and experiment indefatigably in the hope of achieving fame.

So the young Marx tried his hand at it, apparently brimming over with the assurance that his intellectual ability would establish him in this medium, too. Von Westphalen, to be sure, was rather discouraging; he thought that Marx's verse showed nothing beyond cerebral elaboration, that he was devoid of a genuinely poetic imagination. Throughout life, Marx specialized in verbal constructions of singular complexity; as a youthful poet his verses were topheavy with metaphorical and rhetorical ingenuity. Von Westphalen showed no interest in them; his daughter Jenny, on the other hand—doubtless for different reasons —thought Marx's poems absolutely marvelous. Sophie told Karl that when Jenny read a new poem of his, she "burst into tears of joy and melancholy." In the situation in which the young people lived, in each other's pockets half the time, with Karl a passionate seventeen and Jenny twenty-one, it was obvious that one classic situation might lead to another.

But as Marx was just finishing his secondary school and was due to leave home for the university, nothing might have happened after all. In the autumn of 1835 Marx passed his final pre-university examination. He had done almost as well as might have been expected—he had distinguished himself in religion and in the classical languages, though he had only just passed mathematics and also, curiously, French, and his marks in the natural sciences were, as usual, mediocre. A comment on his German composition has some interest for posterity. The subject set Marx was "Reflections of a Youth Before Choosing a Profession," and the professor, after criticizing Marx's characteristic verbal exuberance and exaggerated straining after the unusual and the picturesque, grants the "richness of thought and the well-planned organization of the material," but concludes by pointing out that the "whole presentation . . . lacks the necessary clarity, often even accuracy; and this is true of the isolated expressions as well as of the structure as a whole." Despite this professional sneer, entirely justified, Marx's essay contains an idea that was later to be expanded into a whole view of life. The essay ends on a pregnant note: "We cannot always take up the profession we feel ourselves suited for; our social relations have begun more or less to crystallize before we are able to determine them." In the reputation Marx was later to establish, this thought, evidently sensible, indeed perhaps obvious, was to be a basic factor.

Though Marx's father wanted him to study in Berlin, the center of Prussian culture, Marx himself insisted on going to the far closer University of Bonn. It had been hard for him to persuade his father, who now, after having been appointed a Royal Prussian Legal Councillor—an honorary title—felt more patriotic than ever, that he ought not to go so far away so soon, but since in any case he was leaving Trier, and thus Jenny, his father may have found the idea acceptable.

Young Marx, at the age of seventeen, was thus flung into the carefree atmosphere of a German university. He instantly began playing the classical role of the scapegrace student, becoming careless about money and running up debts—in short, sowing his wild oats. He was arrested by the police for "noisiness and drunkenness at night," and was also punished by the university. He seemed to be doing no work at all, and on top of all his classical misbehavior, it turned out he had been leaving Bonn and going off to Cologne, where he was involved in a curious and mysterious incident—he fought a duel. Not a duel in accordance with the ritualistic and glamorous mystique of the German student duelling with sabers, but a quite serious duel with pistols. Though Marx's life has been gone over with a fine tooth comb, this incident has never been explained. There was a state investigation; when Marx left Bonn University, a note was entered in his report that in Cologne he had been found with "forbidden weapons," i.e., firearms. This was, of course, regarded as a very different affair from playing about in the old-fashioned student manner with foils and sabers, which was thought to improve a young man's morale. Firearms of any kind, with their political implications, were bound to alarm the authorities.

Their apprehensions were due to the swelling current of political liberalism. The aristocratic and monarchic restoration following Napoleon had implied, of course, the suppression of all the various subversive ideas that after kindling the French Revolution had spread insidiously or openly, even after the Revolution had shrunk back on itself. The democratic current as it affected Europe at the beginning of the nineteenth century was aimed at destroying the exclusive political role of the monarchs. Even where there was a parliament, as there was in France, it did not represent much more than the very thin topmost layer of the population, exercising a scarcely discernible restraint over the decisions of the ruler. Elsewhere in Europe, monarchs were for all practical purposes absolute. They not only made the laws on their own authority, but also, naturally, laid down what was to be said and printed in public.

By the beginning of the nineteenth century something began to show up in politics that had already made itself manifest in economics. Throughout the eighteenth century, governments—that is monarchs—who before had been very powerful in economics, had gradually been dislodged from their controlling positions by the swelling tide of economic liberalism, culminating in the Industrial Revolution. The competition of countless individuals in business seemed to have resulted in an unheard-of prosperity for at least the upper levels of society; there was a natural tendency to project the benefits of economic liberalism into the sphere of politics. Because of the practically universal censorship in Europe, this democratic current took the form of various "secret societies," all interested in the restriction of the monarchs' monopoly of power and in a greater role for the ordinary "citizen."

This activity was not confined to ideas. While older people with democratic inclinations might limit themselves to thinking their own thoughts and occasionally publishing them in clandestine publications, younger ones would often lay their hands on actual firearms.

It was no wonder that authority on the European continent felt a little nervous. In July 1830, after all, there had been another echo of the French Revolution. The streets of Paris had been occupied by a mob and the Bourbon dynasty thrown out. A new dynasty, represented by King Louis Philippe, disguised as a sort of democrat—"the Citizen King"—had replaced it.

Such events merely made the secret societies that were agitating against absolutism still more radical. It was obvious that the idea of restricting absolutist authority implied the possibility of abolishing it altogether and establishing a republican form of government, for which the way had been paved not merely by the French Revolution but by the lasting stability of the former British colonies in America. The success of the United States in maintaining a democratic and republican form of government buttressed the confidence of the youthful democrats in Europe. Dissident Europeans were convinced not only by the example of the Marquis de Lafayette, who had been one of the inspirations of the July 1830 uprising in Paris, but by the celebrated book on American democracy written by Alexis de Toqueville, which was avidly read throughout Europe. The democratic movement in Europe was, in fact, growing rapidly enough to alarm police departments everywhere.

In Marx's case, his possession of "forbidden weapons" meant nothing—as a young man he does not seem to have paid the smallest attention to politics. Throughout the year he spent in Bonn he showed no interest even in his studies of law, in which he was supposed to specialize with a view to following in his father's footsteps. During this year of diversion, in fact, he apparently did not even spend much time writing, which had been his favorite pastime— his wild oats consumed all his energies. By the time he returned home, after a year spent in Bonn, his father and he had to agree that it was a year largely wasted.

So he was meant for Berlin after all. The elder Marx took some pains to look into the social situation in Berlin, get his son appropriate letters of introduction, and settle on a course of studies that would constitute a middle road between law and Marx's own more romantic interests. While preparing for Berlin, however, Marx himself made a vital decision—he and Jenny von Westphalen, long since in love, made up their minds to get married.

This decision was a tremendous shock to the Marx family, partly because it was, from a purely social as well as personal point of view, a very remarkable coup for young Marx. Not only was Jenny four years Karl's senior but she was already being courted by a variety of distinguished older men, all quite capable of providing her with an appropriate background and way of life. Young Marx was young, and not to mention his Jewish antecedents, he had no prospects at all except that of making a living, possibly as a lawyer, many years in the future.

Jenny was a considerable personage in the provincial society of Trier. Not only was she known as "the most beautiful girl in Trier," but her noble lineage made her socially desirable. It was only natural for the elder Marx to be rather apprehensive that such a match would disrupt relations with Jenny's father, now an old friend.

In these circumstances, Karl's decision to study in Berlin became still more alluring to his father. A long separation! Just the thing to cool off the young couple's ardor, or else, on the other hand, prove their love. The elder Marx saw the young couple and put it to them. It was agreed that Karl would leave at once and not return during the period he was to spend at the university in Berlin. Thus in all probability he would not see Jenny for three years.

The separation of the two young people was as painful as might be expected. In the autumn of 1836, at the age of eighteen and a half, Marx arrived in Berlin. He quickly found a room in a house that, according to a marker, had once been lived in by the celebrated poet Lessing.

CHAPTER II

Intellectual Beginnings: Hegel: the Young Hegelians

Berlin was typical of Prussia, which had long since ceased being one of the hopes of European liberals, as it had been in the generation after the defeat of Napoleon, and was now the rather stuffy political monopoly of a monarchy more firmly entrenched than any other government outside Czarist Russia. It was impossible to express in public any democratic opinion at all, while the army, which guaranteed the established order and was dominated by the Officers' Corps—a practically impenetrable stronghold of the nobility—gave Berlin society the atmosphere now universally, and perhaps unfairly, associated with the word "Prussian." In addition, the temperament of the sovereign, a great-nephew of Frederick the Great, was in complete contrast with his forebear's religious indifference. Royal piety pervaded public life.

In other respects, the government was extremely fair and the officials remarkably uncorruptible. The legal system functioned smoothly and justly, and even though the censorship forbade all praise of democracy and any talk against religion, criticism was possible as long as it was carried on discreetly. For that matter, if someone wrote a book longer than 320 pages, it was legally exempt from control—in major tomes an author could express whatever opinion he cared to. This was quite in harmony with Prussia's already highly evolved university system, based

on a comprehensive network of grammar schools throughout the country, even in the tiniest hamlets.

Marx paid no attention at first to the political atmosphere in the capital. He was perhaps inclined to a mild
form of "liberalism," which in effect meant little, and as
far as its influence on his thinking was concerned, nothing
at all. His primary interest at the time was still his work,
for he was determined to control his own destiny in a
sensible way. Though he conformed superficially with social customs and called on all the people recommended
to him in his father's letters of introductions, he made no
lasting connections. What seems to have been a characteristic aloofness governed his first period in Berlin. As he
was to indicate, it was he who "repulsed" many friendly
advances.

This time he was a diligent student. He was a regular
attendant at university lectures, including some on criminal law given by Eduard Gans, the principal luminary at
the university after Hegel's death in 1831. A converted
Jew celebrated for having spearheaded the general movement of conversion among the emancipated Jews in Germany, Gans noted Marx's "immense industriousness." But
though Marx devoted a great deal of his energy to his
legal studies, he thought of them at this time as a mere
adjunct of his true goal—to become a poet.

Poetry was the vehicle for all his energies. He spent
most of the day and the night writing; it was his paramount ambition.

He wrote indefatigably, burning, it seemed, with desire
for Jenny von Westphalen, creative zeal, and worldly ambition. In only a few months a huge accumulation of manuscripts displayed the result of his passionate devotion.
He had filled two thick notebooks, "The Book of Love I,"

and "The Book of Love II," both dedicated to his "dear, eternally beloved Jenny von Westphalen." There was a third notebook, "The Book of Songs," and a fourth—untitled—dedicated to his father. He also translated some of Ovid's verse from the Latin and composed a poetic dialogue, a comic novel, and a classical tragedy. After several months in Berlin, he had proceeded far enough with the novel and the play to send his father a good many sections of them.

Around this time his father's health began declining, and partly through panic at the thought of leaving his numerous dependents—a wife and eight children, none of whom could make a living—and partly, perhaps, because he was impressed by his son's determination, the elder Marx also became convinced that a poetic career might not be such a bad idea and would at least provide his son with a livelihood. In a way, the career of a talented poet was easier than almost any other. It took years to become a lawyer, while most poets made their mark as adolescents or at least as very young men. Marx's father went so far as to propose a subject for an extended literary work, so that Karl could "make a name for himself as fast as he could." He suggested as a worthy subject an ode on an episode from Prussian history, perhaps with the battle of Waterloo as a background, "patriotic, full of feeling, and worked out in a genuine German spirit"—this was to "be enough to make you famous."

It was too late; young Marx's feelings had changed. Rather abruptly, he became utterly discouraged with his prospects as a poet. He had been sending out manuscripts to various periodicals. They were sent back to him without a single, even perfunctory, qualification of the rejection. Perhaps his common sense, buttressed by hopelessness, opened his eyes to the plain fact that despite his cerebral powers he simply had no poetic talent. He expressed this unmistakably by mentioning his "generalized and shapeless feelings." "Nothing is natural," he wrote. "It is all rhetorical reflections instead of poetic thoughts."

And it must be admitted that poetry, which, after all, can be and has been written with some degree of success by countless mediocrities, somehow eluded Marx's grasp. He felt bitter despair at the sudden insight into his lack of talent, especially as it meant the end of his hopes for fame and he did not have the consolation of any other occupation. The letter from his father suggesting a majestic ode on Prussian history arrived when his disappointment with himself was already complete. For a while he thought of falling back on the far less exalted domain of literary criticism, he wrote rather grandly to his father that he had been assured the cooperation of "all the famous men in the field of aesthetics" in launching a magazine devoted to dramatic criticism. Nothing came of this either. At the age of nineteen, Marx was alone in Berlin, dependent on an allowance from an ailing father, with no idea of what to do with himself.

After the collapse of his poetic hopes, Marx seems to have returned to his former spendthrift life. His father's letters were again full of complaints that he squandered money far in excess of what even "the wealthiest" spent as students. The elder Marx was declining rapidly; his ill-health cost money. In addition, a younger brother of Karl's had died of tuberculosis, and in order to have another taken on as a merchant's apprentice, his father had to pay the merchant a premium because of the boy's mediocrity. Also, the five girls had to be married off without dowries—at the time difficult or impossible.

Thus Marx's father, now dying after Marx had been in Berlin for about a year, was suffering in all respects. His complaints about his son's extravagance grew more and more bitter, particularly as he was aware that the quality of selfishness he had first complained about in his letters to Marx at Bonn was becoming increasingly evident. On top of a lack of consideration in money matters, his father complained, he was disquieted by Karl's transparent hypocrisy in trying to slip back home in order, obviously, to see Jenny before the three years were up. Marx put on an excessive display of affection not only for his father, which was plausible, but also for his mother, whom he would praise quite out of proportion with his known feelings for her. He also seems to have exaggerated the amount of work he had done during the first part of his stay in Berlin, listing fabulous amounts of reading and writing. But this is difficult to prove, in view of the ability he showed later on in life to accomplish unusual feats of industry.

In any case he claimed to have consumed all of Hegel from end to end and "most of his followers" too. This alone would be enough to occupy a lifetime. He had translated from Latin a great deal of Tacitus, and from Greek, Aristotle's *Rhetoric;* he had applied himself to learning Italian and English from grammars. He also maintained that he had written two works of his own of a scientific nature—a "philosophy of law of almost three hundred pages" and a "new system of metaphysics," both of which he had been disappointed in and had burnt.

He claimed he had done all this in a single year. His father refused to believe him. His father was, moreover, a little perturbed by Marx's somber references to himself as the target of mysterious tragedies. Impatiently simple-minded in his view of personal behavior, Marx's father found his son's tragic posture in the face of the world "disgusting." He called it "weakness, indulgence, self-love, and vanity."

Marx's father came to his end amidst increasing sorrows, with a deep concern not for his only gifted son's mind but for his character. His death in March, 1838, some twenty months after Marx settled in Berlin, left Marx in a sort of spiritual limbo, with no material prospects of any kind.

Yet he had already found a haven in his study of Hegel. It was to provide him with an anchorage for many years.

By the time Marx arrived in Berlin, the influence of Hegelianism at the University and its intellectual satellites—the Universities of St. Petersburg and Moscow and, of course, countless German universities—was simply overwhelming, to a degree that nowadays would seem inconceivable. Hegel exercised the most extraordinary influence over the educated classes of his own country and over whole generations of Europeans—with the exception of England and France.

Later called by Marx "the world-philosopher of our age" and without doubt the most influential thinker of the epoch, Hegel had so impregnated the thinking of his time that all educated people, at least in Prussia, regarded themselves as Hegelians of one kind or another. The only way to distinguish between them was to split up the concept "Hegelianism" into "Left" and "Right" Hegelians, "Young Hegelians," and so on. Hegelianism was all the more widespread because one of its basic tenets was the concept of the State being by its nature preponderant over the individual. This not only characterized the Prussian regime as such, but was accepted by practically all thinking people, including those who were democratic in their ideas about the State. Hegelianism was supple enough in its mechanisms to span all society.

Marx's immersion in Hegelianism was total, yet though he was steeped in it at an early age, he had already been formed to some extent by his father's milieu. Even though he was to lose faith in the potency of pure reason in influencing action, he was to remain a rationalist all his life, with an unshakable conviction that people could achieve perfection. He believed that history could be understood in its inmost recesses and considered its course inherently progressive, tending toward a rational ideal. Consciously, he was always to detest—despite his own passionate nature but in harmony with the ideals of eighteenth-century rationalism—all forms of emotionalism, sentimentality, supernaturalism, fantasies, and so on.

Philosophical rationalism, popularized by eighteenth-century French and English thinkers, retained a formative influence on his mind. Since it converged with Hegelianism on some points, it exercised a harmoniously restraining influence on him even after he was swayed by the romanticism of Hegel and the systematism of classical German philosophy. Perhaps it was this underlying philosophical influence that inspired him to apply Hegelianism to the events of the real world, as he was to attempt to do in his celebrated inversion of Hegel later on in life.

Marxism was to be so indebted to Hegel—though its followers have sometimes chosen to play down Hegel's role—that a glance back is necessary to put Hegelianism in perspective.

The predominance of Hegelianism had come about through the evolution of a purely intellectualist position in philosophy, promoted among the Germans by Gottfried Wilhelm Leibnitz and his many followers, who undertook to demonstrate that an altogether coherent and dogmatic metaphysical edifice could be created through the use of the reason inherent in all thinking creatures.

This was a form of pure rationalism that was systematically attacked in England, as well as later on in France, by the most important philosophers of the age—Locke, Hume, and afterwards Bentham. They all denied the existence of any innate intellectual faculty that could determine fundamental truths. They claimed that the intelligent use of man's ordinary physical faculties supplied him with the primary empirical information on which all real knowledge of the universe is based. Reason was thus not the *source* of knowledge, but a mere coordinator of information supplied to it, from which it could then draw deductions. French philosophers in the eighteenth century, such as Voltaire, Diderot, and others, attacked the rationalist position in their own way—some of them admitted that there might be some knowledge that could be perceived without the senses, but all agreed that there was no evidence for the primordial, incontrovertible truths that the older rationalists claimed to be in possession of through reason alone.

Pure rationalism was attacked for setting up canons of infallible authority—unique interpretations of man's universe that could be regarded as authoritative, such as Aristotle or the Bible. The later rationalists felt that an interacting combination of experience *and* reason was required, for example, to show that human beings were not "naturally" slaves, as Aristotle, appealing to pure reason, had taught simply to defend the institution of slavery in his own day or that man was not "naturally" vicious as the authorized interpretation of religious texts maintained. On the contrary, it could be demonstrated that man was "naturally" good, that reason was implanted in all thinking beings, and hence that the source of human afflictions was itself human, namely ignorance compounded by material interests. If people were allowed to realize their true potentialities they would soon achieve a state of bliss.

The basic tenet of this kind of rationalism, with its em-

phasis on empirical enquiry, was that reason could be
used to explain and therefore control the world—only
lack of knowledge had prevented this in the past. Unhappiness and poverty were thought to be the result of ignorance, both of the world of nature and the nature of
man. If reason were installed as the guide, a new age would
be ushered in. The main obstacle to this age, which human beings, who were inherently rational, would naturally
bring about, was the existence of a vested interest opposed
to the installation of a harmonious society, namely the upper classes, who ruled through various cover arrangements
and institutions, such as monarchies, churches, armies, and
aristocracies. The upper classes had a direct interest in
obscurantism and in the erection of a dogmatic edifice to
keep their subjects in a state of confusion and hence obedi-
ence.

   Yet, while reason was the sole and sufficient guide, it
was necessary for men to study the natural world to achieve
a proper education. Physical environment was an essential
factor in understanding human beings, who were endowed
at birth with the faculty of reason. Everything in man
could be explained by the study of physical influences.
An extreme example of this empiricism was a famous book,
Man the Machine, by the French materialist La Mettrie,
which generated a furor. La Mettrie's views, though somewhat extreme, were also held by the editors of the French
Encyclopaedia, Diderot, d'Alembert, and others, all of
whom agreed that the principal difference between men
and animals—and for that matter plants—was that men
were self-conscious and had the gift of reason, enabling
them to create moral values and attain their ends.

   This philosophy raised a serious problem: if men were
totally determined by their natural environment and in-
born character, how could they exercise any choice, that

is, have free will? But this contradiction was simply a new form of the classical conflict between free will and the divine prescience, in which God was replaced by an all-determining nature. To the rationalists, free will was at best an illusion, human behavior was determined by external circumstances, and the individual behaved as he did because he had no choice. It was impossible for individuals actually to make decisions, regardless of what they thought, since the constraints of nature could not be evaded.

Nevertheless, many radical intellectuals of the eighteenth century disregarded this perhaps unreal logical conflict and believed in a sort of creed that emphasized the perfectibility of man on the basis of reason. People, they held, could be extricated from the bog of millennial oppression and misery; the good things of this world distributed more fairly—mankind could be *made* happy.

Since the phenomenal advances of Kepler, Galileo, Descartes, and Newton in the natural sciences during the previous century had fascinated the imaginations of countless intellectuals, nothing could be more natural than applying their methods to the study of society in the attempt to liberate mankind from its social fetters. Voltaire and Rousseau are the two most celebrated advocates of the new humanitarian religion. Together they created a new universe of language and thought, aimed at improving man in accordance with his underlying nature, when freed of the trappings of traditional oppression and obscurantism.

These new ideas, all rooted in a general disaffection from the social order, conquered whole generations of European intellectuals. The idea that inquiry could and must be free, that its sole criterion was the truth, and that the truth would inevitably prevail because of its very nature, had a shattering effect not only on the fabric of traditional thought but on the actual constitution of society. Its followers may be said to have directly formed the generation that carried out the French Revolution. That generation's moral stance, as well as its political ideas, has created a substantial and quite unconscious portion of the legacy of all democrats, liberals, and socialists—all those who believe in the natural rights of man and mankind's right to apply reason to the construction of a better world.

In Germany, however, the French, or Franco-English combination of rationality and empiricism ultimately collided with a new and profoundly anti-empirical movement. By the end of the eighteenth century, Germany, after having been shattered and almost disintegrated by the Thirty Years' War, had begun evolving a native school of thought, essentially independent of the French school that had become the model for the whole of Europe.

Napoleon's wars put the seal on the Germans' inferiority to the French in the field of philosophy by adding the bitterness of defeat in battle. A patriotic reaction to the Napoleonic wars began what was expressed most systematically in the new "romantic" philosophy, associated particularly with the names of Fichte and Schelling, of the generation after Kant. As the educated classes in Germany were still very small, philosophy acquired an inordinate importance for the intelligentsia, almost becoming an aspect of patriotism.

Through criticizing the would-be scientific empiricism that had been popular in France and England, Germany developed a philosophy of its own—a bold, all-encompassing metaphysical historicism launched by Herder and Hegel. Hegel generalized this into an imposing metaphysical system, which presented Europe and the world with a systematic alternative to an empiricism the Germans felt was shallow, insipid, and ultimately trivial.

It was Herder who, irritated by the rationalism, cosmopolitanism, and egalitarianism of the dominant French philosophy, applied the concept of "organic development" —as it came to be known—to the study of peoples and civilizations. This concept involved the idea that people were formed by some broad pattern of life, without which no individual phenomenon could be meaningful or even exist. Beginning with a concentrated study of German origins and perhaps influenced by the rapid advance of national self-awareness in Europe, Herder tried to create a portrait of the German "spirit" transcending the senseless events of a meaningless and merely chronological sequence.

Hegel generalized this approach far more comprehensively—indeed universally. He was utterly skeptical of the value of radical empiricism, even in the natural sciences. He seemed to feel that the conditions studied and described by natural scientists had been chosen capriciously to begin with and, in any case, represented no more than a tiny sampling of the possibilities. He thought that radical empiricism was completely pernicious to the study of human history and society.

Hegel had a sort of dual approach to history. On the one hand, he believed that the activities of peoples who are in the same stage of development are linked to each other in such a way as to form a pattern that gives each "period" its own unmistakable and unique character. On the other hand, he felt that any complex of events is an inevitable stage in a process of development that in time not only consummates the development of its predecessor but also embodies in its own substance forces that are bound to

emerge and effect a transition to a still later stage. Thus
it is impossible to grasp the nature of any given epoch unless one considers it in connection with the stages preceding and following it, for an epoch contains the seeds of its
own future. In short, "great oaks from little acorns grow"
—an oak cannot be understood without understanding the
acorn and vice versa.

This doctrine is very ancient, preceding even Aristotle.
The philosopher Leibnitz had extended it to encompass
the universe, saying that there was no such thing as ac-
cident and that everything was interconnected. This, he
believed, was why the empiricists were unable to describe
anything accurately. All they could do was mention a
sequence of events or states—either connected or not—
whereas the only way to explain the universe was to demonstrate its *necessary* evolution as an organically integrated
entity.

Hegel took this basic concept and applied it to history
in the broadest sense. For him an explanation was not
just a description or enumeration of events related to each
other in a purely external way, but a demonstration of
the rational grounds for any given development—that is,
the *reason* something occurred as it did. Hegel believed
that events had a purpose, function, or process that could
be rationally perceived. An event had to be the result, in
short, of man's or God's intelligence or of men fulfilling
something beyond themselves. While French empirical
materialism might be applicable to purely static situations,
it could not explain anything dynamic. It could at best
describe differences but not explain why things actually
changed.

Hegel's mind, powerful and industrious, developed his
system into a vast edifice. It probably would be beyond a

very short book even to outline his philosophy, but general structure seems clear.

Hegel thought that all mankind was in a state of absolutely irresistible ascension. The motor behind this irresistible upward movement or progression was a scarcely definable spiritual force, which at various times Hegel called the World Spirit, the Idea, the Absolute Idea, or simply the Absolute. This Absolute was what kept mankind moving upward. But the ascension was not in a simple direction—that is, it was not *merely* upward but upward in a sort of zigzag. The zigzag was formed by the "dialectical" interaction between all the qualities predicated of the Absolute. One thing or idea—the two were synonyms for Hegel—would be negated by another thing or idea, and the combination would create a third thing or idea on a "higher" level. The process did not merely fuse the first two things or ideas but related them to each other in a dynamic way that brought about the upward progression.

In a general way this sounds simple enough; indeed, it is. But it is obvious that when the concept was applied to the world of either material reality or thought—for Hegel, again, synonymous—the ambiguities were endless. They were naturally enlarged on by countless disciples, since it was possible to analyze any aspect of life by means of this simultaneously infinite and concentrated apparatus of thought.

One of Hegel's basic statements has become celebrated —often it is the only thing remembered about him. "What is real is rational, what is rational is real." Everything in reality is defined by its position in the rationality of the universe; thus, to be in reality at all, as Hegel understood the word, a thing must be rational by definition.

Put this way, to be sure, it is obviously no more than

a tautology. Hegel is simply using "real" and "rational"
interchangeably. This is apparent if the word "real" is
changed to "existent"—Hegel clearly did not mean that
everything *in existence* is real. Reality was quite a different category from existence, and Hegel himself had to
correct his initial statement when the tautology was complained about.

Yet even then it was difficult for him to abandon the
definition. Intellectually he agreed that existence was far
below reality, was an inferior order of being, but in practice he had a tendency to speak as though the existing
world were somehow justified from a rational point of
view, too, merely *because* it existed. As Hegel grew older
this tendency made him a conservative in social affairs—
i.e., in favor of the status quo, as something in existence
—and caused him, strangely enough, to deify the Prussian
State as the terminal stage of what the Absolute had been
driving at for aeons.

There was also some difficulty—as there was, after all,
bound to be!—in the definition of the Absolute. Put
baldly, it sounded very like a synonym for God. Hegel
himself had written that world-history was the autobiog-
raphy of God, who revealed himself in the successive unfolding of history. The conclusion of one of his major
works, *The Philosophy of History,* is: "God rules the
world. The content of his dominion, and the carrying out
of his plan, are world-history."

The relationships between the phrases used by Hegel to
refer to this moving force in human destiny—the Idea, the
Absolute, God, etc.—gave rise to endless dispute. In some
respects, Hegel's Absolute, insofar as it could be detected
as differing from God, had more power over human affairs.
Generally religious thinkers have refused to make man a
complete pawn in God's hands: even while agreeing that

an all-powerful God can by definition force people to do anything He really wants to, most religions reserve a place in the cosmos for the exercise of man's free will.

In Hegel's system, on the other hand, everything in human life seemed to be encompassed by his Absolute Idea. He believed that mankind was being driven toward a predestined goal that it was powerless to change in advance and could not even understand until after the goal had been attained. Each stage traversed in mankind's irresistible ascension was apparent to the human mind only after the event.

The dialectic was even more subtle. Since it was the actual contrivance that provided the dynamics for the entire progression, the difficulties in explaining its method of functioning were of paramount consequence.

Hegel did not invent the dialectic, which goes back to the Greeks. But before him the conception of the dialectic was applied simply to thought or language. It was regarded as a method of arguing or thinking that ultimately led to the establishment of a truth that was quite outside the method itself and independent of it. The Greeks had held the view that human thought proceeded by a never ending succession of the "thesis," negated by the "antithesis," which in its turn was negated—and elevated—by the "synthesis." The process of thought was defined as dialectical in and for itself.

Hegel transported this intellectual modality into the fabric of the universe, into real life. He saw the progression in events as in its nature dialectical. Everything, by creating out of its inner being its own opposite, carried history forward in dialectical stages, zigzags. Hegel considered this the "law of motion" of history, and because of its inherently infinite scope, applied it to all fields of knowledge as well as to all events.

Among Hegel's disciples, however, there were many who accepted his "system" as a whole but nevertheless considered it too pietist in its essence, for it was obvious that Hegel's Absolute Idea could scarcely be disentangled from God. Their dissatisfaction was heightened by Hegel's growing conservatism in social and political matters. Accordingly, those of his followers who had been influenced by the spirit of "modern science" felt that Hegel's system was marred by having incorporated a religious element that was superfluous and should be dislodged.

Hegel's system could be exploited by the pietists in public life who believed that the status quo had to be maintained both in society and in religion. Theirs was one way of interpreting his celebrated proposition that "whatever is, is rational." On the other hand, the believers in "modern science" could also find an inherent sanction for change in Hegel's idea of dialectical progress.

Thus the Hegelian camp, which included practically all thinking Germans, and for that matter Russians, naturally split into a conservative and a progressive wing. The conservatives, by pinning their faith on the rationality of the real, found reasons for supporting the status quo. What had survived had by definition passed the test of rationality simply by being in existence as the end-product of the historical process. In this sense, Western culture, as Hegel himself had said, was a higher stage, perhaps the ultimate synthesis, of its forerunners, the Oriental and Greco-Roman civilizations. Hegel used this concept to justify his feeling that the Prussian State was the highest achievement of man, the ultimate embodiment of Western values. It would therefore be pernicious to act against this stage of perfection.

The progressives, or radicals, took the opposite point of view, equally justifiable, of course, by Hegel's texts. For them what was real must be rational. The specific actuality of any institution might be full of shortcomings and imperfections. For these radicals, such an institution in the authentic, metaphysical sense—for them the only meaningful way of contemplating events and things—was not *real* but happened to be in existence at a given, fleeting moment. Hence it could legitimately be transformed to accord with its true, rational nature.

Thus a correct interpretation of a particular institution had to distinguish between its actuality and its potential reality. If an individual could elevate himself beyond the level of mere existence and apply sound critical metaphysical methods to the study of the institutions of his own time, he would be able to further genuine progress toward the genuinely real more quickly.

Hegel had, after all, claimed that reality consisted of a process, of a universal effort, to achieve self-consciousness, and this process was itself perfected by the actual increase in the degree of human self-consciousness. He had also, for that matter, always emphasized the tension inherent in the dialectical conjunction of opposites, so there was no reason to imagine that progress would be particularly painless, tidy, or smooth. Indeed, a crisis was indicated in the very assumption of a dialectical progression, for if one thing engendered its opposite and the opposite that grew within it was destined to burst out, the jump upward to the following stage was bound to be somewhat explosive. Hence explosive progress could be looked for both in nature and in human society.

It seemed obvious to these radical disciples of Hegel, the "Young Hegelians," that the job of the true philosopher was to push the revolutionary process of true history forward by his special critical faculty—in other words, by intellectual warfare on existing institutions.

This was a little difficult, as the authorities were on the alert for any signs of social or political disaffection. Some Hegelians launched a flanking movement for cover; the first struggles against Hegelian orthodoxy and the status quo were made in Christian theology, in a continuation of the so-called Higher Criticism of the Bible for which German theology was already celebrated.

In 1835, a critical *Life of Jesus* was published by David Friedrich Strauss, a disciple of Hegel's, who rejected the Gospels out of hand as part fiction and part mythology. He dismissed the whole theological purpose of the Gospels as simply another stage in the evolving self-consciousness of mankind. As for the texts themselves, he rather arbitrarily maintained that they were unreliable though historically significant.

Strauss's book produced a hurricane, not only in traditionalist circles but also in his own milieu of Young Hegelians. It was true that the life of Jesus had been an object of study for a generation, after having been left untouched for some eighteen hundred years, but Strauss's book brought it to the attention of a relatively broad audience, while his revolutionary implications concerning the life of the supposed founder of Christianity—traditionally a dogmatic system—had the effect of a bombshell in deeply pious Germany.

But although the book inflamed normative opinion, it provoked an even greater extremism. Another Young Hegelian, Bruno Bauer, attacked Strauss's book from a point of view that was still more radical. He maintained that Jesus had never lived at all and that the Gospels were nothing but fiction. In accordance with Hegel's system, he regarded the Gospels as the highest expression of the stage reached during their time by the evolution of the Absolute.

Strauss's book on Jesus, in spite of the storm it raised, was essentially superficial, according to Bauer. He had been unhistorical enough not to make the effort to distinguish between the relative values of different parts of the Gospels but had lumped them all together, simply listing the numerous contradictions between them and using the mythologizing "consciousness" of the community as an explanation. Strauss's main point had been, according to Bauer, that anything that violated natural law could not have happened, but this also made it impossible to explain discrepancies between things that were plausible—for example, that there had been a man called Jesus, who lived in Galilee and was crucified in Jerusalem. If the documents were not to be thrown out altogether, or accepted altogether, they must be critically distinguished between.

Because of these problems Bauer called Strauss's method "mysterious" and even in its own way religious. He himself regarded the Gospels as just like any other human document and looked for the key to discrepancies in the aims of the individual biographers. The result of his work, which made him fall foul of the authorities, was that he denied not merely the divinity of Jesus but his actual existence. In addition, since he maintained that the evangelists were simply people who created the notion of a God—much as the Greek gods had been invented by poets like Homer and Hesiod—nothing in the character of the Gospels served as "testimony" to anything.

The dispute between the two Hegelians, Strauss and Bauer, was not a matter of mere pedantry. Strauss felt that he was living up to the spirit of Christianity by liberalizing it philosophically. He was part of the powerful tendency in German theology that claimed—very naively, as we can see today—to be deepening our knowledge of Christianity by learning more about Jesus the man. Bauer, on the contrary, was persuaded that by destroying the historical foundations of Christianity, by wiping out the reality of Jesus as an historical and *a fortiori* divine figure, he was also destroying religion.

Strauss in his own way was acceptable to many theologians and helped promote a strand in Protestant theology that was to conquer all rivals. After all, Strauss assumed that all four Gospels had independent authority—thus they could be considered powerful testimonials to *some* factual truth. Even if Christianity were reduced to what all four Gospels seemed to agree on, a great deal was left for the pietists. Bauer claimed to demonstrate that all four Gospels were in reality variations on one report, with three versions distorted to further a specific writer's aims. Only one "witness" was left, and his account could be torn to shreds because of his ignorance, gullibility, and tendentiousness. Bauer's position led to a radical atheism, which concerned the police.

Ordinarily, of course, these squabbles on a subject altogether beyond the masses would not have interested the police, but since both sides to the dispute held views that were subversive politically as well as religiously, they tightened the censorship. The only arena for the lively discussion of all the issues touched on by the controversy remained the universities, where a considerable degree of academic freedom was still possible.

At the time of Marx's arrival in Berlin, only a few years after Hegel's death, the philosophical milieu at the University of Berlin was thoroughly entangled in the political aspects of philosophy. When Marx abruptly cast aside his hopes of becoming a poet, he gravitated in a very natural way to these radical intellectuals, the chief opposition at the time to the conformism that dominated this center of the Prussian bureaucracy.

Marx's belief in human perfectibility and his positivistic attitude toward the pragmatic value of studying the natural world through observation interested him in law as a good field for the demonstration of any philosophy of history. Under the influence of Eduard Gans, he encountered the massive tug of the Hegelian system; he was at first so tormented by its challenge that he spent nights unable to sleep and days unable to work, locked in a struggle with the philosophical Master Builder whom he regarded as his opponent. He even fell ill and had to leave Berlin to recuperate. Despite his father's lengthy admonitions to pull himself together, get back to real work, and forget sterile abstractions, he plunged still further into a study of Hegel on his return. His boast to his father that he had managed, reading night and day, to get through everything Hegel had ever written may have been true. After three weeks of renewed effort he announced a complete conversion. A parallel with St. Paul is, perhaps, unavoidable.

He indicated this conversion by starting to hang out with some Young Hegelians in a sort of free-thinking association of intellectuals called the Professors' or Graduates' Club. He was to spend the next three years of his life in this milieu.

These "free spirits," as they called themselves, met in cafés and beer-cellars, wrote subversive poetry, and aired their hatred of the King, the Church, and conventional society.

Hegel's thought was complex enough to nourish countless disciples, especially since in the nature of things it

was not dependent on "proof." The idealists, to whom
nothing in the universe was real but the Spirit, which
manifested itself in Ideas and in turn could be communi-
cated by words, could construct a system that encompassed
everything because the symbolic nature of language makes
infinite abstraction possible. And since it was not necessary
to demand any concrete demonstration of the Spirit, the
wrangling over interpretation was interminable.

Marx was now living on a small amount of money left to,
his mother. He seems to have been paralyzed by his self-
acknowledged frustration as a poet. After his father's death,
he slumped into idleness. He did not even write, which
in view of his sustained literary outbursts during adoles-
cence and afterward may have indicated a sort of suspended
animation.

He retained a student's status, but in the unsupervised
life of a German university this meant almost nothing. He
kept saying, with increasing vagueness, that he was really
planning on a career as a professor, but he fulfilled none
of the conditions for such a career. For three years he
went to the university simply to collect the most indispensable papers at the beginning and end of term, and
sometimes he did not even bother. He had slipped into the
fringes of the student milieu—that is, the students who,
while clinging to their status, did nothing much beyond
chat with each other about all the latest ideas. He spent
half his time in cafés, which in Europe provide marvelous
meeting places for anyone who wishes to sit about in a
cozy atmosphere, reading the latest newspapers free, sip-
ping a beer or coffee, and chatting with friends. There was
no charge for sitting around—for intellectuals it was an
ideal institution.

Most members of the "Professors' Club" were much like
Marx—older students who were a little casual about their

studies—but many of the older men, in their late twenties, ceased coming to chat quite so often and began to settle down in an academic career involving philosophy.

All the members of the Professors' Club were philosophers, each one cultivating a different parcel of the vast terrain on which Hegelianism had staked a claim—the universe itself. Hegelianism was capacious enough for everyone, and the Professors' Club, which consisted of people who thought of themselves as disciples of the Master, busied themselves in their talk and writing with advancing the Master's technique in one direction or another. The results depended on various interpretations of his somewhat obscure utterances, which were necessarily cryptic because of the combination of the vast area taken in by his "System" and the inherent ambiguity of the logic that underlay the system.

Marx's introduction to the singular career he was to make his own was thus via the transmission chamber of the Hegelianism dominant in Prussia at the time. At the Professors' Club, some of whose members were well-known, he was at first a neophyte because of his age, but his conversational powers made him stand out sufficiently for some of the older men to notice and discuss him.

As more of a regular visitor than some of the older students and prospective academicians, he began to make his mark on this milieu. His intelligence, wide reading, polemical vigor, and above all, perhaps, his bent for rhetoric and logical analysis made him a natural member of the coterie.

It was at this loosely organized "Club" that Marx first met and quickly grew quite intimate with some other leaders of a group that today might be called a vanguard. He met Bruno Bauer and his brothers Edgar and Egbert, one Köppen, who had written a history of the French

Terror and was also an early student of Tibetan religion, and Max Stirner, who had given birth to a radical individualism of his own. Marx was to fall out violently with all these men and denounce them with remarkable savagery, but for the time being he was, despite his youth, accepted by them as a welcome acquisition.

Marx completely abandoned his legal studies, as he had his poetry, and immersed himself in philosophy, the only subject that he felt had real significance. He determined to become a lecturer in philosophy at some university. To accomplish this, he and Bruno Bauer set about launching a ferocious atheistic campaign that was to go far beyond the mealy-mouthed moderateness of some of their fellow Hegelians.

Books attacking the traditional assumptions of Christianity helped kindle a generally anti-religious mood that reached a special intensity among the Young Hegelians. The shadings varied considerably—some became violent atheists, others merely wanted to curtail the influence of organized religion on society. Marx cut out a certain position for himself, claiming that he could restore Hegel's prestige by demonstrating that Hegel himself, properly understood, was a complete atheist. Hence his system did not conflict with their anti-religious feelings.

Thus, by the age of nineteen, Marx had impressed his companions, such as Köppen and Bauer, as well as Arnold Ruge, the well-to-do editor of a philosophical periodical designed to be a mouthpiece for the Young Hegelians. Struck by his conversational abilities and polemical brilliance, these men asked him to write, but for the time being he could not organize his thoughts systematically enough. He had not yet, it seems, worked his way through the Hegelian system. He spent his days and most of his nights chatting in the coffee-houses and reading.

By the time he was twenty-two, he had done an enormous amount of reading, but he was well aware that he was in no sense trained and had not the smallest prospect of a livelihood or a profession. A short visit to Trier made it clear to everyone, including his mother, his elder sister Sophie, and especially Ludwig von Westphalen, Jenny's father, that after five years of study he had made no decision about his future. Since he now was secretly affianced, he obviously had to start thinking of a career. His family were fairly comfortable, but he could not live off them indefinitely. When he went back to the cafés of Berlin, it was with a nagging sense that he must bestir himself, for even his conversational companions in the Professors' Club were expecting something of him. Köppen, engaged for some time now on a massive work on Frederick the Great as a free-thinker, had been trying to persuade him to pass an examination for a doctor of philosophy degree that might ensure him a job. Indeed, Marx's name first appeared in print in the dedication to Köppen's book.

Urged on by all his older friends, Marx gradually began assembling the material for a doctoral dissertation. It was to be a comparison of the philosophies of two classical authorities—Democritus and Epicurus. He began writing it in fits and starts without, apparently, getting very involved. His friend Bruno Bauer, enthusiastic about a concrete prospect he had for an actual professorship—in theology, of all things—at the University of Bonn, also encouraged Marx. He promised to help Marx get a university post as soon as he had ensured his own and also to collaborate with him on a campaign of atheism in a new periodical. Bauer felt so certain of his own professorship that Marx was quite sure he would secure an instructorship for him immediately.

The problem of a degree was solved with remarkable

ease. Instead of sitting about waiting to be graduated from the University of Berlin, about which Marx had, after all, been completely lackadaisical, or following Bauer's alternative suggestion that he obtain a degree from the University of Bonn, where the professors were "second-rate," according to Bauer, Marx discovered that he could get one quite easily—by mail—from the University of Jena.

It was as simple as that. Marx sent off his finished dissertation to the philosophy department of Jena in April, 1841, a month before he was twenty-three, and got his Ph.D. a week later. He was now legitimately entitled to call himself Doctor Marx. Since he had a degree, he might have been thought to be on the threshold of his career. The problem was—what career? His hopes were still centered on Bauer's assurances of an academic post. He still had some time to spare, but not much.

He was given a party at a café frequented by the Professors' Club. It signified his farewell to the milieu in which he had spent so much time chatting and reflecting. Now he was to leave it for good, physically and, shortly afterward, spiritually.

CHAPTER III

Journalism: A Conversion
to Socialism: Paris

As there was nothing more for him to do in Berlin, Marx went home to Trier, to await word from Bauer that he had been given an instructorship.

Meanwhile he prepared himself technically for the post by publishing the required scientific work, since so far all he could claim as an academic publication was his dissertation on the two Greek philosophers that had earned him his doctoral degree. He used this and had it printed at his own expense, with the addition of an exceptionally warm, effusive dedication to his future father-in-law, whom all his life he was to regard with an almost idyllic tenderness.

The dissertation was never printed, for Bauer's behavior at Jena had most disastrous consequences not only for his own career but for Marx's.

The atheistic campaign with which Bauer and Marx had been hoping to startle their intellectual world had taken the form of a sort of hoax. The hoax made it appear that a pious anonymous Lutheran attacked Hegel, charging him with atheism and with undermining law, order, and morals, and basing his allegations on quotations from the Master's texts.

The joint work by Marx and Bauer attracted just enough attention to destroy Bauer's, and hence Marx's, chances for a university career. Bauer was kicked out of his university post immediately and could not help Marx, his

junior, get a job at all. Both he and Marx were embittered
by the whole episode. Apparently it had not occurred to
Bauer that a theological faculty might not appreciate one
of its members advocating systematic atheism.

Marx was terribly depressed by the collapse of his
academic hopes. He and Bauer, perhaps unreasonably, considered themselves martyred by the fanatical obscurantism
of the theologians of Bonn as well as by the pietists in
the Prussian Ministry. They thought they had been vic-
timized by a scandalous conspiracy. Marx's hostility
toward anything to do with religion, already powerful,
was reinforced by his bitterness at what he regarded as
outrageous treatment.

But an opportunity of a different kind very quickly presented itself. It marked the end of Marx's academic ambitions, however they are to be assessed, and launched
him on a career of superior journalism that, by immersing
him in "real life," precipitated the curious fusion of social
involvement and dynamic abstraction that was to char-
acterize his career.

A newspaper called the *Rhine Gazette* had been founded
in Cologne at the beginning of 1842 by a group of businessmen, who, in the conventional manner of their class at
the time, were economic liberals, opposed to the monop-
olistic rule of the Prussian government. The newspaper
had been started to counterbalance another, older newspaper, the *Cologne Gazette,* which was also liberal but had
an overridingly Catholic slant that made it the mouthpiece of the predominantly Catholic Rhineland. The
Rhine Gazette was founded, accordingly, to oppose the
Berlin government on specific economic grounds while
remaining sympathetic to Prussia as such, quite unlike the
Cologne Gazette, which was not only Catholic but also

anti-North German in general and had a decided penchant in favor of Catholic France.

The businessmen easily got the required license from the government; the actual management of the paper was left to intellectuals.

A newspaper at that time, consisting as it did of lengthy articles and correspondence by volunteer contributors, did not need much professional editing, though of course it needed some. In the case of the *Rhine Gazette,* two sons of the businessmen who had put up the money were delighted to do the editing. These young men, Georg Jung and Dagobert Oppenheim, illustrated the transition from businessmen to intellectuals that has been conventional in the Western world for generations. The young men were intellectuals and students of Hegel, though professionally they were about to become lawyers, and had even been part of the Young Hegelian milieu in Berlin. They at once set about getting contributors from among their former philosophical cronies.

In this way, the *Rhine Gazette,* independently of its shareholders' attitude, came to be the organ of a Young Hegelian coterie. The Berlin material was to be supplied by Bauer, Arnold Ruge, Köppen, and several others. Various other members of the coterie, scattered throughout the provinces, were to provide the rest.

Thus a paper was started that, though theoretically the organ of a segment of the Rhineland bourgeoisie, was actually run by amateur journalists and sectarian philosophers.

Marx was also asked for a contribution. He promised one but did not send it in until the paper had been running for five months. It was the first time anything of his had been published, and he was still sunk in the in-

dolence brought on by his disappointment over his academic hopes. It also took him several months to satisfy another request, by Arnold Ruge, to send in an article on
how a recent slackening of the Prussian censorship by
King Frederick William IV had not given the press
genuine freedom.

Marx's apathy was compounded by the death of Jenny's
father, who had been his principal protector. Though
Marx's engagement to Jenny had never been discussed
with him, his silence was taken to be the assent that was
indispensable in enabling the young couple to cope with
Jenny's aristocratic family. On top of this, as soon as von
Westphalen had died, after a protracted illness, Jenny's
mother decided to leave Trier.

Young Marx found himself separated once again from
Jenny. He also faced a highly disagreeable and classic
family situation—what was he going to do with himself?
Both his mother, in her simpleminded way, and his more
sophisticated sister agreed that a young man of twenty-four
who was not rich had to do something for a living. His
mother had been left no more than a small pension, and
on this she was obliged to support a large family.

The upshot was that after several months of bickering
Marx's mother and sister cut his allowance and finally
stopped it completely. The long drawn-out argument,
embittered by Marx's assumption that his family were
really "wealthy" and that it was his mother's "rascalities"
that were undermining him, made it difficult for him to
concentrate on writing. Both the young men editing the
Rhine Gazette were disappointed, since they had been
counting on Marx's reputation.

It was at this point when Marx, completely compromised by his association with Bauer in their little

theological hoax, met a man who had a perhaps decisive effect on his career.

Moses Hess, some six years older than Marx, was a Jewish writer from Cologne, the son of a businessman. He was a kindhearted and sincere social radical, and his philosophy was a curious mixture of traditional Judaism, current humanitarian idealism, and some Hegelian ideas. Much admired by young intellectuals, he had recently become a convert to a novel doctrine that had made a powerful impression on many French intellectuals—a new philosophy called "socialism" or "communism." (At this time, and for generations to come, the two words were synonymous and were used interchangeably.)

Hess had been asked, with great deference, by Jung and Oppenheim to give his opinion on various journalistic matters. Naturally he was introduced to Marx.

He was bowled over. This is how he described Marx to a friend: "He is the greatest, perhaps the one genuine philosopher now alive and will soon . . . attract the attention of all Germany. . . . Dr. Marx—my idol's name —is still very young (about twenty-four at most) and will give medieval religion and politics their *coup de grace*. He combines the deepest philosophical earnestness with the most mordant wit. Imagine Rousseau, Voltaire, Holbach, Lessing, Heine, and Hegel fused into one person—I say fused, not tossed together—and you have Dr. Marx."

Though Marx looked down on Hess, partly because Hess had an ardent proselytizing nature and was not much of an original thinker, and partly because Hess was also very much of a Jew (in fact a very early and far-sighted forerunner of Zionism), he was impressed. Hess also had a seminal influence on a young German radical, Friedrich Engels, who was a couple of years younger than Marx and was destined to become his partner in a lifelong enterprise. Both Marx and Engels were later to soft-pedal their debt to Hess, calling him a simpleminded though harmless bore.

Socialism was to fill Marx's life; it may be illuminating to recall the stages by which he progressed from ignorance and indifference to total commitment to it.

Modern socialism, whose origins are doubtless to be found in the upheaval of the French Revolution, was the outcome of a ferment of ideas aimed at the disruption of an existing social order. French thought kindled the idea of socialism and generalized its application to all human society.

Socialist ideas ultimately made their way to Germany, but there was a slight delay before they had an effect. In France, however, different views of a rearrangement of society had taken shape in the first few decades of the nineteenth century.

A characteristic schematization of reform was associated with the name of Charles Fourier, who had conceived a notion, strange to us, perhaps, that all mankind would be better off if it were completely reorganized in what he called "phalanxes." Each of these would be made up of precisely 810 men and 810 women. Fourier had made some complex calculations about the characterological types into which people are biologically divided. Each phalanx was supposed to have its own land and its own capital and congregate in a palace called the "Phalanstère." This somewhat formal idea engendered a whole social movement that had a marked influence on European thought.

A French aristocrat and army officer who had run through a large fortune, the Duke of Saint-Simon, devised a complex system of socialism that was mingled with the ethical teachings of what he understood to be Christianity. Among other things it abolished all rights of inheritance.

The movement, though begun in France, was not restricted to it. In England a highly successful textile manufacturer and businessman, Robert Owen, had not just published works outlining a reform of society—notably *A New View of Society* and *The New Moral World*—but had actually made an initial attempt to translate his ideas into reality. He had devised a "social system," aimed at a gradual transformation of the world into a vast cluster of factories and villages based on cooperation and had founded such societies both in England and in America. These factory-village complexes were meant to serve as models to be imitated everywhere. Owen not merely raised the standard of living of his own factory-workers but managed to increase his private fortune threefold, enabling him to devote still more of it to his idealistic enterprises and to his belief in the perfectibility of society. For the first time, Owen demonstrated the potential of cooperation between capital and labor. His efforts were a milestone in the history of socialism.

It was to be of some interest that these three variants of social reconstruction—Fourierism, Saint-Simonism, and Owenism—despite their differences, which were important, shared a common belief in the idea of "guaranteeing" something by some social device rather than allowing things to be managed through free cooperation between individuals.

Because of this social guarantee, embodied in all approaches to the social problem, the words "socialism" and "communism" made their appearance after the turn of the century. Before their origin was even known, the words were already current in the general discussion that raged among intellectuals. Robert Owen had coined the words in November, 1827, in his own paper, using the terms "we communists or socialists."

It is curious to recall that these two words were coined by a rich businessman.

At this point in Marx's life, while he was still marking time as a sort of unemployed amateur philosopher, Hess's support was very helpful. Hess's prestige among the Cologne intellectuals was so great, and his opinion of Marx so high, that his unqualified endorsement of Marx fortified the confidence of Jung and Oppenheim.

The *Rhine Gazette* was nothing very remarkable, as far as its actual content was concerned. It was a middle-of-the-road organ that mentioned fashionably democratic ideas in veiled terms. Many other newspapers did the same— since the political censorship had softened up, it was not particularly risky.

The paper was actually distinguished not by its specific content but by its unflaggingly cantankerous, scornful, and arrogant tone, which was hidden and sublimated in the most magnificent Hegelian rhetoric. The transcendentalism of Hegelian language made it sound superior to mundane methods of expression. Thus, up to a point, the paper could more easily combine its vaguely radical attitudes with a sort of majestic incomprehensibility—or at least specialization of language—that muffled its punch except to the small coterie of Hegelian intellectuals. The paper dismissed non-Hegelian attitudes as imbecilities and fell into a habit—later to be generalized by the evolution of "Marxist" polemics—of assuming that, since its opponents could not be the cretins they appeared to be, it was necessary to scrutinize their real motives.

Another element in the *Rhine Gazette's* outlook was atheism. It was this obsession of the contributors, in fact, that made them fall foul of the censorship. For though the new king, a sort of mystic, had been relatively indulgent in politics, religion was regarded by him and therefore by the censor as absolutely unassailable. As the contributors began tucking into their articles all sorts of irrelevant sneers at religion, they gradually began to inflame the censor. Their sneers even irritated the paper's Catholic rival, the *Cologne Gazette,* which started to insist, surprisingly, that the censor be still more severe!

In addition, the Berlin contributors, Marx's former cronies from the Professors' Club, had meanwhile become somewhat interested in the new socialist ideas that had been making so much headway in France. The *Rhine Gazette* began publishing whole sentences, paragraphs, and even entire articles whose socialist purport was quite unmistakable. Oddly enough, this did not irritate the government at all, because from its aristocratic point of view, there was nothing remotely reprehensible in taking something away from middle-class manufacturers, aggressive businessmen, and commercial parvenus, and handing it over to other, perhaps even more faithful, subjects of the crown—the masses of the people. Since it was the businessmen, after all, who had been susceptible to all the chatter about democracy, the government may have found it amusing that they should now be embarrassed by more extreme slogans.

Marx himself was startled at first by all the socialist talk, and initially reacted to it with extreme distaste. It was only after his departure from the Berlin Professors' Club that socialist ideas were acclaimed by the Young Hegelian coterie in Germany.

The socialist agitation associated with the names of Fourier, Saint-Simon, and Robert Owen had actually subsided a little in France and England by 1830. From an economic point of view, things had improved. Despite the general poverty, there had been some evidence of a rise in the level of wages. In England, too, some steps had been taken, in the teeth of liberal "laissez-faire," toward helping the working-class—Parliament had passed a law in 1833 against child-labor in textile mills, the most notorious of abuses. The working-class itself had developed a hopeful attitude toward legislation.

There had also been a decline of interest in socialist ideas from a purely doctrinal point of view. The initial zeal on behalf of the novel formulations of Fourier and Saint-Simon had slackened off considerably, and Owen's more practical innovations had not proved very successful. In France both the Fourierists and the Saint-Simonists had become almost ecclesiastical—the Saint-Simonists actually described themselves as a church, and one of Saint-Simon's followers called him a union of Moses and Jesus. Thus, in France, socialist doctrine was relatively neglected in the 1830's.

By 1840, however, a new wave of interest had sprung up and this time flowed into Germany, where it was to have the most widespread and profound results. Three Frenchmen and a German Jew produced works in that year that were to have an explosive effect on the German intellectuals, especially the Young Hegelians.

Pierre-Joseph Proudhon was the son of a brewer who had gone bankrupt. After earning his living as a printer, he went on to immerse himself in the study of society and came to hold a radical view of what he regarded as the basic question in social life—property. His attitude was summed up pithily: "Property is theft."

Another radical writer was the former Governor of Corsica, Etienne Cabet. He described in some detail, in a way that would strike us today as science-fiction, a never-

never land in which society had been completely reorganized to achieve general happiness. The ideas in Cabet's
book, *A Journey to Icaria,* were confined to it, and he was
successful only in making everyone in his dreamland
happy.

Another book was written by Louis Blanc, a radical
journalist in Paris, also in reduced circumstances—his
father had impoverished his family through unwise speculations. Blanc's book was called *The Organization of Labor*
and contained an ingeniously elaborated scheme for the
improvement of life in general.

Hess, while still in his twenties, had also published a
book called *The European Triarchy.* This discussed the
general reform of society with a view to abolishing the
poverty that had oppressed mankind for so long. Hess
maintained that economic factors were far more important
than political factors and that mankind could not be
emancipated without the prior liberation of the working-
class. His main point was that a world in which economic
inequality and exploitation could exist was not a world
where justice could be achieved, and hence that all the
efforts of intellectuals to reform society were inherently
futile. He thought private property was the root of all
evil, and therefore that property, both private and national, had to be abolished. This would entail, of course,
the elimination of all national borders. A new international society could then be built up on a collectivist basis
with reason as its foundation. Hess propagated his views
with unflagging zeal.

The works of these four men, appearing in the wake of
the pioneer efforts during the first third of the century
by Fourier, Saint-Simon, and Owen, gave the Young
Hegelians a tremendous stimulus. Their endless speculations, debates, and wrangles now had a singularly rich sub-

stance to batten on. By linking an attack on God—that is, on the ecclesiastical foundations of society—with an attack on poverty—that is, on the basic condition of the bulk of humanity—there was obviously no limit to the possibilities for both discussion and ultimately, perhaps, action.

The general poverty of mankind was emphasized at this time not just because it was considered a basic, constant condition, but because it was associated with the birth-pangs of the industrial revolution. The fact that technological advances made it possible to make goods much more cheaply seemed to entail the depression of the workers who made the goods. There had been a fantastic increase in wealth as a result of recent technology, typified by new machines and factories, but most of the workers in the modern factories, handling the modern machines, were poorer than ever. They were steeped in the most abysmal poverty imaginable—a new kind of industrial poverty that blighted human relations as much as it heightened human suffering.

It could not be denied that the factory workers were far worse off, actually more miserable, than their predecessors, the craftsmen and artisans. Not only were their wages lower, but they worked longer hours and in far more dis-agreeable circumstances. The standard of living was so low that even children, often no more than six or seven years old, would be put to work for a pittance in some frightful workshop for nine and ten hours a day.

The new machines and factories had the most disastrous effect on the organization of the working stratum of the population. The guilds regulating relations between crafts-men and artisans and their employers had, to a large ex-tent, safeguarded, with their ancient rules and customs, the well-being of their members. They were now bypassed or destroyed by the spread of the machines. The labor market was flooded by masses of untrained workers barely able to work the modern machines, whose efficiency depended on their being so simple that anyone could run them. The machines made fortunes for their owners, but at the time they seemed to depend on the misery of the men who worked them. The swiftly evolving industrial working-class—the "proletariat," as it had begun to be called in France—was hardest hit of all the strata of the population, and for a while seemed the most defenseless.

The despair of untold millions was summed up by the singular phenomenon of the "Luddites"—bands of English workers led by a mythical General Ludd—who for years had been smashing machines, the obvious cause of their distress, in a systematic guerrilla campaign. In retaliation, the destruction of machines had been made a capital offense.

It was these birthpangs of modern capitalism, the frightful distress of the industrial workers at the end of the eighteenth and beginning of the nineteenth centuries, that had first stirred up the initially theoretical interest in socialism or communism of Fourier, Saint-Simon, and Owen. And it was on their theoretical fantasies that the more down-to-earth, or at least more doctrinaire, writers of 1840 now constructed their philosophy.

The Young Hegelians had been swamped by this flood of new and revolutionary ideas. It had the most extravagant effect on them. They did not restrict themselves to publishing their views in the *Rhine Gazette* and elsewhere, but turned their lives topsy-turvy. The Professors' Club had been succeeded by the "Athenians," who called themselves "Freemen"; these Young Hegelians suddenly began badgering the ordinary Berliners. They would launch fantastic parades through the streets and start brawls all over town in public places like theaters, cafés, and for that matter brothels. All this was done under the leadership of Bauer, who thought it immensely entertaining. Other members of the coterie, like Köppen and Ruge, dropped the group completely.

Marx thought Bauer and his followers had taken leave of their senses. He found their scandalous public behavior quite distasteful. He also considered their newly revealed socialistic effusions in the *Rhine Gazette* completely absurd. He had, in any case, started to rebel against the literary style of his philosophical companions—a style that was characterized by a remarkably dense compound of pedanticism, arrogance expressed in a frantic straining after rhetorical effect through impenetrable paradoxes, and contrived epigrams. It was a tortuous prose, tormented by puns and alliteration and probably designed to be only partially understood. Marx's own prose at this time was a splendid example of this curious school of philosophical writing, but in comparison with his peers it was a model of clarity. He was to "settle accounts" with them some five years later, turning on them all with ferocity in a massive work devoted to their total destruction.

In May, 1842, Marx was ready to publish an article—his maiden effort—at the age of twenty-four. His first three articles, unsigned in accordance with custom, attacked both the Prussian government and, more especially, religion. His second article defended the Prussian throne in a rather outmoded dispute about the "ecclesiastical controversy in Cologne" with arguments drawn from atheism. The whole article was suppressed. An attack on the sacrament of marriage in a following article was totally cut out.

The articles were really no more than a way of annoying the censors, since after nine months of existence, the sales of the *Rhine Gazette* amounted to no more than 800 copies. Its rival, the Catholic *Cologne Gazette,* had a circulation ten times as large. Yet the authorities were finally irritated out of their indulgence toward the pretentious, arrogant, and indiscreet writing that characterized the tiny paper. Their problem was made worse by the feeling that they had not licensed the respectable businessmen of Cologne to attack religion. So the question of the license, granted to the businessmen only for a trial year, began to worry the youthful editors as the end of the year came into view.

It was just this that was to give young Marx his opportunity to do something besides write a few articles. He had already told the editors that the difficulties of the newspaper could be blamed on the little "clique" of Berlin "windbags," his former boon companions, and when the editors told Marx that the government had hinted to them that their license would not be renewed under the present current management, Marx recommended a policy of extreme prudence—as nothing should be printed that might annoy the government, the management must be changed.

The implication was obvious: Marx looked like a natural replacement. He was given a brief interview by the owners of the magazine; after only a few hours of consultation, they offered him the editorship-in-chief.

Thus, by the middle of his twenty-fifth year, in 1843, Marx was at last in a position to participate actively in the tussle of views that was being carried on in advanced circles in Germany. After only four articles for the *Rhine Gazette* and another two for Arnold Ruge's periodical, he had been offered the management of a daily newspaper.

As the new editor-in-chief, he sent a letter to the government on the future conduct of the paper that was a model of prudence and dignity. While Marx denied in principle that the government had any particular right to fire the editor-in-chief, the latter had been replaced. He also agreed that though in religious matters it was easy to produce free-thinking quotations from the works of none other than Frederick the Great, the paper would nevertheless steer clear of "clerical and religious subjects," unless it had to deal with them because of political circumstances or because of articles in other periodicals.

His letter also pointed out that the *Rhine Gazette* had been very pro-Prussian in general and had highlighted "North German science" in contrast not only to French "superficiality" but also to "South German theories." The paper had done its best to "introduce the North German and Protestant spirit into the Rhineland." In short, Marx displayed diplomatic qualities not generally associated with his temperament.

He then found occasion to establish his thoroughgoing antipathy to any form of "socialist" or "communist" ideas, which had only recently begun infiltrating the world of German thought. To make a clear cleavage between the *Rhine Gazette* and another organ of opinion (the Augsburg *General Gazette*) Marx stated unequivocally that the *Rhine Gazette* could "not even grant any theoretical validity to communist ideas, much less desire their practical implementation, or even consider them possible."

Up to this point Marx had been successively a poet and a philosopher, with perhaps a special bent for abstract legal problems. But the necessity of taking up an attitude on socialistic or communistic ideas, which initially he was quite hostile to, meant that he would, finally, have to study them seriously. For the first time, he began to read the new literature, starting with Proudhon.

From a practical point of view, as editor-in-chief, it was now also important for him to clarify his relationship with his former Berlin cronies. Having been instrumental in replacing the former editor-in-chief, the tempestuous Dr. Rutenberg—to whom he referred at one time as his "closest friend"—Marx wrote a violent reply to a letter from the "Freemen" in Berlin in which he was asked why he was abandoning the views they had previously held in common.

Marx was remarkably unambiguous. He rounded on the "Freemen" completely and broke off all relations. He denounced their "vague arguments and highfalutin phrases," and vowed to block any "smuggling in of communist and socialist dogma into casual dramatic reviews" —he called it "immoral"—and promised to censor everything they wrote more remorselessly than a real censor. He made a point of publicly dissociating the *Rhine Gazette* from the Freemen, who had actually written half of it up to then. The whole of the Professors' Club, including his one-time mentor and friend Bruno Bauer, was now to be denounced as an enemy.

Marx had a marvelous time as editor-in-chief. The lethargy that had plagued him periodically as a young man, attacking him in between bursts of enthusiasm and activity, left him completely. He flung himself with singular energy into the work of writing, editing, and corresponding.

There is a curious description of Marx by an assistant, Carl Heinzen, in his memoir; it is not very friendly. Heinzen describes Marx at this age as puny, with jet-black hair and a sallow complexion. His forehead was rather low, Heinzen tells us, and in "his small, dark, short-sighted eyes there shone an intelligent and malicious flare." His mind was "amazingly penetrating," but his character was in all respects unpleasant. Heinzen relates that Marx became very agreeable over some good wine. When they adjourned to a tavern every evening to relax over a drink, Marx would become merry and unaffected, although otherwise he was, in Heinzen's words, "an unreliable egoist and a lying intriguer," "swayed by envy" even more than by "his own ambition." Over one bottle after another, Marx would play about with the repetition of the same, rather odd joke, according to Heinzen—turning to someone at the table, he would repeat, again and again, the same sentence: "I'm going to annihilate you!"

This period as an editor was probably one of Marx's most pleasant interludes, but it lasted only a short time. He had taken it over in October, 1842, after the newspaper had been in existence for just ten months. It went on splendidly for another few months, until almost the end of the trial year. He had run it with decorum, and the censor had even said that "the tone of the paper is undoubtedly much calmer." Marx had been expending immense energy, running the paper with great highhandedness, while the people under him were delighted to let him do the bulk of the work. Though the tone of the *Rhine Gazette* continued to be very vigorous, he had never overstepped the bounds set up in his letter to the authorities.

From their point of view, of course, the newspaper had had a slightly checkered career. Published by impeccably respectable Rhineland businessmen, it had, under the guidance of some young intellectuals, specialized at first in long muckraking attacks on the Prussian censorship, the Federal Diet, and on landowners in general. It had not been popular, but it had managed to annoy the authorities as it acquired a small reputation throughout Germany, while the shareholders were startled by the newspaper's intransigent tone on so many subjects. But since the paper was very liberal on economic matters, sponsoring free trade and the economic unification of Germany—

both cherished goals of the rising middle-class—nothing was said. The Prussian authorities were also influenced by their desire not to vex the provinces, only recently annexed. Marx's policy of moderation was very reassuring to them.

Then Marx went too far, perhaps because he overestimated the apathy of the authorities, as well as of the newspaper's shareholders. He launched an attack on two particular subjects that were the focus of intense feeling in the Rhineland: the impoverishment and exploitation of the grape-growing peasantry in the Moselle province, and the severe laws against the stealing of wood by poor people in the local forests. Marx took both issues as a springboard for a ferocious assault on the government, which was made up of landowning gentry. He was later to say that it was his reflection on the background of these apparently simple thefts of wood by poor people that led him to his major theory—"historical materialism."

In any case, the Prussian government, cautiously sounding out the public sentiment in the Rhineland, began to tighten the screws on the *Rhine Gazette*. For a while Marx played a sort of game with the censorship; he squeezed through its meshwork some scarcely veiled articles on both democracy and republicanism. Though the censor was replaced by an official who was stricter, the game might have continued if Marx had not gone overboard by including as a target of his polemics the Czar of Russia.

Czarist Russia was regarded by all liberals at this time as the absolute incarnation of intellectual obscurantism and political repression. It was quite routine to attack it as the source of strength for all reactionary forces in Europe, which could look to the Czarist autocracy as a bottomless well of moral and material support for their own repressive policies.

In a number of leading editorials, Marx attacked Russia, at this time the leading partner in the current alliance between Russia and Prussia. It came to the eyes of Czar Nicholas I himself, "the gendarme of Europe," who instantly expressed his annoyance to the Prussian ambassador, who in turn passed it on to the King of Prussia.

This was not the only cause of friction between Marx and the government. He gave vent to his anti-clerical feelings by printing a letter—unfortunately filched from the Ministry in Berlin!—about a plan for a new divorce law in which the king was interested. Marx was incautious enough to print the actual document, despite the fact that it had been stolen, and appended an article with a clear-cut atheistic bias.

The authorities lost patience very suddenly. The King of Prussia, at a cabinet meeting held just three months after Marx had taken over the editorship, withdrew the license that enabled the "whore on the Rhine" to carry on her business. The more or less cat-and-mouse game that had been played with the paper during the preceding year was over, and though the authorities were broadminded enough to allow the paper to go on appearing until the first quarter of the new year was over, out of consideration for the shareholders, Marx's brief journalistic career seemed definitely ended.

The suppression of the paper caused something of a sensation not only in Prussia, but wherever such things were taken seriously in Germany. The mere fact that the government had suppressed it appeared to imply that the contents had been violent enough to require suppression. Because of this classical aspect of inverse propaganda—suppression heightens sales—the little newspaper, which had boasted only 800 readers before Marx, had 1,800 readers when the government issued its first policy ultimatum before Marx became editor. It increased its circulation still more substantially during the remainder of the three-month period it was allowed to live on. Petitions signed by thousands were sent to the king, and such a commotion was kicked up by the suppression of the *Rhine Gazette* that in spite of Marx's bitter disappointment at the loss of his position it created a sort of heroic nimbus around his personality.

Marx skillfully helped arrange this nimbus himself, for through his initiative an article appeared in another paper presenting him as the hero of the suppression. The article was based on material supplied by Marx, and the impression created by it, as well as by the distortion of the politics behind the suppression of the paper, started a legend about the heroic democratic radicalism of the *Rhine Gazette*.

Yet it is clear that the actual sequence of events had far more to do with Marx's atheism than with any real interest he had, at this time, in democracy. Marx always had an immense intuitive feeling for the value of legends, and the legend of the *Rhine Gazette*, while exalting Marx's personal "heroism" in running the newspaper, blurred both his initial posture of compliance with respect to the censorship and the fact that when he took over the paper he was still hostile to socialism. It was he who had suppressed the socialist attitudes fashionable among his former cronies in Berlin.

Marx transformed himself into a martyr as a result of the suppression of the *Rhine Gazette*. His feeling of martyrdom, expressed in a fury of rage against the bourgeoisie, against the Prussian tyranny, against practically all institutions extant, was now to be linked to a complex of ideas—socialism—that he had been reading about since he had become editor.

Throughout 1843 he worked with unusual zeal, reading

the works of French socialists and immersing himself in recent French and German history and also in the history of art, both ancient and modern. He seems to have been searching for socio-historical material with which to support his view of the essentially explosive force of Hegel's intellectual categories, despite Hegel's personal political attitudes. Together with so many other Hegelians, including the Russians, who also looked up to the Master, he regarded Hegel's categories as constituting—in the phrase of the celebrated Russian political journalist Herzen—the "algebra of revolution," in the sense that with proper coaxing the revolutionary processes imminent in nature could be extrapolated by reason, which could then further them through conscious, critical thought. As Herzen had written, old Hegel himself had been "too frightened openly to apply" them in the "storm-tossed ocean of politics." Instead he had "set them afloat in the tranquil inland lake of aesthetic theory."

Marx was to change all this, and his discovery of the vehicle that would transplant Hegel's categories from their celestial arena to the blood and dirt of reality was to be made within the next twenty months. Between the spring of 1843 and somewhere short of the end of 1844, the whole of his future career was contained in embryo. In few careers is there such a clearly marked-out period of incubation ending in the emergence of a personality. One might liken the twenty months to the chrysalis stage of Marx's life. When he emerged from the chrysalis at the end of the twenty months, he was the Marx that is familiar to posterity.

But in April, 1843, by now almost twenty-five, Marx was still no more than a fairly well-known political journalist with a slight halo of martyrdom. He was known as a stormy petrel specializing in attacks on reactionary regimes, but he still had no *special* goal. He had not yet formed his own approach to events, he was not yet a socialist, and he had no job. He was almost in the same position as he had been after leaving his student days behind him in Berlin.

Marx at this time had nothing whatever to tie him to Germany—he had never had the smallest interest in his family except for his father, and now that his father was dead and he had no way to express his ideas and feelings, there was nothing to stop him going. He was bored and irritated by his former Berlin associates and by the whole Young Hegelian milieu. Not only had he shaken loose from their ideas, which seemed to him pretentious, shallow verbiage, but he also loathed the scandalous extravagance of their private lives. Wilful bohemianism now repelled him. All his life he was to detest it as a sort of playing up of middle-class conventions precisely by flouting them. For him, bohemian affectations revealed exactly the same vulgar philistinism as the customs of the middle-class itself.

But a Young Hegelian connection, Dr. Arnold Ruge, was now to prove of decisive importance. Marx wrote to ask Ruge whether he could think of some job for him abroad, since he wanted to leave not only Prussia but Germany. Ruge also was having some administrative difficulties. His own periodical, the *German Yearbooks,* had been ruined by the King of Prussia when the *Rhine Gazette* was suppressed. Though published in Saxony, and hence outside the direct power of Prussia, the magazine obviously needed access to Prussian readers. After it was forbidden entry, its fate was as good as sealed.

Ruge combined the atheism he continued to preach, in the characteristic Young Hegelian manner, with the democracy then becoming modish in oppositionist circles. He had spent six years in a Prussian jail for advocating democracy, and though he had become more cautious in

Saxony, he made no bones about his basic beliefs. His reputation as a democrat was heightened by having recently published an essay, *Reaction in Germany*, which had made something of a sensation.

Its author was a young Russian aristocrat, Mikhail Bakunin, writing under a pen name. Bakunin was a physical giant, a geyser of energy and emotional magnetism. He was already famous in the fashionable drawing rooms of Berlin and Dresden and had become notorious for preaching a coming revolution in Europe—a revolution based on freedom and democracy. Bakunin was later to become celebrated as the apostle of pure anarchism, based on the utter annihilation of all traditional institutions. His essay in Ruge's *German Yearbooks* helped finish the magazine, but since it was a philosophical organ, it did not cause nearly as much commotion as the suppression of the daily newspaper Marx had been editing.

In any case, Ruge, despite his negative opinion of Marx's character, regarded him as a potentially useful contributor, especially as he had been thinking of starting up his *Yearbooks* somewhere else. He settled matters quickly and found a publisher who said he would print the magazine in France or Belgium if Ruge contributed a fairly substantial sum toward it, some 20,000 francs. By June, 1843, everything was arranged. Marx was to be paid 1,800 francs a year, plus additional fees for his own contributions. The combined salary would enable Marx to live adequately, though modestly.

Once Marx had made up his mind to leave Germany, it was necessary for him to settle his marriage to Jenny. Their engagement had lasted already for some seven years, and he had been away from her almost all the time. With his future seemingly anchored, at least for the moment, in Ruge's plan for collaboration on a periodical abroad, the marriage had to be decided on once and for all, and the opposition of Jenny's family had to be circumvented or overcome.

During their engagement Jenny had suffered from a variety of qualms; Marx had been tormented by her indecisiveness. Now, however, her mind was made up, and she did all the battling needed. Her determination was irresistible. With some help from a rather bohemian brother—Edgar, whose name was to appear later with Marx's on some socialist publications—she fought tenaciously against her whole family, who were appalled at the idea of being associated with a rank outsider like Marx, now known as a radical, an atheist, and at best a middle-class Jewish ne'er-do-well. Another brother in the von Westphalen family was destined, after all, to become the Prussian Minister of the Interior. To safeguard the social situation that would make this kind of appointment possible, Jenny's mother did her best to change Jenny's mind.

It proved impossible, and Jenny's mother submitted very gracefully. The same month the *Rhine Gazette* closed down, Marx married Jenny, and since he had no means of support until he could work on Ruge's periodical, Jenny's mother invited them to stay with her in her house in Kreuznach. She put them up for five months after their marriage.

Jenny was Marx's youthful and indeed his only love. She was to devote her whole life to him and to his activities. Her family's opposition to the match had done no more than heighten her loyalty to Marx, to whom she remained subordinated throughout her life, a subordination based on love, unqualified admiration, and faith. She had, in addition, an intensely jealous nature. Marx in his turn never wavered in his own attachment, except, perhaps, for a "domestic" love affair he was to have much later on with their servant. Throughout his life he was proud of Jenny's beauty, her origins, and her intellect. Her charm and wit were unusual, and her devotion, soon to be tested by Marx's adverse circumstances and become the foundation of their life together, was extraordinary.

Marx's new venture converged with the development of his relationship to Moses Hess. He had been looking down on Hess for some time, calling him the "communist rabbi," partly because of his slightly comical appearance— "tall and scrawny, with kind eyes and a rooster-like curve to his neck"—and partly because of his benevolent, sermonizing manner. Hess spoke very mildly, full of manifest goodwill, about abstract ideals like love, justice, humanity, and so on.

Hess had been making converts to his ideas on socialism for some time, and in that winter of 1842–43 he had converted a German bourgeois, Friedrich Engels, who was a couple of years younger than Marx. Engels, described at this time as "a slender youth with a look of almost boyish immaturity"—a look he was to retain for many years— was the son of a solid textile manufacturer in northern Germany. Since he was supposed to become a businessman, he had never gone to a university but had started working for his father at the age of seventeen. He was an incredibly energetic student on his own, however. He consumed books in all fields and wrote with stupefying fluency in all sorts of literary styles. He was, moreover, systematically rebelling against the stuffy, lifeless Protestantism of his father's household.

In his leisure time Engels hung out with the Young Hegelians. On a trip home to Barmen he had met Marx, though only fleetingly, as Marx was suspicious of his intimacy with the Young Hegelians, with whom he was in the midst of breaking off.

Hess had had a remarkable triumph in converting Engels on this visit. He was delighted at having made the "most enthusiastic communist" out of such a talented young man, while Engels was to acknowledge Hess as having been "the first to make communism plausible to me and my circle."

Now, after Marx's disappointment over the fiasco with the *Rhine Gazette,* Hess found him also receptive to his missionary zeal. Hess, who had been in Paris, where he had met all the authors of the books that had appeared with such success in 1840 as well as countless other intellectuals and was brimming over with the fashionable concepts of socialism and communism, now preached all his basic ideas to Marx. The root of all evil was to be found in money, profit, and property. To uproot this evil all society must be reconstructed from top to bottom. Hess was able to tell Marx all this not just as an abstract speculation but as the reflection of a bona fide movement among intellectuals in France, the homeland of culture.

In these discussions Marx, while moved by the news of this intellectual turbulence, missed an element that from his Hegelian point of view was essential—its inevitability. Like Hegelians in general—after all, Hess, too, was a Hegelian—Marx had to be convinced that something was desirable not simply because it had moral value—an essentially capricious notion—but because it was rational—rooted in reality. Thus movements in human affairs could not be brought about because someone thought they were necessary, or sensible, or meritorious: they happened because they *had* to happen. The concept of a thing bearing within itself the seeds of its own destruction meant that one cycle of being, or one stage of history, could be terminated only after it had exhausted all its potentialities. Then, and only then, could such a stage of being or history succeed in negating itself to ascend to a still higher stage of being.

Hess had to agree that this was certainly so, and that the new stage of socialist society could come into existence only because its preceding stage, the property-owning social order, was definitely finished. But Hess had not proved this, and until it could be proven, it was bound to be regarded as no more than a sentimental utopia. Hence Hess's version of socialism, filtered by and modified from the ideas of the new school of French socialists, was still unacceptable to Marx, the rigorous Hegelian.

There were, of course, also temperamental differences between him and Hess, whose nature was rather conciliatory, whereas Marx's nature, as Hess recorded, had more of a "disintegrating" force. Characteristically, Hess was moved by compassion for suffering mankind on an emotional level, a feeling quite alien to Marx, who was preoccupied with tracing the logical consequences of applying his basically Hegelian system-making to social life. Emotionally he was inspired more by the idea of an ultimate reversal of values than by the elevation of the meek in spirit. Initially he was not moved at all by the purely social indignation of, say, a later rival like Lassalle.

Yet in one way or another Marx, after the *Rhine Gazette* fiasco, and in contradiction to the promise he had made just before the debacle to look into the new communist ideas before annihilating them, became a convert to those very ideas. By the summer of 1843 Marx was considered by those who knew him best to be already a socialist, which at the time did not imply any necessary distinction from a democrat. The differences between the two approaches to society were still blurred.

While Marx was staying with his mother-in-law, Ruge

wrote him that it had been decided to move the new periodical to Paris. The title was to be changed, appropriately enough, to the *German-French Yearbooks*. The periodical was to be put forth as the organ of an "intellectual alliance between the Germans and the French," and the masthead would read "published by Arnold Ruge and Karl Marx."

The idea of such a spiritual alliance between the Germans and French, each leavening the other with seriousness and brilliance was novel and regarded as rather explosive. It was supposed to attract the most brilliant contributions from the most famous writers and thus stimulate a wave of interest in both countries.

Accordingly, in November, 1843, at the age of twenty-five and a half, Marx emigrated to Paris with Jenny. Because he was known to some extent as a journalist and was considered a liberal with a rather acid pen, it was assumed that he had left Germany because of his excessively vehement belief in democracy.

In Paris he was to undergo his final and most radical transformation, to emerge the figure that he was to remain the rest of his life. His stay there was decisive, both intellectually and emotionally.

But it is ironical to reflect, on looking back at his career from our vantage-point, that Marx's activities had a unity at this time that they were to lose as the result of the exile he was to be forced into a few years later.

For up until his exile, Marx's activities were fused into a unity of "theory and practice," as he liked to say, that afterward would not be possible. Exile would bring out his scholarship, his erudition, and his intellectual qualities in general but prevent him from being the man of action that his espousal of socialism made him for a time. Exile greatly magnified the intellectual side of his nature and heightened the importance of his role as the inspiration of action in others—it was to curtail his own.

Ruge had been thoughtful enough to rent a little house for them in the Faubourg St. Germain, but his very friendliness was to prove a slight embarrassment to Marx, who had already, after all, shifted the intellectual base of his collaboration with Ruge without Ruge's awareness. Ruge was not a socialist at all. On the contrary, he thought the ultimate goal that socialists were leading up to would end in a mere "police and slave state." In this opinion he distinguished himself from the many enthusiasts for whom the two varieties of thought, democracy and socialism, were deeply akin. Ruge was already persuaded that they were not only different but incompatible.

The first issue of the *German-French Yearbooks* came out a few months later, in February 1844. It had proved impossible to get any famous writers to contribute to it, so the whole issue was filled with articles quickly put together by Hess, who was still not well-known, and by the young Engels, who was not known at all. Of the famous Germans, in fact, only Heine, who had a European reputation, was persuaded by Marx to send in a contribution, and that turned out to be a poem. Of everything that appeared in the magazine, only Marx's articles were important, and they were important chiefly from the point of view of his personal development.

Marx's two articles were on Hegel's philosophy and, oddly enough, on the Jews. During his stay with Jenny's mother in Germany, Marx had begun thinking through his own approach to socialism. The two articles embodied, in a somewhat inaccessible way, the beginnings of his own formulation. Though we now can see that the articles laid down perhaps the most important points in Marx's formulation of his views, the articles themselves mentioned socialism only as a sort of digression. Neither Hegel nor the "Jewish question" seemed a springboard for discussing socialism—the article on Hegel had all the abstruseness of such articles, while the one on the Jews was so filled with a peculiar vituperative, abusive quality that it made a curious impression of paranoid extremism.

The essay on the Jews was a spirited retort to one by Bruno Bauer, who had attempted to demonstrate that before the Jews had the logical right to claim social emancipation they had to be baptized. Marx said that the Jews no longer existed as a racial or even a religious group but had been squeezed into a purely economic category because of the way they had been handled by their neighbors. Thus they could be emancipated only when the whole of European society was regenerated. Baptism would simply mean the replacement of one set of chains by another, and mere political liberties were too superficial to be of any value.

Marx seems to have been determined not to be bothered by any references to his personal origins. His essay represents an attempt to settle the question, as far as he was concerned, once and for all. He was declaring, in short, that the Jewish "problem" was simply fictitious—a mere mask for real social afflictions that when finally alleviated or healed would obliterate the whole Jewish dilemma. It was his last formal statement on Jewish affairs, and though his writings were to contain countless references, generally acid, to individual Jews, he never showed anything but hostility to all Jewish institutions and kept himself strictly disengaged from any indication of sympathy with Jews.

In his article, Marx identified the Jews, as he was to do later on, with what he regarded as the very essence of the

bourgeoisie—money. "What is the secular cult of the
Jews? Bargaining. What is their secular God? Money." He
wrote this at a time when the overwhelming majority of
the Jews in Europe lacked the remotest connection with
money-making. Millions of them, in Eastern Europe,
were practically out of touch with the beginnings of the
capitalist process in Europe. In the West, the Jewish elite
—the artists and writers—had already turned their backs
on it. Thus the idea of using bargaining to sum up Jewish
life seemed very one-sided, and the fact of Marx's origins
made his concentration on the financial aspect look a little
obsessive.

The article on Hegel is important in a study of Marx,
since it indicates the beginning of a definitive break with
his former master. It took him a few years to break with
Hegelianism formally, or, at any rate, in his own mind. He
was to do so through creating a system of his own that
laid the foundations of an actual movement, based on its
own dogmatism and a definite scheme of political activity.
It led to a revolution of action and ideas that still domi-
nates a vast segment of the human race.

Yet despite the superficial irrelevance of the two articles to a formulation of Marx's view of socialism and
despite the fact that they attracted no attention when they
were published, they contained four points scattered about
that were to remain the cornerstones of Marx's evolving
theory.

The first point was the insistence on inevitability as
the justification of the new order. The property system
was bound to decay beyond redemption before it could be
replaced by the next stage. As a Hegelian, Marx therefore
felt bound to demonstrate that the property system had to
go because it was time for it to go. He summed it up: "The
system of commerce, money-making, property, and human

exploitation leads to a breach in present-day society that the old system is incapable of healing."

This bald statement, of course, however persuasive it seems intellectually, or perhaps emotionally, would obviously need to be backed up by some sort of data in order to carry conviction. Many contemporary socialists, including the religiously minded Saint-Simon, had made the point that the transition to a better order would take place in the natural course of events—for a Hegelian, of course, that was just so much ABC. So far Marx had never looked at a book of economics, a study that had made a significant beginning only in the generation before. Yet even before embarking on the study of the facts and figures presumably contained in this bourgeoning science of economics, Marx thought it quite safe to claim the appropriate inevitability for his prediction.

The second point that he took as his own, and to which he remained fairly faithful, on the whole, for most of his career—with some significant later modifications—was that of armed revolution.

He phrased it in a formula that became classic: "The arms of criticism cannot replace criticism by arms. Material power must be overthrown by material power."

It is true that some socialists had made much of the idea of overthrowing the status quo by armed force. Even in England the radical wing of the Chartist movement, to say nothing of the extremist, machine-destroying Luddites, advocated the use of force. On the other hand, the socialists of Marx's own time were firmly against the idea of force. All of them—Saint-Simon, Owen, Proudhon, Hess —believed that the new, morally superior social order would come into being peaccably, through the progress of the forces of goodness within the hearts of men. Hess put it perhaps most touchingly (or sentimentally, depending on how one looks at it): "No social class would be so heartless as to leave fellow-men in misery if it could make them all happy."

Marx thought this preposterous sentimentality. He believed that human beings had material motivations, and therefore were quite incapable of doing anything because of mere ethics and were bound to behave on the basis of economic interest. Hence, since the material interests of the propertied classes were threatened by the inevitability of the new order, it seemed quite obvious to Marx that the only lever for effecting a change in society was force.

It is true that this formula contradicted—from a purely logical point of view, irreconcilably—the idea of inevitability. Putting it succinctly, if a revolution in the social order was inevitable, why was force necessary? Conversely, if force was actually needed, what was the point of calling the transition inevitable?

Force implies resistance; resistance implies the possibility of success. Both together imply doubt as to the outcome. Thus socialism cannot be called inevitable if its arrival is in doubt; the need for violence implies that its arrival is *not* inevitable.

The logical—and practical—contradiction between these two concepts was to lead to basic difficulties throughout the socialist movement in which Marxism was to play a preeminent role. It could never be resolved, in theory, since it was rooted in a logical contradiction, and in practice it could be solved only be finding various rationalizations for choosing one concept over the other in implementing a political program. Its practical resolution was perhaps to be found in the interaction of character and circumstances rather than in the application of any particular "theory" to events, despite what different theoreticians maintained.

But regardless of the logical difficulties and practical problems arising out of the contradiction, which were to trouble the socialist movement for decades and which have never, in fact, been resolved, Marx soared above the problem and embraced the two extremist and irreconcilable formulae simultaneously.

A third point he plumped for revolved around the role of the "proletariat." This had been a subject of discussion for some years, ever since the French Revolution, during which it had become apparent that in addition to the three estates comprising the country before the revolution— the nobility, the clergy, and the middle-class, or bourgeoisie—there was another group—the bulk of the people—that owned nothing at all and had no stake whatever in the country beyond their own persons. This group had been named, in the conventional erudite manner, after the most miserable social group in ancient Rome, whose sole function was to produce children (*proles*). The definition of this social group had led to an endless amount of theorizing about what the relationship was between it and the rest of society.

Different people in a given society have stakes in it of different value. Rewards and deprivations are obviously not allocated equally. The basic problem can be loosely summed up by asking whether the differences are irreconcilable—that is, whether one class is bound to lose when another gains—or whether another state of society can benefit all classes more or less equally or at least fairly.

The idea of a conflict between classes, which was to become a cornerstone of what was later to be called "Marxism," was a commonplace. The question was really one of degree—just how far did that conflict go?

For some decades the most important French socialists had been maintaining that the conflict between classes extended over a relatively minor zone, beyond which the common interests of all classes in society were joined together. Their main point was that the reform of society, the transition to socialism, would benefit everyone equally even if some were still too blind to see it. Only a few men thought that the rise of the lower class inevitably implied the destruction of the upper class.

Marx now adopted an extreme version of this theory of social irreconcilability. He laid it down that the proletariat's opposition to the rest of society was not merely "unilateral" but "multilateral"—there was nothing *whatever* connecting the proletariat with the rest of society, *no* interest shared in common. Hence the antagonism of the proletariats to the rest of society was in effect universal. No one could help them, and they must in consequence "free themselves."

Marx had never actually seen any members of the industrial working-class and was not, in any case, particularly interested in psychology, yet now he laid it down, as a concomitant of the unique role assigned it in the class war that was to usher in the new order, that the proletariat, in contrast with all other strata of society, possessed an unspoiled "naive folk-soul." It was in the grip of "total injustice" and "universal suffering." Its "chains" were "fundamental." His identification with the proletariat—perhaps with the idea rather than with the reality—was to be a permanent feature of his general theory. Later on he made attempts to support this basic attitude with concrete data; he never deviated from it as a principle.

Most important of all, for an understanding of Marx's later development and the general course of Marxist socialism, was his fourth point—the scientific nature of the whole struggle.

This idea of science was fundamental, not just in the

assertions that would be made by Marx and all his followers, but in the emotional tug that the novel formulation
exercised over so many temperaments and minds. It was
the claim of scientific validity for his theories that gave
Marx a special emotional position in the world of socialism
and his followers, perhaps, a feeling of election.

For it was this claim of scientific precision, scientifically
established inevitability, scientific necessity, that enabled
Marx to bridge the gap between the facts and his predictions. So far there had not been a trace of any proletarian
involvement in the theories that had been formed about
society as a whole and about the proletariat specifically.
All this theorizing had been done by intellectuals of one
kind or another—middle-class, lower-middle-class, occasionally aristocratic. The whole notion of a world not
based on private property but governed by ethical principles of a new sort had developed independently of the
proletariat. The very conception of this property-less society had been contrived by millionaires and the sons of
millionaires, by manufacturers, businessmen, intellectuals, and noblemen. It was obviously not a movement *of*
the lower class, *of* the proletariat but a movement that
had been conceived by the superior classes in society *on
behalf of* the working-class. Insofar as the working-class
had been active as it had been in organizations and trade-
unions—it had not concerned itself with changing the
social order as such. It was simply bent on improving its
own condition within the general framework of society
as it existed.

Hence the idea of the proletariat "freeing itself" could
actually be understood only in the sense of a certain kind
of organization—that of an army headed by the general
staff, the intellectual leadership. Thus it was this philosophy, ultimately rooted in Hegel, that was to constitute the

executive head of the army, whose ranks were made up of
the proletariat, as yet unconscious of its crucial historical
role.

Philosophy, queen of the sciences, was to be the
architect of a new order, and the scientists, or philosophers, were to be in charge of the transition to the new
order and of the order itself.

This predilection for science was common to all the
socialist thinkers. It was only natural, after all, for them to
believe that their thought was founded on the observation
of phenomena and on the methodical deduction of conclusions from these observations. Moreover, advances in
the natural and exact sciences, and in the technology based
on them, had been so staggering that intellectuals in all
fields were mesmerized. Even unequivocal emotionalists
would lay claim to "science" to sanction their own work;
the three principal French socialists had all been zealous partisans. Saint-Simon's views constituted the "science
of universal gravitation." Fourier's notions were "the
sure science." Proudhon spoke of mankind's task as the
construction of "the temple of science." In short, the adora-
tion of "science," which in our own day has reached unprecedented heights—the word itself has somehow become
iconized into an object of reverence—was already installed
as the basic element in any theory intended to influence
the minds of intellectuals.

In this respect Marx was quite conventional. What was
to be unconventional in his own approach was the con-
sistency and the firmness with which he held to the view
that it was his system alone that was *really* scientific,
whereas the theories of other socialists were so much sentimental twaddle.

The curious thing about this period in Marx's life,
which was crucial for his future career, was that though

he had only just been converted to a belief in socialism, he never deviated from these principles, formulated when he was twenty-five years old. His four principles—inevitability, force, the uniqueness of the proletariat, and "scientism"—which, in view of his youth and more especially, of their initial appearance in a random, digressive form in two unimportant articles, might have been considered a demonstration of youthful bravura, were in fact the foundations of his later system.

It will be seen that Marx's attempt to associate the qualities of inevitability and scientism with his own tentative formulation of socialism was a reflection of his Hegelian roots. The attempt foreshadowed his famous later remark that he had, by turning Hegel upside down, put his feet on the ground, by placing him not in the sphere of ideas but in the real world.

Marx's philosophical transition from the pure idealism of Hegel to his own claim that the victory of the proletariat was to be the ultimate triumph of German philosophy was triggered by a philosophical work published in 1843.

Theses on the Hegelian Philosophy, by Ludwig Feuerbach, was read by Marx in the full flush of his hatred for the hairsplitting abstractions and subtleties of his former Young Hegelian cronies. Marx, who now had a violent aversion to his old milieu, found Feuerbach's attack on Hegel interesting as an instance of the materialism he had come to long for by way of contrast to the excessive abstraction of Hegel and most Hegelians.

It had been one of Hegel's primary claims that everyone living in a given cultural epoch was infused somehow with the same "spirit," which displayed itself in all the ideas and institutions of that epoch. Feuerbach dismissed this as rubbish. He asked, quite simply, what the spirit of an age could consist of except the sum of the phenomena that constituted it. Feuerbach maintained that this claim meant that the phenomena were determined by themselves—an evidently silly tautology.

Nor could this label be taken as a pattern or model of some kind. Such labels, like "the Greek genius" or "the spirit of the Renaissance," were abstractions that might prove handy rhetorical devices for referring to vast complexes of events but were not in themselves real elements of the real world. Feuerbach felt that the more traditional view, which explained events by the people who were their primary causes, was inadequate. On the other hand, it was far more sensible to highlight the role of people, who at least existed, than to talk about purely abstract personifications of ideas.

According to Feuerbach, Hegel was correct in stressing the shallowness of the view that people were primary in causing historical events, since this theory failed to explain how a result could be derived from the mere interaction of a large number of individuals. Hegel was certainly right in seeking some underlying common element, or force, that could make history understandable.

But Hegel's final system was also a preposterous fiasco, Feuerbach said, since it ended up with no more than a mystical substitution of the Absolute Idea for the old-fashioned personal God of Christianity—if that Idea was not to be understood as a rhetorical tautology for the events it was supposed to elucidate.

Feuerbach, a materialist, went in the opposite direction. Agreeing that a common factor of historical processes was needed, he found it in the sum total of the material conditions that determined both the behavior and the thought of the men who lived in those conditions. Their idealistic illusions were caused simply by the absence of various things on earth—namely, justice, harmony, unity. They simply projected these into an ideal, transcendental sphere, which they then called real in order to comfort themselves. Then to comfort themselves further they worshipped this nonexistent delusion.

To explain the delusion, accordingly, the material short-comings of the epoch had to be elucidated. Human psychology was rooted in the material condition of mankind. In his loathing of any form of transcendentalism, Feuerbach resorted to the most simple-minded, coarse explanation of all behavior. In its crudest form his doctrine was summed up in the German pun: *Der Mensch ist was er isst* (human beings are what they eat).

Feuerbach's materialism was expressed very primitively, but it made an immense impression on Marx and later on Engels, perhaps because it demonstrated that all "ideologies" (illusory intellectual structures) are no more than psychological excrescences of genuine miseries that they are meant to alleviate and compensate. And even though expressed with a sort of earthy exaggeration and forthrightness, the contrast with the ethereal dogmatic constructions of the idealistic Hegelianism of the 1830's gave Feuerbach's book a quality that was refreshing enough to convince those steeped in idealism of its social effectiveness.

Marx at the age of twenty-five was still a radical and an idealist, a dogmatic Hegelian. The Absolute Idea of Hegel had come to seem to him so much verbiage, but the *method* whereby Hegel had established his system meant something to him and his generation. They felt it was up to them to apply this priceless method of Hegel's to real things in the real world instead of to mere figments of the mind.

Marx had thus taken his first and most decisive step in anchoring Hegelian abstractions in the real world. By plumping for the basic categories of scientism and inevitability, he had linked his own social views to the dynamics inherent in what for Hegel had been a purely ideational progression, and so laid the foundations for an approach to the life of society—human history—that would demonstrate, with "scientific certainty," that a certain order of things was bound to come about in a certain way.

To be sure, he lacked what might have been considered vital—a cogent demonstration based on observable facts. So far, his theory, while "scientific" in its claims, still lacked the confirmation of facts and figures. It lacked a proof. But since he was convinced of the essential truth of the theoretical formulation, he was sure that proof was bound to be forthcoming as soon as someone began looking for it. The seeker, of course, had to have a serious enquiring mind guided by the scientific principles established in Hegel's philosophy.

This purely theoretical evolution was now to have an effect on Marx's personal life. With the *German-French Yearbooks* he once again, for the second time, fell foul of the authorities. What made it all the more grotesque was that of the almost hundred thousand Germans then living in Paris the only one who seemed to have read the issue of the Ruge-Marx periodical that called for armed revolution on behalf of a socialist theory was the Prussian ambassador. He faithfully reported Marx's views to his government.

The Prussian government took a somewhat subtle stand on socialism. In many ways the authorities were in favor of its theoretical expression, since it might split up the democratic opposition to the Prussian monarchy. On the other hand, it was obviously out of the question to talk about armed insurrection—this was banned, as common sense proscribed.

The results were disastrous for Marx personally. Not only was an edict of arrest put forth against him if he ever set foot in Prussia, but the importation of the issue was forbidden. Practically the entire supply of the magazine that had been sent to Prussia was seized at the frontier, which ruined the magazine financially. The *German-French Yearbooks* expired.

Marx was once again in a highly embarrassing position. He was stranded in a foreign country with no money, no connections, and a wife now pregnant and not very well. The one bright spot for the household was the arrival of a peasant girl, sent by Jenny's mother. This girl, Helen Demuth, had been brought up by Jenny since childhood and was utterly devoted to her mistress. She was to remain with the Marxes all their life. Her last name—which means humility—symbolized an unquestioning loyalty that was one of the chief props of Marx's home life. It was in fact she who, much later, was to bear Marx an illegitimate child in circumstances that are still somewhat obscure and have often, indeed, been denied. At this time, however, she merely increased the size of the small household— an extra mouth to feed.

Marx's relations with Ruge became envenomed when he insisted that Ruge put up the money required to continue the magazine. Ruge refused on financial grounds and on principle. Since he had never intended to associate himself with an extremist socialist position, he could see no moral point in struggling to subsidize another issue of a magazine containing Marx's now unacceptable views.

Marx took the whole matter in a highly personal way. He considered that Ruge had lured him away from the comforts of his mother-in-law's home in Germany and was in some moral sense responsible for the prosecution of the enterprise. Ruge took the view that Marx was not only unreasonable but full of "hatred and insanity," a "fanatical egoist." The upshot was that Ruge, who had been regarded for years by Marx as a dear friend and older confessor—there were sixteen years between them—was now a hated enemy.

Marx's desperate need for immediate cash had to be satisfied by donations, which were sent in by his mother-in-law, a Dutch relative, and Georg Jung, of the days of the *Rhine Gazette*. In 1844, at least, enough money came in to see Marx through the year, primarily from Jung, who took up a collection among the former stockholders of the *Rhine Gazette*.

His financial problem was acute. It turned out to be insoluble and remained so for the rest of his life. The year 1844, when Marx turned twenty-six, was a turning-point —from then on, as long as he lived, he was almost wholly dependent on charity for the support of himself and his family.

CHAPTER IV

Marx Becomes a Full-fledged Socialist

In the 1840's, Paris represented a unique cauldron of novel ideas, feelings, and activities. The French capital was a magnet for a whole galaxy of European intellectuals, poets, writers, painters, and musicians, as well as an endless number of theoretical reformers who had been granted political asylum in France by the indulgent regime of Louis Philippe. The 1830's and '40's had seen a general reaction throughout Europe, and Paris, traditionally celebrated for its hospitality to ideas and people, was a mecca for homeless intellectuals. In Paris they were not ignored, as they were in London. Once they had taken the trouble to learn French, a natural language for all educated people at the time, they were enthusiastically welcomed to the various artistic and social coteries.

The spiritual atmosphere of the period was passionate and idealistic. Intellectuals of opposing views were emotionally united against traditionalism, oppression, and perhaps above all against philistinism—the dumb acceptance of the status quo. There was a vehement concentration on personal emotions and on revolutionary and humanitarian attitudes. The interchange of ideas and theories was livelier than it had ever been before. Indeed, not since the Renaissance had there been such a concourse of distinguished, eccentric, gifted, and passionate personalities gathered in one place. The Habsburg and Romanov regimes kept producing huge new crops of political exiles

every year, who gravitated to Paris. Expatriate colonies
from all over Europe attracted the admiration as well as
the compassion of enthusiastic Parisians.

The talk was torrential and the production of books
and pamphlets staggering. The atmosphere was one of universal idealism. The cause of freedom, however interpreted, was taken for granted by men who believed themselves to be acting on behalf of mankind and not merely
of some specific movement or group. In 1830, a political
victory had checkmated, at least for a while, the reaction
following the French Revolution. Humanitarian slogans
retained the perhaps simpleminded attraction they were
not to lose until the failure of the 1848 political upheavals.

The mood of humanitarianism was given a special savor
by the early advances of the industrial revolution that—
just as in England, though in a more circumscribed way—
was swiftly transforming the economy and society of
France. Financial activity was turbulent. There was a sort
of parvenu ruling class composed of great financial complexes, which enveloped a government of cynics in a web
of intrigue and corruption. At the same time, the small
numbers of industrial workers were in a state of turmoil,
because of the abuses of individual employers and the industrial revolution.

The combination of the intellectual exchanges, govern-
mental corruption, and large-scale social changes produced
a situation of optimism for all those wedded to the idea of
reform. It also, of course, stimulated the opportunism of
ambitious individuals. Writing was not yet so demone-
tized as it has since become. Authors could evoke great
enthusiasm, and political journalists, above all, heightened
the atmosphere of crisis, transition, and opportunity. The
legend of intellectual vitality, social turbulence, and pas-

sionate idealism that was created by the Paris of the 1830's and '40's was to survive even the disappointment of 1848 and its aftermath—it has lived on to our own day.

Though Marx was rather immune, even hostile to the emotional atmosphere, it was in many respects an ideal medium for him. Even though penniless and dependent on charity, he could devote himself to his reading with a greater sense of purpose than before. He plunged into a study of socialism, which, it was now clear, he was determined to make the chief arena of his activities. It was almost as though he were choosing a profession. Jenny was rather dubious, but from Marx's point of view, socialism or communism was not a harebrained concept but, in a sense, practical. Socialism was in the air. Almost a banality in the most aristocratic salons in Paris, it was espoused by many fashionable people in Paris, including millionaires. And if it was true that it was destined to arrive because of its sheer inevitability, a perfectly good case could be made out for getting on the bandwagon.

Gripped by the extraordinary energy he was capable of when involved, Marx set to work mastering an enormous amount of material.

He became fascinated by the problems of the French Revolution. The basic question was why it had failed. Why had the restoration of the Bourbons been possible, to say nothing of Napoleon's success in establishing an Empire on the groundwork of the bourgeois revolution? Were there some underlying, fundamental social laws? The rationality made so much of by the French Encyclopaedists obviously explained nothing—they had simply been wrong in ascribing so much effectiveness to the powers of reason. On the other hand, the Hegelian response to the question was meaningless: to say that the revolution had failed because the epoch had not yet reached the stage when it could be successful was ridiculous, since the only criterion was the occurrence itself.

Marx plunged into the problem. He absorbed the torrents of French polemics that had been appearing ever since the revolution itself, but he foundered completely. He mastered the material but found no answers in it. He changed course a little—after reading the literature of politics he turned to the literature of economics. For the first time he began to study economics systematically, as he was forced to descend from the heights of abstraction to specialized information.

He filled one notebook after another with abstracts from economic writers, the English writers Adam Smith and David Ricardo, the Frenchman Jean-Baptiste Say, and out-and-out socialists like Proudhon. These were elementary, the sort of books read by students nowadays in their first term, but they marked the beginning of his enquiry into why the present order *had* to be dislodged from history by the succeeding order.

Marx was impressed by the sensible, cool, unemotional lucidity of the French and English writers and especially by their references to empirically observable fact. The aversion he had already formed to the bombastic rhetoric of the Young Hegelians was reinforced by the admirable ability of the French and English economic and political writers to combine the observation of real phenomena with the construction of general theories, often ingenious. It reinforced his penchant for naturalistic observation and turned him still further away from the fogginess of Hegelian abstractions.

He was also much impressed, in a general way, with the superiority of the French to the Germans, particularly in the field of political thought. He decided that the Germans were the most backward of all civilized peoples and at present were no more than a mirror of the French and English past. From this stand, it was easy to claim that all Europe would be emancipated once Germany was; Marx thought Germany was to Europe what the proletariat was to society as a whole.

But though he admired the realistic coolness of the French and English economists and political writers, Marx was distressed by what he regarded as their lack of historical perception. He thought they lacked *system*. This defect made it possible for them to pick and choose from many observations and possibilities, modify, add to, and subtract from their generalizations and show a deplorable bent for the eclecticism he had always regarded as pernicious.

Marx always had violent, clear-cut ideas, deduced, it seemed to him, with incontrovertible logic from premises that in the nature of things entailed their conclusions. He conceived the historical process as allowing for no significant variations or as a framework that had to be in a certain shape and not in another.

Marx felt that the classical economists reasoned as if the categories of behavior they were dealing with were somehow timeless. Instead of accepting this as a convention of the period, he assumed that it was a defect of the method of reasoning itself and that it made impossible a genuine insight into the peculiar historical conditioning inherent in any given epoch. From his point of view, an appeal to the timeless moral idealism of man rather than to the inevitability of the unfolding of historical stages was just a form of sentimentality.

The French and English economists, then, were unscientific. Yet he found the moral flavor of their work very agreeable, with its dedication to logic and empirically ascertained data. Obviously, in a broad sense, they were on the side of reason and against the claptrap of traditional thought.

Since Marx had already plumped for the proletariat as the flag-bearer of his own concept of history, it was natural for him, despite his reserved nature and a perhaps fundamental inability to get on with people on a simple, personal basis, to want to know some real proletarians. Even though he considered philosophy the executive organ of a coming transformation of society, it was, after all, the proletariat that was to carry out the orders of philosophy. The idea of historical progression in Marx's mind by its very nature required an agent. It had to be implemented by the social force he had deduced from his philosophical construction.

He began going to meetings of French workers, held in tiny gathering-places wherever bourgeois intellectuals had managed to get hold of workers to indoctrinate with some form of socialism or other. Like many people with no great interest in other people's personalities, he was immensely impressed by the workers, who hitherto had been to him no more than an incarnation of an idea.

Marx lapsed into the most extraordinary sentimentality on his initial contact with real workers. He wrote about them with a strange effusiveness—"in their toil-worn faces" he saw "the nobility of mankind shining forth." And he added, "One must have seen their thirst for knowledge, their moral energy, and their tireless drive toward development to have any idea of the human nobility of this movement."

Later on, after Marx was embarked in a political struggle, he was to change his attitude, referring to ordinary workers rather rudely, but in this honeymoon period of his life he was still smitten. It gave him pleasure to believe that the instrument he had selected as the agent of social reform was more high-minded than other people, of whom he had, it is true, a very low opinion.

At the meetings of French workers a young and unknown foreigner could only sit and listen, but there were also some German workers in Paris, members of the "League of the Just." This organization had been founded only a few years before in Paris and had branches elsewhere. Its aim was to make socialists out of Germans working abroad in accordance with the old German tradition of wandering journeymen. The founder, Wilhelm Weitling, was a most unusual phenomenon, a white crow—a socialist who happened to be a proletarian. His father was a French officer, who had been stationed in the Napoleonic army of occupation in Prussia, where he had lived for a while with a servant girl and then vanished. Weitling had been a tailor's apprentice and had succeeded somehow in educating himself. He left Prussia when he was called up for army service and had been a wanderer ever since. One of his two books described a Christ-like figure patently modeled on himself, a communist and revolutionary to boot. Officials in Switzerland had failed to find it edifying, and Weitling was at the moment serving a short term in jail.

Marx faithfully attended the meetings of the League of the Just. Though called proletarian by Marx himself, there was nothing really proletarian about it. The society simply consisted of a number of old-fashioned, almost medieval types of German artisans—watchmakers, cobblers, carpenters, etc. They were not the contemporary workers in modern factories to which the word "proletarian" generally referred.

A handful of such artisans would meet in a small room in a Paris suburb, Vincennes, and listen to talks on socialism by a bourgeois intellectual, a physician from Danzig. The number of people at any given meeting was pathetically small, varying between ten and at the most twenty, but they stood in Marx's mind for the vanguard of a great army. By this time Marx had grown the great beard that has indelibly fixed his face in the minds of posterity, and despite his youth he was looked up to by these somewhat simpleminded journeymen as a great scholar. They listened to him with attention. It is difficult to know just how much his ideas, then in the process of formation, actually persuaded his listeners, but in view of the potential they represented in his mind, he was bound to take seriously what Ruge referred to contemptuously as the "one-and-a-half journeymen."

In looking for flesh-and-blood workers and trying to find a social basis for an idea, Marx had accomplished something very unusual. He had described a full circle between an idea and its realization by following the path of logic wherever it led him. After deducing the necessity of the proletariat from his elaboration of his idea of history, he had actually gone into the streets and found some proletarians, or at least some artisans who might pass as such. Thus, in spite of his almost complete detachment from ordinary human relationships, his abstract mind had forced him into the thick of society, looking for a flesh-and-blood army to parallel the development of the ideas in his head.

He met Proudhon around this time, in 1844. Proudhon was now the most famous socialist in Europe, and he thought it his duty to learn something about Hegel. He had been told of the young Dr. Marx, who could explain it all, and received many lengthy lectures from him, often lasting far into the night. Marx behaved toward him at this time with great respect, though only a few years later he submitted Proudhon to a devastating polemical onslaught.

Marx also met the gigantic Russian nobleman whose name had become a byword for upheaval, Bakunin, by this time no longer a democrat but a "whole-hearted communist," converted by Weitling, who had met him in Switzerland. Bakunin was a remarkable force of nature. Quite without means and a dilettante in all subjects, he had an extraordinary magnetism that apparently made him the focus of attention wherever he appeared. He had, in addition, an extraordinary linguistic gift that he exploited on behalf of his volcanic rebelliousness. Not only could he learn a language rapidly for ordinary purposes, but he had the ability to use it for his own brand of flamboyant rhetoric so quickly that within a short space of time he would be haranguing multitudes in the most emotional, infectious manner. He was in all respects the very opposite of Marx; their relations were marked by a revulsion to each other that had an almost chemical basis.

Later on Bakunin was to say that in spite of his admiration for Marx's erudition and devotion to the proletariat, "there was never any real intimacy between us. Our temperaments did not allow it. He called me a sentimental idealist; and he was right. I called him morose, vain and treacherous, and I too was right." Bakunin also wrote:

M. Marx is by origin a Jew. He unites in himself all the qualities and defects of that gifted race. Nervous, some say, to the point of cowardice, he is immensely malicious, vain, quarrelsome, as intolerant and autocratic as Jehovah, the God of his fathers, and like Him, insanely vindictive.

There is no lie, no calumny, which he is not capable of using against anyone who has incurred his jealousy or his hatred; he will not stop at the basest intrigue if, in his opinion, it will serve to increase his position, his influence, and his power.

Such are his vices, but he also has many virtues. He is very clever, and widely learned. In about 1840 he was the life and soul of a very remarkable circle of radical Hegelians—Germans whose consistent cynicism left far behind even the most rabid Russian nihilists. Very few men have read so much and, it may be added, have read so intelligently, as M. Marx. . . .

Like M. Louis Blanc, he is a fanatical authoritarian—triply so, as a Jew, a German, and a Hegelian—but where the former, in place of argument, uses declamatory rhetoric, the latter, as behooves a learned and ponderous German, has embellished this principle with all the tricks and fancies of the Hegelian dialectic, and with all the wealth of his many-sided learning.

Nevertheless, each respected the other. Marx was careful to stay on formal good terms with Bakunin. In any attempt to influence society he obviously had to have allies, though his temperament, imperious and self-assured, required subordinate personalities, the only ones with whom he could assume his natural position as a commanding personality.

So far the only bona fide subordinate he had found was Jenny. Witty and intelligent, she had for him the natural devotion of a loving wife. But at just this time, in connection with some articles in the luckless *Yearbooks*, Friedrich Engels, who had been cold-shouldered by Marx before in Cologne, came to Paris from his father's textile firm in Manchester, England.

Engels, still looking "boyishly immature," had been leading a peculiar life in Manchester, which was a natural headquarters for a textile business. To keep up appearances in the offices of his father's firm, he played the role of a model fox-hunting squire in Manchester local society. At the same time he led a secret life in the slums of the city, where he lived with a red-headed Irish working-class girl, Mary Burns. He had in mind a book on English working-class conditions. After putting on old clothes, he would mingle with all the workers he could find. He and Mary Burns lived together as husband and wife, and he would go with her to visit working-class friends, keeping an attentive eye on everything. He had been writing, with his characteristic fluency, articles in English for the Chartist press and in German for various socialistically minded papers in Prussia.

Quite independently of Marx, Engels had come to hold certain views that harmonized with Marx's whole attitude. With his typical impulsiveness, he had formed a definite opinion that England was on the eve of a socialist revolution. He had proved to himself three things: the imminent destruction of British exports by the industrial development of countries outside England, the consequent worsening of the already miserable conditions of the English working-class, and the concomitant indifference of the cruel upper classes and their degenerate parliament. Any question of giving the population the vote was simply laughable, since universal suffrage, implying the dominance of the masses, naturally meant the end of private property. Hence, as Engels wrote in 1844, there was absolutely no way out for the English bourgeoisie but to be confronted by an inevitably successful proletarian revolution. As he put it, "the ground beneath their feet is bound, with the inevitability of a mathematical law, to swallow them up."

This formulation, with its emphasis on scientific predictability and inevitability, was bound to appeal to Marx. It coincided admirably with his own views. On many other crucial points, too, their views dovetailed completely.

Thus, when Engels came to Paris in 1844 and met Marx, there were already many links between them, and after only a few days of animated talk, they had become an intellectual and practical team.

Aside from their intellectual harmony, the relationship was based on the total subordination of Engels to Marx's personality. He instantly felt the power radiated by Marx. Apparently without the smallest resentment, he clung to him at once as a completely superior person. As he himself was to say, "I am meant to play second fiddle." Engels was, in fact, a sort of pupil of Marx's, in the sense that he was willing to receive his spiritual sustenance from him without any feeling of competition. He repaid Marx by his devotion, his common sense, his gaiety, and very soon by supporting him materially.

Marx, whose thin skin was made all the more sensitive by an almost complete inability to establish an emotional footing with anyone, and who was at all times jealous and suspicious of any reservations about himself and his ideas, had found, for his part, an ideal companion and friend and an able ally.

Engels's own gifts were very considerable, though from a certain point of view superficial; he was like a skillful journalist. He could digest enormous masses of data very quickly and write about them with unusual clarity. He made no particular claim to originality, but he nevertheless could see the point of other people's ideas and perceive their practicability. His initial contribution to Marx's thought was characteristic of his later share in their joint enterprise—he gave Marx the concrete data about the actual conditions of a real society. This furnished the material evidence for the broad generalizations that were the natural medium for Marx's abstract mind. At heart a bookworm, Marx tended to apprehend things, after a considerable time lag, on the basis of books, which, after all, could not give a complete description of social reality. Engels produced the concrete underpinning for Marx's theories. This was all the more essential because Marx had long since broken with mere abstraction in philosophy and required a firm structure. Marx required facts, without which his social philosophy was bound to remain an abstraction hanging in the air, and Engels required an intellectual pattern, without which facts have no impact.

Their meeting in Paris in the autumn of 1844 led to an instantaneous fusion of personalities and aims. As Marx was to say years later, it was the start of their "running a joint business." Their partnership lasted as long as they lived. For all practical purposes they were a single person, an intellectual team doubtless unique in history.

Another basic stage of Marx's development, during his two years in Paris, was the establishment of what may be called his polemical style. Beginning with a curiously violent attack on his former colleague Ruge, and continuing to a systematic onslaught on all his former associates among the Young Hegelians, he molded the somewhat tortuous philosophical style he had inherited from his Hegelian studies into a slashing weapon that combined the qualities of the scalpel, the rapier, and the bludgeon.

He had just undergone a near-tragedy—his beloved wife had almost died giving birth to a daughter. He had resumed his struggle with the mountain of economic material he had been studying in his quest for the socio-economic demonstration of the broad historical thesis he was trying to formulate.

It was a relief for him to take time off to rupture relations with all former associates. His irritation with Ruge
over the fiasco of their joint magazine was vented with remarkable savagery when he saw an article by Ruge in a
new little bi-weekly German newspaper published in Paris,
the *Forwards*. Picking one or two sentences out of Ruge's
article—on a revolt of pauperized weavers—Marx spun a
comprehensive attack that ran to about ten times the
length of Ruge's effort. It was so disproportionate to its
target, and so obviously the result of personal venom, that
its conclusion, which boiled down to an exhortation that
Ruge stop writing altogether, gave Marx the nickname of
the "calf-biter."

He also took time off from his research into economics
to deliver a massive blow at the whole school of Bruno
Bauer and Bauer's friends. While in Paris, Engels had
dashed off a slight journalistic attack on Bauer and his
newspaper, the *General Literary Gazette*, apparently in
order to please Marx, who had been sneering at Bauer
in their lengthy conversations. After Engels had gone home
to his father's town, Marx took up Engels's little sketch,
which amounted to some twenty pages of relatively good-
natured abuse, and expanded it into a sustained, virulent,
and almost obsessive attack on Bauer and everything Bauer
represented to Marx. It was an extension of the feelings
that had been accumulating in Marx ever since he had
abandoned the coterie of the Professors' Club in Berlin
and had turned violently against the peculiar literary style
affected by the Young Hegelians.

Marx put his formidable energies into the total destruction of Bauer. He was subjecting all eight numbers of
Bauer's paper to painstaking scrutiny when he received
word that the paper had quietly folded through lack of

response and that Bauer was now desperately poor and in a hopeless condition. Marx was thus attacking a symbol for a whole group of people, but he was immersed in his polemical fury and paid no attention. He was so intent on tearing to shreds Bauer as well as all Bauer's associates that he enlarged Engel's meager sketch from an article to a massive book of some 350 pages.

It was Marx's first book, a notable experience for a young man of twenty-six. Marx sold it immediately to a German printer, who insisted that Engels's name precede Marx's on the title page, on the theory that the combination of the well-known Engels family with the name of Marx, already known as a martyr of the *Rhine Gazette* fiasco, would ensure sales in the Rhineland.

The title of this first opus of Marx's was *The Holy Family*; its sub-title *Bruno Bauer and His Accomplices.* It was such a painstaking and incredibly overblown polemic that Engels was not very enthusiastic about it, especially as the title was also guaranteed to vex his pious family and perhaps even more because he had not, in fact, written any of it.

The polemical style associated with Marx may be said to have been established in these two works. His chief official biographer, Franz Mehring, generally rather pious, describes that polemical style as follows: "Whenever the debate becomes heated, it degenerates into logic-chopping and carping . . . of the most trivial kind" characterized by "running a figure of speech into the ground; giving the silliest possible meaning to his opponent's speech by a literal or distorted interpretation, and indulging in exaggerated, unbridled expressions."

Engels, meanwhile, had been filled with enthusiasm by conditions in Germany. He thought socialism was making such rapid progress that it must be just around the corner. He reported that there were communists everywhere, not, perhaps, among the small industrial working-class, but surely among the bourgeoisie and the intellectuals. Even the chief of police in Engels's home-town was a communist! The literary world was simply steeped in it—all the reviews and newspapers were filled with communism. The former sponsor of the *Rhine Gazette,* Jung, gave a similar report of the fantastic progress being made by the notion of communism—in bourgeois circles.

Things were going so rapidly, indeed, that Engels, who had always loathed "filthy commerce," determined to forget it altogether and begin agitating in public. He and Moses Hess joined up in an attempt to spread communism in the big towns of the Wupper valley. They began holding meetings everywhere. In Engels's words, everyone "from the financial aristocracy to the shopkeepers, was present"—everyone except the proletariat. The rallies started with the playing of harps, followed by recitations of poems by Shelley. Then Hess or Engels would address the crowd, describing the misery of society and the vices of the bourgeois organization of society. The meetings would go on for hours, often till dawn, but even though the speeches occasionally bordered on the subversive, the crowd included so many respectable people—district attorneys, judges, a chief prosecutor, etc.—that there was no real danger. It was not too much to say that the proletarian movement was leaping ahead, except among the proletariat. Engels's enthusiasm was boundless.

There was only one thing lacking, in fact—a sound philosophical foundation for the rapidly spreading political movement. Concretely this meant that the bold schema already outlined by Marx in general terms had to be given the solid substructure of factual evidence, a proof that the historical progression predicted by Marx was rooted in objective reality and not in his own mind.

The proof had to demonstrate that the status quo was not merely collapsing but must inevitably collapse because of its very nature. This could be proved no longer by abstractions, which Marx was very skillful at arranging, but by concrete socio-economic data. Marx directed his reading toward outlining and anchoring his basic theme. He had promised Engels to write a book proving what they had so quickly discovered they agreed on. Now Engels was enthusiastically, perhaps too enthusiastically, calling for an actual book. Marx's attacks on Ruge and Bauer, though lengthy, had done nothing for the movement.

Engels had been so zealous that he even had found a publisher for the unwritten book, who insisted on offering Marx an advance. Though hesitant, since he had not yet found the "proof" he was looking for in books, Marx accepted the advance. A title was agreed on, *The Critique of Politics and Economics,* and Marx plunged into his researches with redoubled energy.

But Marx grew more and more discouraged by the mass of factual economic data that he had been accumulating. It seemed to lead nowhere. He was in a mood of extreme pessimism; he felt he was bogging down in a swamp of facts that he was incapable of organizing into a general intellectual structure.

It was at this point, when Marx was fed up with economics, that he had a flash of dazzling illumination. It preoccupied him for days and kept him pacing nervously back and forth in his room, smoking like a chimney. His nights were so restless that he could hardly sleep. But finally he confided to his wife, who had been bearing patiently with him as usual, that he had just made an absolutely marvelous discovery, of cosmic dimensions. Jenny at first thought he had discovered the "proof" that the present social order was bound to collapse, but Marx's enthusiasm ran far beyond that.

He had found the motor that enabled him to use Hegel's system of thought by transposing it from the heavens of abstract thought to concrete social conditions. In a sudden vision, as he expressed it to Jenny, he saw that Hegel, that "colossal old boy," had been quite correct in analyzing the forward movement of history through the resolution of the dialectic tension between negation and negation but had misconceived the motor of the whole operation. That motor could not be found in the self-unfolding, or self-realization, of the Absolute Idea, but in something observable and hence verifiable.

Instead of looking for discoveries within the sphere of economics, instead of finding a proof that economics works in such and such a way, Marx decided that economics was itself the motor of history.

This discovery, which took shape in Marx's mind as a sort of culmination of the thought he had already outlined in the first essays in the *German-French Yearbooks* on Hegel's *Philosophy of Right* and on Bauer and the Jewish question, was never expounded by Marx in a systematic way. It occurs in a somewhat splintered form in the casual articles he wrote from the age of twenty-five to twenty-eight, and then is simply assumed as the background in everything he wrote later on. He did not conceive it as a unique invention—that is, an independent philosophical system—but regarded it as a scientific method of socio-historical analysis and, also, in political agitation a groundwork for strategy. He was aware of its slightly haphazard quality, though he, and especially Engels, were to think of it as a sort of actual science that would enable a foregone socio-historical conclusion to come about if the right strategy, also scientifically deduced, were applied. He was later to complain that his followers had no business turning his practical method into a system.

He indicated the evolution of this idea still further in *The Holy Family,* and most fully in an introduction he wrote when he was twenty-eight to *The German Ideology,* which he composed with Engels as an extravagant blast against a whole range of long-forgotten authors. In this introduction, which is unwaveringly Hegelian in its structure, Marx makes an attempt to show that there is a unitary process in human history whose laws can be discovered—laws that do not entail each other in the manner of the Hegelian self-realization of the timeless Universal Spirit (or God). Marx, still in agreement here with Feuerbach, regarded the Hegelian self-realization as a piece of hocus-pocus, a form of inaccessible metaphysics, unverifiable and hence unscientific.

On the other hand, the attempts of various Young Hegelians, such as Bauer, Ruge, and even Feuerbach, to replace the defective structure of the Master by their own contrivances were also doomed to failure, Marx thought. While they claimed that their criteria, too, were rooted in flesh-and-blood human relations, they were no more than abstractions, of a slightly different kind, that explained nothing.

The laws governing history must be sought in a medium where they could be observed, analyzed, and verified. Since they had to do with human history, they must be found in the environment of men, in the dense mesh of interrelationships that constituted the fabric of human society. Hegel's genius in demonstrating that the upward progression takes the form of a zigzag was borne out precisely when his theory was transposed to real society, in which progress was bound to be staccato. When the tension reached the critical phase, it would lead to a cataclysmic explosion.

The conflict that Hegel had seen only in relations between ideas must be sought instead in relations between men, and these must be understood within the context of civil society, which was established by conflicts between economically conditioned groups of people, or classes, themselves defined by their relationships to the forces of production as they existed at any given stage of history. In short, men's collective behavior was dictated by their economic relationships, whether or not they were aware of them. This did not imply, to be sure, that men's motivations were dependent on a desire for material gain, as many opponents of Marxism and even some of his followers have sometimes maintained, but simply that their behavior was ultimately conditioned by the over-all economic pattern of a specified society.

Marx did not regard this theory as new, for as Jenny pointed out to him, no one had ever denied that economic factors were *important*. Marx struck a novel note—a note that was to prove essential for the movement that sprang up in his name—by deciding that economic conditioning, expressed as a reflection of the class struggle revolving around the forces of production at any given stage, was the overriding and ultimately—despite all illusory appearances—the sole cause.

This tremendous contention, to be sure, had to be proved; it was a cardinal problem. How could everything in human affairs—law, morality, ethics, metaphysics, philosophy, the whole life of the human spirit—be shown to arise from economic conditioning? The basic point was made even in Marx's initial conversations with Jenny, as he read aloud to her from the *German Ideology*. Marx readily granted that verification was necessary, but he was perfectly certain, since his theory was so convincing, that it was a matter of time and hard work.

His quest for proof had moved from a narrow field—showing that the propertied society of the time was doomed by its nature—to the far broader one of demonstrating the "Law of Motion" of all human history. He admitted that he was at the outset of the quest but nevertheless overflowed with enthusiasm at the certainty of the results that would be achieved. The cause of socialism would be advanced if scientific demonstration proved that it was not the wishful dream sucked out of some thinker's fingertips but was laid down by the scheme of natural laws.

Marx felt confident and blissfully happy about his discovery. Armed with this confidence, he was to make one mistaken prediction after another, but he never lost his faith that the "scientific" theory of economics as the basic cause of human history was not only his distinctive achievement but one of the most remarkable products of the human mind.

Thus Marx's full intellectual character had already unfolded itself by the time he was twenty-six; nothing substantial was ever added to the structure of his thought.

CHAPTER V

The Road to Exile: Belgium: 1848

In January, 1845, when Marx was twenty-six and a half, he was expelled from France. His expulsion had nothing to do with his activities, but was a ricochet arising out of a diplomatic imbroglio.

The little German newspaper *Forwards* had been imprudent enough, on hearing of an attempt on the King of Prussia's life, to make some offensive comments—to hope that the aim would be better next time. The Prussians asked the French to shut down the paper, but the French, after ironically offering to try the editors of the newspaper in public on a charge of incitement to murder—obviously embarrassing to the Prussians, since it would involve examining the King's private life in detail—compromised by deporting all foreigners who had ever contributed to the paper.

This was no more than a diplomatic evasion, for such orders, in accordance with the French tradition of flexibility, were made to be circumvented. None of the foreigners was compelled in fact to leave. Heine and Ruge simply "arranged" things.

Marx chose to yield to the police order, though some of the radical foreigners protested that it was rash to allow the police to get above themselves by having their orders obeyed.

Nevertheless, Marx decided to leave for Belgium. Paris meant nothing in particular to him. He could just as well carry on his work elsewhere, and since he had convinced himself that socialism could be achieved, in accordance with the laws of history, only by an uprising of the proletariat, all that was left for him to do was to help organize that uprising as quickly as possible.

Marx's personal biography now begins to be integrated with the history of the socialist movement in Europe; it is, in fact, indistinguishable from it. The intellectual preparation for his new role was finished. His philosophy of politics was rounded off, his strategy was, so he thought, laid down, and the only thing that remained for him was political struggle.

He was sure that there were imminent prospects for a radical upheaval. All over Europe young men interested in politics were in a state of effervescent expectation. Many thought great things were in the offing. Marx's high spirits were linked to a theory that these great things would occur within a brief period of time. His vast, cosmic concept of history was in the service of an optimism that he did not lose until the last part of his life. Throughout his active career it made him hopefully predict one cataclysm after another.

He arrived in Brussels with his whole family—his wife, Helen Demuth, and the one-year-old baby Jenny. Engels immediately started to collect money for him, also impressing Jung and Hess into this urgent assignment. It was around this time that Engels began automatically assuming personal responsibility for Marx's material support. He not only collected funds but renounced in Marx's favor some money due him for a book he had written in 1844, *The Condition of the Working Class in England.* Most important of all, Engels moved to Brussels, after a decisive falling-out with his "fanatical and tyrannical" father, who, though reconciled to his son's leaving the family business, could not endure his radical convictions and, more particularly, his intimate association with Hess. Engels had been offered a small but adequate allowance if he agreed to leave town. Thus for a while he became a sort of remittance man and moved into a flat next to Marx in Brussels.

Their spiritual union was now reinforced by a remarkable coincidence. Engels had arrived at practically the same conclusion about the "laws of motion" governing all history as Marx. The whole economic interpretation of history, as revealed to him by Marx, dovetailed very neatly with the ideas he himself had been working out. Marx was to acknowledge this without the smallest hesitation, though Engels, true to his role of second fiddle, gave Marx the primary credit. In any case, they talked the matter through for several days, and soon polished their joint theory to the point where, for the rest of their lives, it remained "our theory."

This joint theory, built on the foundations of Marx's blinding insight in Paris, was now honed by the two men into a rounded-off system of historical philosophy, to be called the "materialist conception of history." The materialistic data they accepted were, to be sure, found only within the sphere of economics, although toward the end of his life Engels was to extend the application of the theory to the natural universe too.

Economics as the primary motor force of human history was now concentrated into the idea of the forces of production—the various devices and processes needed for human survival. Marx and Engels conceived of society as a sort of edifice in which the foundation is provided by the productive forces, which establish the general socio-economic system, which in its turn generates everything else assumed to be the ethical and intellectual life of mankind—the state and its laws, ideas, ethics, religion, political behavior, and so on.

Thus it is the productive relations of a given society that determine its economic structure; this forms the "real basis from which, in the last analysis, is to be explained the whole superstructure of legal and political institutions as well as religious and other concepts." This was Engels's formulation. In view of the endless difficulties with which the theory was to meet, it is perhaps wise to recall that a way out could always be found in this simple phrase, "in the last analysis."

The joint theory created by Marx and Engels attempts to explain the total structure of all human society, including all aspects of behavior and ideas. Moreover, it provides an explanation of how society changes.

Since society does change, it is evident that change also begins on the groundwork of the productive forces. This is where the Hegelian dialectic comes in, now "materialized," as it were, by Marx. Technology evolves through natural adaptation. As it changes, the forces of production gradually grow beyond the bounds set by the economic system they once created. Hence the productive forces outgrow their own shell, and because of this the given economic system starts to decompose. This is one of the "seeds of destruction" that any system bears within itself. A second seed is to be found when the oppressed class—the proletariat, in the case of the current European bourgeois system—which is essential to the running of the system, finally pounds away at the whole structure and brings it down.

The end of the system is described in the joint theory through various metaphors, all similar—the system "explodes," "dissolves," "is burst asunder." The process is so elemental, so embedded in the nature of things, that there can never be any question of modifications, for instance, by the ruling class to ensure the survival of the system. On the contrary, the system is completely destroyed "by the blind, violent, destructive work" of productive forces that *must* destroy their own handiwork.

In this way both seeds of destruction—the productive forces and the proletariat, the human agent of the upheaval—contribute to the transformation of one social order into its inevitable successor. This naturally involves the total transformation of the society as a whole, including its spiritual superstructure, with all its ideas and feelings.

Their theory was regarded by Marx and Engels—at this time, it should be recalled, respectively about twenty-seven and twenty-five years old—as applicable to all history past and present. And, in the present, it seemed to them to imply, since the signs of socialism were all around them, that socialism was about to arrive as a demonstration of the eternal, and therefore current, validity of their theory. It was obvious to both men, in view of the current growth of technology—i.e., inventions like the steam-engine—and the fact that the forces of production had consequently outgrown the bourgeois system, that the conditions were ripe for the explosion of the present system by the "midwife" of the new order—the proletariat.

The concept of dialectic progression also fitted in here. The proletariat negated the bourgeois system and thus engendered the higher synthesis—a new social order. And precisely because the productive forces had achieved such a high level of technological efficiency, it was possible, "for the first time," to eliminate the regime of private property.

This in itself was just another aspect of the inevitably higher level of the coming new order. Technological efficiency had arrived at the point where, again for the first time, it was now possible—not merely desirable, or praiseworthy, but *possible*—to usher in an age of justice and happiness. All forms of oppression, inequality, and poverty would finally be eliminated. The forces of production, in short, would ascend to a level at which humanity could at last be happy.

All previous history would then be demonstrably not real history but pre-history. The real history of mankind would begin only after the introduction of socialism—the highest stage of history. The potentialities of the new technology would ensure the end of other stages in history. History, in other words, would have finally negated itself, as far as development was concerned. It would become absolute.

It is, perhaps, difficult to see why a process woven into the fabric of the universe should suddenly come to a stop at a particular stage of human development, however rich this stage may be in potential, but neither Marx nor Engels ever bothered to make specific predictions—which in any case they thought a childish enterprise—about what would happen after the Great Transition. This gap in their theory—at any rate this cut-off point in their historical speculation—was to present some of their partisans with great difficulties, notably the triumphant Bolsheviks in 1917. But all that lay far in the future.

The whole theory, extended, ramified, and polished by the two young men in Brussels in early 1845, did not contain any single element that was new in itself, but constituted an original approach to the history of mankind that was to prove singularly influential. By establishing each link on the basis of a single interpretation and systematically disregarding other possible explanations that would make their own theory of causation at best partial, they created a rigorous chain of reasoning in which each link had one essence. *Only* economics, *only* forces of production, *only* class struggle, *only* proletariat . . .

Thus the chain of reasoning had a remarkable unity of effect, as well as a unique magnetism for many intellectuals in succeeding generations. True, if a link were demolished, if it could be shown, for instance, that human behavior was not conditioned *exclusively* by the economic background, or that the "bourgeoisie" could improve its situation by becoming aware of it, or that the proletariat might not necessarily develop its class consciousness to the point where it would insist on "bursting asunder" bourgeois society, or simply, for that matter, that there were other possibilities inherent in a developing bourgeois society, then the whole chain of reasoning would, of course, snap.

It is illuminating to note that one element in this theory, worked out so rapidly by the two young men, had an objective validity—namely, the technological possibility of producing an economy of abundance in the world. Marx and Engels thought that this element elevated their theory above a mere sentimental *longing* for a better world.

Yet it is clear that this objective element did not necessarily imply the rest of the theory at all. It could quite easily be maintained, and of course has been maintained, that the very possibility might well imply a slackening of tension in the class struggle. Since there would be more for all, there might be less greed on the part of the few— this was in harmony with the idea of people being conditioned by the economic framework of society. As commodities grew cheaper, they might become accessible to all society. Hence the poor would not get poorer at all but richer, as far as having more of the necessities of life.

Historically, this is what has happened in Western industrial countries, and insofar as there remains a large
segment of the population that has not participated in
the increased wealth, it might be claimed that the political
action of an advanced electorate at the polls, for instance,
might bypass the need for a transition to socialism at all.

One of the things about Marx and Engels's theory that
made it so attractive was its analytic method—the dialectic.

For even though both Hegel and Marx thought the
dialectic rooted in reality—a different reality for each, to
be sure—it was most effective in the realm of debate. It
created a universe of discourse that could be taken to be
a universe of reality.

If anything can be split up—dialectically—into differing
and conflicting elements and recombined—dialectically—
into still other differing and conflicting elements, it is
possible to use the dialectic to discuss anything and make
sense.

The only proviso is that one has to be intelligent.

Thus, an intelligent person, in discussing, say, the sociopolitical and historical material that was to form the substance of later Marxism, is perfectly capable of carrying
on the conversation through the dialectic, which, because
it is inherently pivotal, can be used with endless flexibility.
The dialectic can be likened to a sort of universal joint
designed to accommodate an endless variety of different
facts, events, and ideas.

The Bourgeoisie, for instance—hypostasized as a logical
entity for one purpose—can always be broken down dialectically in any specific political situation and become a
great variety of entities—petty-bourgeoisie, Big Capital,
comprador bourgeoisie, rentier bourgeoisie, finance plutoc-
racy, big landowners, middle landowners, smallholders,
poor peasants, and so on.

An indefinitely extensible classification, from a practical, polemical point of view, can provide an intelligent person with enough elements to talk sense about a situation and still sound as though he were using the dialectic. It enabled Marx himself to write penetrating political analyses on occasion, not because the dialectic used his mind as a tool but because his mind, coping in a commonsense way with a complex of facts, made use of the dialectic as a rhetorical technique.

The converse, alas, is also true. The dialectic in the mouth of a fool makes him more foolish. This has been demonstrated by the silly predictions and consistently wrongheaded analyses made by Marxist spokesmen for generations, notably with respect to the rise of Hitlerism and the "class struggle" in Western Europe and America.

For intellectuals, of course, the dialectic has been a great game, appealing to analytical acumen and verbal facility. Moreover, since its scope is infinite—being applicable, as its defenders maintain, to all phenomena—it can be used as a prism through which the entire universe can be inspected.

The combination of these two factors—the pivotal quality of the method and its infinite applicability—has made the study of Marxism practically boundless, and the literature of it and about it remarkably voluminous.

Marx himself never thought of "Marxism" as a comprehensive philosophy. Engels tended to, and was to claim to have demonstrated its applicability even in the exact sciences. An evaluation of such a claim is quite beyond the scope of this book; perhaps it can be put in perspective by Albert Einstein's shrug of the shoulders when he said that Engels's studies in physics were of no interest either for physics or for the history of physics.

Yet the overriding effect of the theory created by Marx

and Engels was to prove compelling. Though it was a mixture of various other elements freely drawn from other
sources—the intellectual structure from Hegel, the dynamic political principles from Saint-Simon, the emphasis
on the paramountcy of "matter" from Feuerbach, and the
stressing of the proletariat from French socialism—it was
more than a mere cluster of separate factors. The motor
force Marx and Engels had found in history, by combin-
ing a Hegelian idea with a factual condition of human
society, gave the whole construction immense power.
As a system of thought, simply because it is all-inclusive, it
has exercised a potent tug over the minds of men, and
hence has become a factor of social change itself.

Marx was proud of having put Hegel "on his feet."
Hegel had been rather scornful of the results of the scientific investigations of his own day, but Marx, since he
considered himself to have established his own structure in
harmony with the empirical disciplines of science, could
consequently pay close attention to all the sciences that
were evolving so rapidly during his lifetime. His feeling,
shared still more strongly by Engels, was that there was no
reason for them not to be incorporated within his own
system.

Yet though their theory has room for the empirical
disciplines, it is quite non-empirical in its approach to
them. The Marxist doctrine of the zigzag movement of
history, of movement in dialectical ricochets, is not a mere
empirical hypothesis whose probability-value can be
changed to the slightest degree by actual observation, that
is, by the evidence of facts, but a basic pattern of thought
that is simply taken for granted as the starting-point for
the whole intellectual process. This is why Marx and all
his followers have always sneered at "vulgar empiricism,"
by which they mean a disregard of Hegel's work in rec-

ognizing that only those connections in the real world have
validity that do not depend on the evidence of the physical
senses.

"Marxism" exercised, the moment it was formulated as
a system, an appeal to the mind that had nothing to do with
a simple experimental demonstration in the field of any
given science. Even if every single conclusion is proved
false—and many claim this—Marxism would continue to
exercise its fascination over the minds of millions and thus
influence history. In addition, one of its underlying fea-
tures—the concentration on the importance of economic
factors—if deprived of its systematic, monolithic primacy,
was in sharp contrast to the very ancient tradition of taking ideas, notions, and speculations seriously in terms of
themselves and disregarding their social roots.

Because of this, Marx's views, though rejected as a
system by many scholars in the following generations,
nevertheless had the most direct effect on all the fields connected with history and sociology, so that for an immense
number of works in both fields his whole approach has
become a commonplace. It has been excised from the
general fabric of Marxism and used as a starting-point for
general investigations just because it is, after all, an obvious fact that the economic background of society is important. The very obviousness of this fact is a sign of the
degree to which Marx changed the direction of thought, as
well as of action in the political sphere. The theory, indeed, was to change the world, and, to that extent, "verify"
itself.

A curiosity of the new construction was that though it
came forth in a fairly polished form from the minds of
Marx and Engels, it lacked any form of proof whatever.
Marx's previous quest for an economic proof of the imminent collapse of the property system now had a goal

that was perhaps still more unattainable; the need for some sort of proof had become all the more indispensable as the mountain of theory grew bigger and bigger. Even if he could dispense with verifying the dialectical process itself, or with a demonstration that the ideas of man are derived from an economic factor in society, the purely *economic* elements—the substructure of the superstructure—were speculations, or rather affirmations. There was not a shred of proof that the economic process in fact worked the way it had to in order to set the whole process in movement. Marx now had to verify far more than he had had to before, when it had been a simple question of finding some proof that the existing economic order was doomed. Now he had to demonstrate that it was doomed *because of* the factors outlined in his and Engels's theory.

In short, the book on economics that Marx had already accepted an advance for was more urgently needed than ever. In the event, no "proof" was ever actually supplied, but at the time Marx and Engels felt it was vital. Both men were sure it was forthcoming, since it was, after all, right there, in the nature of things.

Before they attempted to find the proof, however, their theory was swiftly transformed into a faith. They began with what was a network of suppositions, a chain of abstract philosophical propositions, which claimed to describe reality yet could not be verified by it, but immediately fell into the habit of calling their hypotheses "laws." These hypotheses were spun out of their heads from general reading and therefore had to be tested, yet Marx and Engels soon began referring to them as a science.

The theory became the basis on which Marx, in accordance with his imperious temperament, began to treat the work of all other socialist and radical thinkers as pure sentimentality—*his* work was scientific, *theirs* illusion. It became a cliché of Marxism, starting with Marx and Engels themselves, to refer to their "laws" as "immanent," "infallible," "compulsive," "absolute," "coercive," or as "natural laws working with iron necessity toward inevitable results." (Preface to *Capital*.) The word "iron" or its equivalent was to become an integral factor of Marxism's attraction—everything *had* to happen the way it was foreseen. This idea was to appeal to whole generations of restive youths and rebellious spirits.

Marx and Engels insisted, in fact, on the status of scientific discoverers. Their discovery was to be summed up as the "laws of motion of the evolution of mankind," as Engels put it. Using a phrase coined by Proudhon about his own ideas—"scientific socialism"—Engels was to declare: "With these discoveries, socialism became a science." All other theories were just "ideologies."

Oddly enough, Marx was reluctant to set down the new doctrine, and never did so systematically. In spite of Engels's insistence that they put the whole of their revolutionary discovery into a comprehensive form suitable to its scientific importance, Marx waited for thirteen years before using it, condensed, as a preface to another book.

It is easy to suggest that Marx's reluctance to commit himself to making an orderly demonstration of the evidence for the majestic architectonics of their intellectual edifice was ultimately based on the common-sense realization that it was not possible. By limiting himself, however, to a two-page condensation of the theory (in his *Critique of Political Economy*), or even by expanding this a little further (in the introduction to his posthumously published *German Ideology*), he could secure for himself a springboard for a savage polemical campaign against his rivals. It was child's play, for instance, to demonstrate that the defense of an idea *as such* was naive, since it failed to grasp the material origins of the idea, just as it was child's play to show that whatever statesmen said about what they were doing was bound to be either a delusion or a self-delusion, for they could not comprehend the economic interests that *really* governed their conduct.

In short, Marx used his theory as a weapon. In polemics he would refer to it as though it had already been set down comprehensively and heap scorn on the heads of those who failed to understand it. The theory could, to be sure, be pieced together by anyone who read the many books, articles, and letters he went on to write. But he never overcame his reluctance to make a coherent, complete, and systematic exposition of his discovery, even though it was, as he said in the same preface thirteen years later, the "guiding thread of all my studies."

The problem in piecing something together from an immense number of sources is that it is difficult to make a demonstration acceptable to critics. It can always be claimed, with some degree of justice, if the idea is not expounded as a coherent whole, that an incorrect or inadequate selection has been made. In the history of Marxism, this was to be the source of the most tortuous, hairsplitting argumentation since the establishment of Christianity. The lushness of Marxist disputatiousness may be traced, perhaps, to this combination of dogmatic statement and imprecise formulation.

The polemical, negative handling of Marx and Engels's theory gave it its principal utility. Marx carved out a place for himself by destroying other theories on the basis of his own. It was essential to him to expose all other writers and thinkers who disregarded the plain fact that economics was the sole motor of history, who overestimated the power of ideas, who persisted in their sentimental illusions.

It was to become a commonplace of later Marxism that it could be *understood* only as having been created through polemical struggles. This was to account for the palpable onesidedness of any specific statement. Marx's failure to formulate his theories in a deliberately systematic way, as a cohesive entity, was to be explained by some apologists as being due to the exigencies of polemics. It was to be said that Marx had forged his intellectual apparatus in the heat of battle, by being obliged to take up different positions against different opponents—*against* the idealism of the Young Hegelians, materialism; *against* Feuerbach's *passive* materialism, the notions of activity and interaction central to Hegel's own dialectic; *against* mechanism, the claim that people make their own history; *against* sentimental rhetoricians, the claim that history is nevertheless made under certain conditions. In this way the elusiveness of the theory as a whole was made understandable, while at the same time it was possible for later polemicists to complain that even opponents who had spent their lives studying Marxism had completely missed the point—a point that a given polemicist, of course, had in his pocket.

All these polemical sorties in Marx and Engels's own life were to be thought of as mere adjuncts of political activity. Marx, now twenty-seven years old, had a theory, an attitude, and a strategy developed, so he thought, by his work in Paris. These had culminated in a complete theory through his talks with Engels during those fateful few days in Brussels. He was in a position to play a political and organizational role. He could now make his entry into real life.

He did something else on his arrival in Brussels that was ultimately to have the most decisive effect on his life.

Partly to put himself beyond the reach of the Prussian government and partly, perhaps, because of his political optimism, he renounced his Prussian citizenship in a formal letter. It was accepted at once.

This piece of youthful bravado, often glossed over, was to condemn Marx to a life of exile.

At the time it seemed a triviality, for Marx and Engels felt that they were on the threshold of major events.

Shortly after their meeting in Brussels, Engels proposed that Marx accompany him on a trip to England, where he had some things to do—among them to take Mary Burns back to Brussels with him. Engels gave him a sort of guided tour around the England of the mid-1840's, which lasted six weeks. Marx had his first taste of the country in which he was to spend most of the rest of his life.

It made a curious impression on him. The combination of English insularity, piety, quietism—even among the radicals he met—was so far removed from Marx's inflammatory attitude toward society that he found it bewildering. He was told by some radical leaders of the Chartists, for instance, that piety was still a matter of course in England. The workers still respected law and order and believed that they could improve their situation by organizing in trade-unions and by influencing legislation. This was all the more puzzling to Marx, for according to his and Engels's theory, it was logically necessary for workers in the most advanced industrial countries to be on the threshold of "bursting asunder" the old order. The English workers were incomprehensibly backward, from this point of view, and useless as a criterion of what was to be done in the political arena.

Marx also met some Germans in London, at the branch of the League of the Just founded by Weitling. This branch was much bigger than the Paris one; it had seventy or eighty workers in it, who were apparently a little more radical than those in Paris. His experience with these workers, however, was irritating, because Weitling himself had come to London after his prison term in Switzerland and had been given a tremendous welcome in working-class circles. He was feted by Englishmen as a comrade and enthusiastically hailed by his own branch. Only a year before, Weitling had been hailed by Marx as the wearer of the "giant babyshoes of the proletariat." On closer examination Marx, now thoroughly equipped with his own theory of the economic groundwork of history, found Weitling a mere babbler of not the smallest use to the proletariat—just because of his success in appealing to its most superficial sentimental attitudes.

The trip to England was disappointing. Afterward, it seemed all the more essential to attract the attention of the world to the theory that so far was still inside the heads of its authors. Marx, however, who, as I have said, was reluctant to commit himself on paper, instead proposed a joint polemical work, in which by way of clearing the field of all opposition they would finish off the extant German philosophers once and for all. It was to be a repetition, on a larger scale, of the savage onslaught on Bruno Bauer and his friends. This work, *The German Ideology,* which consumed an enormous amount of time, partly because Marx's handwriting was almost completely illegible, did not see the light of day during the lifetime of its authors. It is a monumental volume, more than six hundred pages, which carries on a sustained attack on totally forgotten authors and works, though the introduction contains the longest exposition of Marx's historical theory. It came out long after Marx and Engels were dead, and was either totally unknown to or quite neglected by his own followers—including, significantly, the architects of the Russian revolution! So the Marxist movement was shaped after Marx's death on the basis of only a part of

BAKUNIN

Marx's anarchist rival—haphazard as a theoretician, potent as a force.

LASALLE

Brilliant speaker and organizer—Marx's most envied competitor.

ENGELS

Marx's lifelong teammate.

his thought. Eighty years, in fact, were to pass before *The German Ideology* was published by a government publishing house in post-revolutionary Russia.

This massive work was a philosophical application of the theory. It was also natural for Marx, in the name of the union of "theory and practice" that was to become the hallmark of the whole movement, to turn the theory into practical political channels. After all, it was the proletariat that was to be the agent for the execution of the inevitable socio-historic process.

Marx took the shortest possible step—he founded a party.

In practice this was quite a simple thing. At some point during the conversations between Marx and Engels in Brussels, they started referring to themselves as the Communist Party, asking some of their friends and acquaintances whether they might like to join it. There was no party of any kind in the German-speaking world at the time, least of all a socialist party. Some friends gladly joined. Since there were no formalities involved in membership and no political program was drafted, there was not much difference between joining the Communist Party and going to a tea-party. That was the original Communist Party.

It should be recalled that the word communist had no special meaning at this time. Both communist and socialist were always identical for Marx. On this occasion, he and Engels had chosen the title Communist Party as a tactical device to differentiate themselves from a socialist party, founded by Louis Blanc, that was already in existence in France.

The group founded in Brussels ultimately grew to seventeen. Its most famous member was a well-known poet called Ferdinand Freiligrath, who took no particular interest in the group beyond lending it his name. Hess was another member, also Marx's bohemian brother-in-law Edgar von Westphalen; there were a number of obscure writers.

None of these members had any connection at all with the proletariat. Until Weitling came over later from London and joined it, and Marx and Engels recruited a couple of typesetters from a German paper published in Brussels, the group never had any proletarians at all. Fifteen of the original communist members were writers, and fourteen of the seventeen were bourgeois.

The newly constituted Communist Party produced its first institution by setting up a Communistic Correspondence Committee, in effect a letterhead under which Marx and Engels began a campaign of writing pamphlets, bulletins, and articles. These were printed or lithographed and mailed out to special periodicals and associations that had indicated some sympathy with socialist ideas. There was a similar committee doing the same sort of thing for the London branch of the League of the Just, but that concentrated on speakers of German.

Marx's aims were much broader. He envisaged an international application for his views, which otherwise would have been quite meaningless. The very scope of Marx's idea—the idea of the International, a uniform movement comprising the common interests of workers of all countries but controlled and guided from a single center—in this case, of course, by himself and Engels—gave it a compelling simplicity. In the socialist competition that was already widespread throughout Western Europe, Marx was making a bid for leadership. He was descending once again into the arena of political action in the hope that he could achieve a commanding position with a system of his own.

He sent Proudhon an engagingly worded invitation to contribute to his Correspondence Committee, but though Proudhon's response was very warm, it contained too much "liberalism" for Marx, who was firmly convinced of the uniqueness of his own method of carrying on the struggle for socialism. Marx never wrote him again. A passage in the letter from Proudhon may be worth quoting, in view of Marx's subsequent violent attack on him and perhaps even more in view of the subsequent development of Marxism as a system:

For God's sake, after having abolished all dogmatism in the first place, do not let us in our turn dream of indoctrinating the people ourselves. Do not let us fall into the contradiction of your compatriot Martin Luther, who, after having overthrown Catholic theology, set about immediately with the help of excommunications and anathemas to found a Protestant one. I applaud with all my heart your idea of presenting all opinions. Let us have a good and honest discussion; let us give the world the example of a wise and far-seeing tolerance; but being at the forefront of a movement, do not let us therefore make ourselves the leaders of a new intolerance, do not let us set ourselves up as the apostles of a new religion. Let us accept and encourage all objections; let us brand all exclusions, all mysticisms; let us never look upon a question as exhausted; and when we have used up all our arguments, let us start afresh, if need be, with eloquence and irony. On these conditions I will join you with pleasure; otherwise not.

In Europe, the years 1846 and 1847 were filled with an extraordinary political fermentation. The dissatisfaction of so many radicals with the political monopoly still in the hands of monarchs of one kind or another kept increasing. A murmur of rebelliousness, more and more openly expressed, could be heard even by non-specialists in all the capitals of Europe; in France especially, under the "Citizen King," the democratic opposition had evolved to the point where it could begin openly challenging the conservative defenders of the regime.

Marx and Engels, stuck away for the moment in Brussels, had their eyes fixed, like so many others, on an imminent revolutionary upheaval. In accordance with their new theory, they were sure the upheaval would develop along the lines their science had enabled them to foresee with gratifying infallibility. As both young men were fired by the general enthusiasm and belief that a revolution was around the corner, the main thing was to get some organizational power so that they could operate more effectively.

This organizational question was felt to be all the more urgent since Marx's literary labors, aside from letters and articles, had been concentrated on finishing the immense *German Ideology*. It proved absolutely impossible to get it published. An admirer of Marx's, Joseph Weydemeyer, who had been deflected out of the Prussian Army officers' corps by a sudden ardor for socialism, and who had proved invaluable in the collaboration between Marx and Engels on *The German Ideology*—if only because of his patience in deciphering Marx's handwriting—held out great hopes that some rich businessmen, whom Weydemeyer had converted to socialism, would not only launch a socialist publishing house run by Marx, but would publish *The German Ideology* as its first offering.

This mood of optimism lasted until the two businessmen actually saw the endless manuscript. A deep chill entered the relationship between them and Weydemeyer and, after Weydemeyer had failed to market the book elsewhere, into the relationship between Weydemeyer and Marx and Engels. The reasons are simple enough—according to Mehring, Marx's pious biographer, *The German*

Ideology "is a still more diffuse super-polemic than the *Holy Family* even in its driest chapters, and the oases are fewer and farther between."

It was at around this time that Marx ceased emphasizing his philosophical status and began referring to himself as an economist, almost exactly three years after first opening a book on the subject. Although he had published nothing whatever in this semi-technical field, he got around the difficulty by referring, somewhat vaguely, to work in progress. Meanwhile the German publisher who had already paid him an advance for a book on political economy kept pressing him, more and more disagreeably, for a manuscript. To cover up his embarrassment, Marx allowed it to become known that his problem was finding a publisher for his book—what he had, in fact, was the publisher but nothing else.

Marx consolidated his control over the minuscule Communist Party he had founded in Brussels with Engels by expelling a couple of other members whose sentimental views irritated him—notably Kriege, a writer who had emigrated to America, and Weitling himself.

His attack on Kriege—following some articles on socialism that appeared in Kriege's little German paper, published in New York—revolved around Kriege's rather utopian idea of allocating agricultural land in America to produce small farmers and, more importantly, around Kriege's "sloppy sentimentality." Marx's attitude on both points is of some interest today; in the attack he developed his own view of the peasants as essentially nothing but small capitalists, who "at first" might have to be offered a reallocation of land in order to have it "ultimately" taken away again. This is of particular interest because of Soviet practice in the first post-revolutionary decade. It was on the basis of the second point—Kriege's senti-

mentality—that the formulation of Marxism as an iron-
hard, unemotional, objective science instead of a wishywashy utopianism was concretized and a contrast made between "emotional communism" and "critical communism."

At the meeting held to preside over the expulsion of
Kriege *in absentia,* Weitling grew very excited in Kriege's
defense. Weitling was himself, of course, a typical "emotional" communist and felt directly threatened. His passionate defense of "emotionalism" made Marx raise the
question of Weitling's own membership, only a couple of
years after Marx had praised him so highly as the proletarian paragon.

Marx's attempt to remove Weitling became a sort of
campaign, in which he was opposed, very violently, by
Hess. Shortly afterward, Marx tried to get Hess expelled,
too—just three years after he was inducted by Hess into
the nascent movement. The attempt was forestalled only
by Hess's resignation.

During the intrigues aimed at Weitling, Engels went
to Paris and managed to turn the members of the organization founded by Weitling against him. The upshot was
that Weitling got so depressed by the campaign being
waged by Marx and Engels that he too emigrated to
America. He was promptly forgotten in Europe.

There was a striking contrast between Marx's theories,
of cosmic dimensions, and his actual organizational pre-
occupations. However these are analyzed, they simply boil
down to a struggle for the leadership of a handful of expatriate Germans in a few capitals.

Yet the contrast is only ironic to us now; at the time,
when so many hopeful radicals were looking forward to
cataclysmic events, it was perfectly reasonable to assume
that even a tiny handful of individuals might become the

spearhead of a vast movement created by titanic subterranean shifts in society. Before the collapse of hopes in 1848, Marx and Engels could legitimately anticipate a rapid growth of the army of which they regarded themselves the leaders. After 1848, with their political activities substantially curtailed, the irony in the contrast between Marx's factional activities and his political ambitions became even more pronounced.

It was always difficult for Marx to work in an organization he did not control. Just as in personal relations he needed subordinates rather than friends, so in organizations his natural position was that of leader—his problem was to find followers. Here his difficulties were in a sense personal.

Temperamentally Marx was quite alien to what may be called the emotional archetype of his era. Men were laying an enormous emphasis on singularity. Heroes were admired with unqualified enthusiasm. Personal sensibility had become extremely fashionable, and cultivated European society was preoccupied, by and large, with the cult of the individual. Great leaders were admired for their achievements and their romantic personal aura. Their accomplishments dazzled their admirers not merely from an external point of view, but because it was assumed that these were the result of intense personal experience.

Marx was quite removed from all this. Outside his family circle he was emotionally rather chilly, without the smallest interest in the psychology of the people he met, worked with, or fought. Socially he was regarded simply as a boor. The sentimentalities of his student life were a thing of the past. As he grew older, he came to look upon personal suffering as self-pampering. In his fight against "bourgeois" society—i.e., society as such—he developed an attitude of deep contempt for anyone absorbed by personal woes in the midst of what he thought of as a battle.

Here is a description of Marx, in his late twenties, by a rich Russian nobleman and literary bohemian, Paul Annenkov, who had given him some money:

Marx belonged to the type of man that is all energy, will-power and unshakable conviction, a type that is extremely remarkable in externals too. With a thick black mop of hair on his head, with hairy hands and crookedly buttoned frock-coat, he had the air of someone with the right and the power to command respect whatever his appearance and whatever he did. All his movements were clumsy, but bold and self-assured. His manners clashed with the accepted conventions of social intercourse; they were haughty, and almost contemptuous. His sharp voice, which had a metallic ring to it, made strikingly radical judgments on the people and subjects he mentioned. Even at this time he did not speak except in judgments from which there was no appeal, and which were dominated by one painfully sharp note. This note reflected his own firm conviction of his mission to govern men's minds and to dictate the laws of their being. Before me there stood the personification of a dictator from the people such as might appear to the mind in moments of fancy.

It was Annenkov, commenting on Marx's attempts in Brussels to dominate the German workingmen's tiny organizations, who coined the sobriquet for him of "proletarian dictator."

During this miniature political campaign in Brussels, directed at nothing more, after all, than the expulsion of a couple of individuals with whom Marx disagreed, both he and Engels lost some of the youthful idealism that had characterized them in the first flush of their enthusiasm for the "proletariat." As they came into direct contact with real people, the things they said about the workers privately began to diverge very substantially from their public statements. With respect to the myth into which they were trying to transform the proletariat, as redeemer of the cosmos, their public references retained a sort of unearthly luminescence. Privately, in Engels's letters, the workers were referred to simply as jackasses, gullible fools, etc.

Marx and Engels had, in this one respect, at least, plunged from their philosophical heights into the practical life of factional struggle.

Yet in spite of everything, Marx's organizational activities consisted, for the time being, of attempting to dominate the tiny field of the German workers' organizations outside Germany, while maintaining his intellectual position through polemical onslaughts on all rivals.

He did this in the midst of increasingly difficult circumstances. Marx had now no possibility of earning a living, nor for that matter did he ever look for a job. But he had a large family—in addition to his wife, the servant Helen, and his first-born, Jenny, two more children had arrived, a second girl and a boy. On top of this, Marx began, at the age of twenty-eight, despite his remarkable energies, to suffer from physical ailments.

Marx was compelled to borrow money from everyone he could—from a relative in Holland, from two brothers-in-law, from his Russian admirer Annenkov. There were only two possible large-scale sources of money—what he referred to as his "fortune," still held by his mother, and the brilliant prospects that would, somehow, open up after the revolution took place. Marx and Engels, in the infectious optimism of the years before 1848, without describing how it would happen, expected the revolution just around the corner to solve Marx's money worries too.

Nevertheless Marx immersed himself with unflagging energy in a torrent of polemics, which arose very naturally out of his conviction that he and Engels alone possessed

the true key to the analysis of socialism, now a respectably
sized movement in Europe. His determination to dominate
this movement made him carry on a systematic campaign,
in articles and letters, to cut off the heads of all possible
rivals and contenders as they appeared.

From a purely polemical point of view his theory had
marvelous advantages. It was very compact, very balanced,
and had tremendous flexibility because of the dialectical
method of discourse, in which all entities could be broken
down, redivided, and recombined in a "dialectical" manner that gave his style immense verve and bite. The basic
structure remained simple: the development of the productive forces was leading inevitably to the smashing of
the old order since the fundamental "law of motion" was
working with iron compulsiveness toward its inevitable
conclusion.

During this period, the chief rival he "settled accounts
with" was Proudhon, who had written a book called *The
Philosophy of Misery*, which he had been imprudent
enough to show Marx, apparently still thinking him
friendly. Proudhon, who had become famous through his
epigrammatic description of property as "theft," had
evolved somewhat beyond this into an attack on the state
as such. For him, the state reinforced the pernicious tendency of the accumulation of capital by fusing economic
control and political authority. He had developed a less
extreme view of property and thought everyone had a right
to a small minimum for his dignity. The state, which
through its power could take even this away, was thus
the principal enemy, according to Proudhon. He also detested competition as injurious and unnecessary. He expressed his hatred of this "unnatural" situation in semi-
Hegelian language that infuriated Marx perhaps even
more than Proudhon's theories themselves.

In any case Marx attacked *The Philosophy of Misery* in a singularly savage polemic, *The Misery of Philosophy*, a play on Proudhon's title. It was perhaps the most ferocious attack by one intellectual on another for centuries.

Marx took pains to demonstrate that Proudhon was practically a moron, totally devoid of the faculty of thinking abstractly, a vacuum he attempted to fill by his mock-Hegelian vocabulary. He thought Proudhon stupid and in particular despised his vague sentimentality and rhetorical exuberance, which he shared with Bakunin, a more serious rival of Marx's. Marx called Proudhon, rather oddly, a "self-taught" economist, although he himself had taken up economics in the same way.

In spite of Marx's attack, however, and even to a certain extent because of the sympathy it aroused on behalf of Proudhon, Proudhon was not only not destroyed but his movement survived and very much held its own—especially in Latin countries—against the later growth of Marxism.

In the period immediately preceding 1848, Marx and Engels shared the general optimism of European intellectuals to such a point that it seemed very obvious to them that the stage of history they had been predicting was about to arrive. In 1847 a tremendous economic and financial crash took place. The stock markets and exchanges in Europe and America collapsed, and by the time the crisis was over, the depression was the worst in history. In addition, it had come only some five years after the preceding crash. It seemed to justify the current political optimism. From Marx's point of view the situation looked singularly "ripe," for according to his theory, things were bound to crash, explode, and be burst asunder whenever the forces of production outgrew their matrix. With economic ripeness, the imminence of socialism, ensured by the activity of the intellectuals guiding the movement, was guaranteed.

It was this depression, Marx thought, that he had foreseen in his theory and prophesied. And since this forecast had been correct and properly deduced from his inevitable laws, it was only natural for Marx to take the second step and assume that with this collapse of markets the whole system was bound to be obliterated through the establishment of a new order after the great proletarian revolution.

It is curious to reflect that ever since Marx's optimism of 1848, his followers, for more than a century, have been hailing each depression or economic collapse as the "final" collapse heralding the dawn of the new order. This assertion has been regularly made and ascribed to the infallibility of the general Marxist theory of social history.

If we cast our minds back to the middle of the last century, in which a feudal or semi-feudal order reigned throughout large sections of Europe, with a bourgeoisie either fully established, as in England and France, or in the midst of a dynamic expansion, as in Germany, with only an embryonic working-class movement in Germany, and with the bulk of English workers indifferent to socialism, it may seem rather odd that Marx and Engels should have been so *sure* of a cataclysmic social upheaval: where were the human beings who could bring it about? We are bound to think that Marx was not so much an observer of events as the prisoner of a logical system. Identifying his own intellectual activity with the activity of society, he assumed that since the logic of his own train of thought was impeccable it must be realized in the social transformation it had set out to prove. This, linked to his youthful exuberance, made his optimism natural.

In 1847, his general theory seemed very plausible indeed; his reputation grew substantially. The Committee of the League of the Just in London, the major branch of the group originally founded by Weitling in Paris, was so impressed by the assurance with which Marx had been predicting what in fact seemed to be happening around them that they sent someone to see him in Brussels. It was Marx's greatest political success so far.

The League in London was not only prepared to accept Marx's doctrine but was willing to take the start in uniting existing "proletarian" forces into a single Communist League. This would take in all extant groups in London, Paris, and Brussels, and, for that matter, all national groups, and so constitute a formidable international organization. It went without saying that in these circumstances Marx was asked to formulate the platform.

Marx was delighted. Engels went to London to attend the first convention that was scheduled to discuss the whole plan of merger. The German delegates were the only *de facto* group—numbering some three hundred people. The representatives of the other groups actually represented no one but consisted of a few random foreigners living in London who happened to speak German. But the whole idea of fusion was greeted with enthusiasm; it was to be set up in final detail at a second congress later on.

What had to be worked out now was the platform, a sort of "credo." Engels wrote out a draft in the form of a catechism consisting of twenty-five questions and answers. Through a curious maneuver, Engels managed to have the text sent to London as though it came from the Paris branch, which had, meanwhile, accepted one prepared by Moses Hess.

By the time Marx himself appeared with Engels at the second congress, it was their draft that was under discussion, though, since Engels was a little dissatisfied with its form, they both said that they had settled only on the content, and the form would be changed.

The change in form had far-reaching consequences. The final draft, written by Marx in Brussels as a radical reworking of Engels's effort, became known as the *Communist Manifesto*. It is one of the most celebrated documents in history.

The document, largely Marx's handiwork, is a series of dramatic and sweeping generalizations. It begins with a lyrical denunciation of the existing social order, proceeds to a chain of interlinked arguments demonstrating that the pernicious status quo is bound to be destroyed by the vindictive forces inherent in the future, and concludes on a note of exhortation that has become the signature quotation of the socialist and communist movements: "Workers of all countries, unite!"

The *Manifesto* was designed to do a number of different things: to recruit new people to the Communist League, to deflect men away from other brands of socialism, and to lay down practical political suggestions on the basis of a philosophical doctrine that would encompass and justify the whole document.

In addition, it had to be very easy to read, in view of the large audience it was aimed at. Thus the *Manifesto* took the form of an elementary primer. It was a popular summary of the cardinal views of Marx and Engels in their late twenties.

The generalizations spanned all history in a categorical, epigrammatic way. They laid it down that one system had always followed another, only to be destroyed in the course of time by the growth of the productive forces and by the revolt of the classes hitherto exploited. Leaping to the current era, they described how the bourgeoisie rose from the feudal system and accomplished fantastic feats, which

Marx and Engels summed up in the most extravagant way. Now, "for many decades," it had been in the process of destruction because of the growth of the productive forces it had itself developed, accompanied by the revolt of its own exploited class, the proletariat. This process of destruction was, as they put it, "going on before our eyes."

Though the structure of the document theoretically rested on a scientific demonstration of a factual situation, the language itself was chosen to appeal to pure emotion. It was not, to be sure, a sentimental appeal to the softer emotions, like love and kindness, which in the work of other socialists had always struck Marx and Engels as wishywashy sentimentality, but an outright appeal to the most violent hatred, in the most far-fetched generalizations—"the bourgeoisie has torn the veil of sentimentality away from the family and reduced it to a mere money relationship. . . ." "The bourgeois sees in his wife a mere instrument of production."

The *Manifesto* violently condemned not only the upper bourgeoisie, but the "lower middle-class, the small manufacturer, the shopkeeper, the artisan, and the peasant" as fanatical adherents of the property idea. In many countries, Marx and Engels agreed, the peasants came to "far more than half the population." At the same time, somehow, "private property has already been eliminated with respect to nine-tenths of the population." On the other hand, the proletarian movement was one "of" the immense majority as well as "for" the immense majority.

The *Manifesto* avoided any discussion of the social order that was to succeed the destruction of the current order. The vistas it opened up simply stopped short with the coming revolution. This omission was never filled by Marx or Engels; later on they called the demand for a solution a pedantic philistine desire for a "blueprint."

The *Manifesto* was a most effective synthesis of many celebrated slogans, taken from many sources. Marat, the theoretician and terrorist of the French Revolution, was the source of two: "The proletarians have nothing to lose but their chains" and "the workers have no country." "The exploitation of men by men" was taken from a follower of Saint-Simon. Indeed, the celebrated concluding line, "Workers of all countries, unite!" was taken from a German student; it had been published a few months before in London.

The *Manifesto,* which in the course of time was to become the most popular socialist document, was an unusual blend of German and French writing. Some of its remarkable rhetorical effectiveness is due to its intertangling German and French thought in a dense melange. It has always had far more of an effect on the European continent than in the English-speaking world.

Nevertheless, despite its complex origins, the present unity, at least from a rhetorical point of view, is striking. Considered as propaganda, it must be the most effective single piece of prose ever written. Indeed, it cannot be understood outside a quasi-religious context of emotion. As a literary work it is regarded as Marx's masterpiece and also Engels's, whose contribution has been much slighted, as much through Engels's modesty as through neglect by later scholars.

The *Manifesto* was finished in the first month of 1848, only a short time before the upheavals began that seemed about to change the whole picture of European society.

On February 22, 1848, the streets of Paris were flooded with crowds of people, in demonstrations that ushered in a period of ferocious turbulence throughout Europe.

Marx himself had been expelled from Belgian territory in the wake of the publication of the *Communist Mani-*

festo. His personal circumstances were easier. On February 10, he had received a sum of money, substantial for the time—6000 gold francs. On the invitation of a member of Louis Blanc's socialist party, who was now a member of the new democratic government in Paris, Marx came to France, after being detained overnight by the Belgian police. He arrived to find Paris in a state of unbridled rapture. Memories of the French Revolution were still inflaming broad strata of the populace; the king had fled without making the slightest difficulty. A new government had been formed that appeared to be made up of a range of luminaries, including the poet Lamartine. Even the working class was represented by Louis Blanc and by an unknown worker, Albert.

Lamartine rose predictably to the occasion with a magniloquent manifesto that was instantly taken up and repeated, quoted, and declaimed everywhere. The boulevards were thronged by an immense concourse of people singing their heads off, all of them democrats of every conceivable shading and nationality. There was no sign of life whatever from the expected conservative opposition. The church published a manifesto pointing out that, properly understood, the church, since its kingdom was not of this world anyhow, was a natural ally of all the forces of progress. Its recent position as a supposed defender of the reaction had nothing to do with its principles, and the church could be counted on to help out with the rectification of social ills.

The enthusiasm was universal. In Paris all the foreign exiles—Germans, Poles, Italians etc.—were agreeing that their own countries would not procrastinate in following the French lead.

The newly proclaimed French republic was ten days old when Marx arrived. It seemed to many that a new form of constitutional legality was about to take root in France. But Marx, strolling about in the exhilarating atmosphere of a capital in upheaval, thought that phase of social organization long since outmoded by the course of events. He was very optimistic about the prospects of a total revolution—a revolution that would discard obsolete democratic ideas and develop in accordance with his predictions. He was particularly elated at the sight of a new kind of organization—the Workers' Guard—marching about. He and Engels indulged in a spate of optimistic formulations that they were to call—fifteen years later— "comfortable delusions and almost childish enthusiasm."

Marx thought the most urgent practical question was that of the elections proposed by the new government. Here the substance of one of his claims—that socialism was not merely *for* the great majority but *of* it—came into conflict with the realities of the democratic process. Even in Paris the proletariat was, after all, a small minority, and a still smaller minority of that minority was even remotely socialist, while outside Paris there was no proletariat at all. It was clearly pointless for Marx to sponsor a democratic election. On the other hand, a few Frenchmen were also against elections, notably Blanqui, an insurrectionist who had just come out of jail and who had invented a slogan that was ultimately to bear some unexpected fruit, "the dictatorship of the proletariat." Marx was delighted with the phrase and later adopted it.

Marx had high hopes of the Germans in Paris, but he had arrived too late to influence them along the lines he wanted to. A well-known, very rich poet whom he had come to know during his first sojourn in Paris, Herwegh, the "iron lark" of democracy, had proposed the organization of a German Legion that was supposed to overwhelm

Germany and either trigger a democratic upheaval or pro-
tect one if it was already going on.

The French government naturally encouraged this—
maybe as a way of getting rid of potentially troublesome
foreigners!—but Marx was completely skeptical about it,
perhaps because he had no control over it. Objectively,
too, there seemed no reason to think it could lead to anything. Marx set about the organization of a rival group,
to oppose Herwegh's. He organized his own communists,
with some additional arrivals from Brussels and London,
into a club of German Workers. Since most of the German
workers in Paris were either indifferent or actively hostile
to any form of socialism, the club was founded ostensibly
to champion democracy, the catchword of the time. Engels was later to make it clear that "in the spring of 1848
the only possible means of getting the ear of the working-
class" was democracy. This little Club of German Workers organized by Marx in early 1848 was the first of the
many "front" organizations invented by Marx and made
familiar by his followers.

By now what seemed like a tidal wave had been spreading from Paris throughout Europe. In Italy, in all the big
cities—Florence, Naples, Turin, Milan, Venice, and even
Rome—demonstrations had been breaking out like a rash.
Any number of thrones were saved from complete collapse only because some democratic concessions were instantly and painlessly granted. Constitutions were being
proclaimed everywhere. In Italy, and later Austria, the
same slogans of republicanism, democracy, and also nationalism were making lightning-like progress. The Habsburg autocracy was shaken, and the question of nationalist
self-determination was raised throughout the ancient empire, on Hungarian, Czech, Polish, and Italian terrain.

Even in Marx's homeland the fortress of Prussian self-sufficiency seemed to have been taken by storm. Berlin was flooded with the usual street demonstrations of people —all sorts of shopkeepers, workers, students, and artisans —yelling "Freedom," "Constitution," and "Long Live Germany!" Barricades were set up. The monarch, Frederick William IV, was frightened enough to order all his troops out of the city. There was bloodshed; countless people died—the king had to uncover his head in front of the corpses of the demonstrators. He was obliged to promise the demonstrators everything they had been asking for— elections, constitution, democracy, even the establishment of a new German Empire that would incorporate Prussia.

From Marx's point of view the difficulty was that none of what was happening seemed to have the slightest relationship to the abstract schema he had become so dogmatic about. None of the slogans was connected with the "productive forces," economic ripening, or any other aspect of his general system. There was not the smallest trace of a proletariat or any modern productive forces in places like Hungary and Italy, where actual revolutionary demonstrations had taken place, while in England, industrially the most advanced country in the world, there was no hint of a revolution at all.

But he was at least in the thick of turbulent events. He controlled an organization, however small, and believed in his compelling view of social transformation. Also, the arena of immediate action had, with the outbreak in Berlin, shifted back to his own country.

Marx was in control of some three hundred intellectuals, semi-intellectuals, and artisans in a number of cities. These were all dispatched to Prussia, and told to scatter throughout the cities. Marx was to go on to Cologne, where as the ex-editor of the martyred *Rhine Gazette,* he would have a reputation at hand. Meanwhile he had been collaborating with Blanqui, who was agitating against setting up any electoral system in France, on the theory that the French were still too unenlightened to understand socialism. He also began working energetically in a nondescript French organization at just about the time that the first copies of the *Communist Manifesto* arrived in Paris, though no French translation was yet ready. Marx began interpreting and explaining the *Manifesto* to this French organization. Eventually he won it over to his own views, no mean achievement considering Marx's difficulties in personal negotiation. This club also came out against elections.

Marx could leave in a mood of confidence. Beginning in April his agents left for Germany, and on April 5, Marx, the commander-in-chief, left. It was the beginning of a sort of communist campaign inside Germany.

In France, however, the campaign led by extremist socialist groups was unsuccessful; by April 23 elections for the National Assembly took place despite the protests of the socialists who had opposed them on principle. An enormous number of people—nine million!—voted in a genuinely popular election—the first election, indeed, held on the European continent on the basis of universal suffrage. The attitude of the inexperienced electorate was unmistakable on two counts: only 200 royalists were elected as against 600 republicans, while of these republicans only a sixth were socialists of any kind whatever; of these, ninety per cent were what Marx called "petty-bourgeois" socialists, i.e., they did not believe in a special status for the proletariat. Hence in Marx's opinion the elections were just as discouraging as he had expected—seven-eighths of the populace had rejected socialism out of hand

and three-quarters had demanded a non-socialist democracy. And this was France—the "ripest" country on the
Continent!

But Marx was now deeply involved in his hopes for
Germany. On his return to Cologne, where most people
still thought of him as a democratic martyr because of the
suppression of the *Rhine Gazette,* he at once put himself
forward as a democrat, veiling completely his recent political and philosophical transformation. As Engels explained it later, it would have been quite out of the question to come forward at this time as a communist, since
that would have meant no more than futile agitation in
some tiny corner, whereas the democratic party was at
least a method of getting the attention of the working
class. It was, perhaps, a curious notion to launch a communist revolution on the sly, but in view of Marx's conception of inevitably evolving social forces it could have
been considered a sensible tactic. It was, initially at
least, quite successful.

The main thing was to found a new newspaper, one
that could be considered to carry on the traditions of the
defunct *Rhine Gazette.* The problem of money was of
course fundamental. Although Engels had found plenty of
enthusiastic communists among the parvenu millionaires
of the Rhineland, what they thought of as communism was
something quite mild—any mention of "armed force,"
Blanqui's "dictatorship of the proletariat," and so on
would have frightened them off. These rich bourgeois
communists, in other words, thought of communism as a
method for the democratic transformation of society.

Some rumors about Marx's and Engels's real opinions
had reached the Rhineland and given rise to understandable difficulties. Nevertheless, some pliable millionaires
were approached, and by May 5, 1848—Marx's thirtieth

birthday—there was enough money to finance the newspaper. It was another success for Marx's strategy of the false front in the class struggle.

Unfortunately, Marx found, despite his conviction that the nature of events was bound to radicalize social relationships, that nothing of the sort seemed to be happening. In all of Germany, in the midst of the anti-absolutist (i.e., democratic) fever that had taken hold of substantial sections of the populace, there had not been the smallest sign of any further split of the democratically minded masses into a bourgeois and a proletarian wing. A little while after Marx had arrived in Cologne, elections were held for a Prussian constitution. Later elections were held in the dozens of little German states as well. Throughout these elections whatever workers there may have been seemed to identify themselves completely with the democratic enthusiasm of the bourgeoisie.

It is true that in Paris things looked more radical, at least for a time. Some of the clubs, one of which Marx had conquered intellectually, made an attempt to establish a socialist republic over and against the democratic elections that had taken place. But even though they actually had the audacity to occupy the parliament building, it was not for long; only a few hours later the elected government was reinstated and things went on as before. Even if the episode were made out to be a harbinger of something more important—Marx did this later—it presaged nothing for Germany.

Hence Marx was obliged to depend on his army of agents. In accordance with the technique of concealment decided on both in Paris and in Cologne, they were supposed to "infiltrate" democratic organizations in Germany and build up a network of secret cells. This notion was conveyed to Marx's followers—often quite simple-minded

—in secret instructions. In theory it was easy, but it was obviously difficult to apply. Once the secret network had been set up, with the agents installed as ostensible democrats in various democratic organizations, they were then supposed to profess dissatisfaction with the degree of democracy in the parent organizations and set up still other democratic associations, under their own control. Hence a network of "front" organizations would ultimately be established that would be guided by "philosophy," i.e., Marx and Engels.

Marx was later to call this, in a letter to Engels, "at bottom nothing but a military plan against democracy." It was obviously a lot to expect from the simple-minded agitators in the field, though in Cologne, where Marx was personally in charge, there was no lack of brainpower to negotiate the maneuvering.

The successful publication of a newspaper, the *New Rhine Gazette,* was invaluable as a programmatic guide. Marx took immense pains to omit any mention at all of communism or socialism in the paper—it was ostensibly no more than an organ of democratic opinion. The articles Marx and Engels wrote for the *New Rhine Gazette* were collected some eighty years later by a Soviet publishing house, they formed a massive tome. The word "communistic" or "communist" is absent from the entire work.

The justification of all this activity remained, of course, Marx's theory, which was his principal political weapon. With respect to Germany, the theory rested on the notion that the Germans, just because they were the most backward of civilized nations, would not be allowed by the necessary evolution of history to do anything halfway. Just because they had lagged so far behind the French and English in accomplishing their bourgeois revolution, they had put themselves in the position of having to take a still

bigger jump forward, and accomplish, instead, a true proletarian revolution. Marx considered the democrats who
represented the newly evolving German middle-class far
too diffuse a political force to accomplish anything substantial even against the decayed absolutist regime. Hence,
to accomplish anything at all, the Germans—that is, the
German proletariat—had to leap over the intermediate
stage in one bound and accomplish the full-scale revolution at once.

The method devised for this was to acknowledge the
claims of the bourgeoisie for tactical purposes by concluding a purely conditional alliance between the proletarians
and the radical bourgeoisie. This would be vital for the
destruction of the reactionary regime, for whereas the
French had overthrown feudalism in 1789 and could thus
take the next leap forward in 1848, the Germans still had
both to eliminate feudalism and to promote the bourgeois
transformation of society. After this, they would catch up
with the more advanced industrialized countries, like
France and England, and be able to keep abreast of them.

After the victory of this purely provisional alliance between the German workers and their fellow-sufferers
among the middle and lower middle-class, the German
proletariat would have to curb the growth of its provisional partners simply by sheer bulk.

Such at least was Marx's theoretical assessment of the
German situation at the time.

Tactically the *New Rhine Gazette* concentrated on dissociating itself from the still strong current of democratic
opinion—sponsored by many socialists and former socialists, like Ruge and Hess—without coming out in a categorical way against democracy as such. It did this by vilify-
ing not the principles of democracy but its leaders. These
—in a manner reminiscent of later events—were simply

lumped together as distorters of democracy for an immense variety of reasons, many of them startlingly trivial.
In recalling this period, Engels was later to remark that
"the scorn and contempt with which we treated our opponents" were the paper's hallmark.

With respect to "national" politics Marx was a sponsor
of German unification and nationalism, from his point of
view quite consistent with his general position. Like Hegel
—and Bismarck—Marx saw in the amorphous condition
of Germany the source of its feebleness and inefficiency as
a society, as well as of its political backwardness. He was not
a nationalist on principle at all. On the contrary, he took
the view that small nations were, except in unusual circumstances, outmoded and historically meaningless anach-
ronisms. Thus it was quite sensible for him to approve in
public the German invasion of Schleswig-Holstein, a province of Denmark. It also gave him added support in German democratic circles, since this curiously pointless invasion of a friendly neighbor was wildly acclaimed by the
leading German democrats, in sharp contrast with the extreme reluctance of the Prussian king to press the war.
The war was considered by the king, oddly enough, to be
a war on behalf of democracy, which was just why he was
dragging his feet about it. The king did not want to annoy
either England or Russia by invading Denmark, nor for
that matter, and perhaps especially, did he want to send
his troops out of the country while so many democratic
disturbances were taking place.

Marx was also violently in favor of an immediate war
against Russia, which as the fortress of European reaction
could be depended on to crush any real attempt at a
democratic revolution in Germany. Such a revolution was
also to serve as a springboard for the fusion of the various
German princedoms into a democratic union that would

then be set off squarely against the Czarist regime, the most solid support in a Europe of the dynastic principle in social organization.

In Marx's wholehearted sponsorship of a war against Russia another factor may be detected. Bakunin had been attracting a great deal of attention because of recent anti-German pronouncements. He had come out for something he called the Slavonic revolution. This was to unite all the peoples of Slavic "race" against everything German, which, unaccountably, Bakunin had now turned against violently. Some have thought that Bakunin's abruptly expressed hatred of the Germans was a reflection of his loathing for Marx.

Marx now took the occasion to turn on Bakunin with his characteristic ferocity. He decided that Bakunin, who had spent most of his career fighting despotism, was in fact an agent of the Czar, and his "Slavonic revolution" a mere camouflage for sinister aims. Though it was always quite impossible for Marx to state his sources for the information that Bakunin was an agent, Bakunin never wholly lost the brand of traitor. The whole argument gave Marx and Engels the occasion, however, to discuss the "Slavic question" thoroughly.

They formulated another "inevitable" law, which justified both a war against the Czarist regime and a justification for wiping out a number of small nations.

Since the Russians as a people had played a progressive role in Asia, Marx and Engels decided, they could legitimately claim their own independence. The Poles, on the other hand, had a right to exist only insofar as they might contribute to the overthrow of the Czar through a national revolt; there would then no longer be the smallest justification for them. The Czechs and Yugoslavs "had no historical future whatever," and could never be anything more than agents of political reaction. In fact, only Germans and Austrians were authentic agents of the progressive principle in history.

Marx never expressed these views as reflections of any feeling he had about these particular nations, though he had a colloquial habit of referring to individuals very often in terms of their national origin. For him they simply represented one principle or another that was organically rooted in the scheme of reality. It might have been accidental that, in its disunified state, Germany seemed to him a natural vehicle for unification as a springboard for a progressive historical development. Yet the fact remains that practically every time there was an international conflict Marx produced a chain of reasoning that supported the German nationalist idea.

Then there occurred a spectacularly bloodstained event in Paris that seemed to justify, for a while, Marx's optimism about the oncoming revolution.

At a vast mass-meeting convened in Paris on June 23, 1848, some 40,000 people, all armed with guns and even cannon, mustered by three dissident democratic clubs— one formed by Blanqui, another by an intellectual, Barbès, and a third that had come under Marx's own influence— were inflamed to rebel against the government. This time the government, though set up by an immature, sentimental liberal movement, felt justified in taking to arms itself; it crushed the uprising in blood. The 40,000, despite the absence of any hope, since they had absolutely no support from the populace, were unaccountably intransigent. They refused to surrender when the National Assembly, elected by perfectly democratic methods, sent out an army against them under General Cavaignac.

There was a shocking amount of carnage. The armed

contest lasted four days, and even though there was no doubt as to the outcome by the end of the first day, the rebels, apparently expecting support from a substantial number of workers, were peculiarly stubborn. They were slaughtered.

It was a clear case; there was not the smallest evidence of any democratic support for the losers. They had come out arbitrarily against the legally and democratically elected government of the most advanced country in Europe, and with unparalleled and incomprehensible obstinacy had forced the slaughter of countless innocent victims.

Marx, on the other hand, had a special problem. He was bound to sympathize with the losers, since it was they who had gone to such lengths against a democratic regime that he was himself opposed to at heart. On the other hand, he could not afford to lose his foothold among the democrats he was doing his best to swing over into his own following.

The issue was all the more difficult for him since it seemed so clear. A democratically elected government had simply been attacked, without even a serious pretext, by a small minority; it had done no more than defend itself.

Marx had to find a riposte to this obvious interpretation of the events, concurred in by democrats not only in France but in Germany.

Marx's unusual boldness and rhetorical ingenuity came to his aid. By shuffling around the elements in the situation, it became child's play for him to represent the government that had just been elected by nine million people as the agent of the bourgeoisie, while the 40,000 rebels became the martyred people of France and the workers to boot. The insurrection had been put down most ferociously by the workers' battalions that had been constituted in

February. To Marx, the workers' battalions, only recently
his heroes of the barricades in February, were now the
"riffraff" of the streets.

But though Marx's effort was a masterpiece from a
purely rhetorical point of view—he succeeded in turning
this rather pathetic, though historically complex fiasco
into the source of another legend—he was incapable of
halting or deflecting the retreat of radicalism that was
prompted by the bloody clash.

What seemed to great numbers of people an attempt at
a violent take-over of the state marked a switch in feeling
not only in France but throughout Europe. The high
hopes of the extremists were frustrated. The turbulence
died down, and there was a return to some form of law
and order.

Marx's organized effort in Germany did not expand,
either in the clandestine headquarters or in the numerous
small democratic front organizations he had set up. His
three hundred agents failed to achieve anything substantial
outside half a dozen cities, and even there they were not
particularly effective. In Cologne and the Rhineland,
where Marx had installed himself and his immediate subordinates, the "Workers' Club" had a few thousand members, but they did not show any serious signs of what Marx
still persisted in thinking of as the "radicalization" that
was bound to arise out of the "deepening" of the conflict.

The proletarian revolution that he had deduced as the
immediate successor to the bourgeois overturn yielded, instead, to the growth of a reaction against the preceding
democratic wave. Yet Marx felt that the only thing to do
was to take control of whatever democratic movement was
left. In the midst of the steady retreat of previously optimistic democratic societies and clubs, he kept attempting

to grow stronger by splitting up the ranks of the remaining democrats.

We have testimony on Marx's activities at a conference of some of these associations in the Rhineland by Carl Schurz, later to become a distinguished person in American life—a senator, general, and Secretary of the Interior. Schurz's testimony helped add to Marx's reputation for intransigence:

Never have I met a man of such offensive, insupportable arrogance. No opinion which differed essentially from his own was accorded the honor of even a halfway respectful consideration. Everyone who disagreed with him was treated with scarcely-veiled contempt. He answered all arguments which displeased him with a biting scorn for the pitiable ignorance of those who advanced them, or with a libelous questioning of their motives. I still remember the cutting, scornful tone with which he uttered—I might almost say "spat"—the word "bourgeois"; and he denounced as "bourgeois"—that is to say as an unmistakable example of the lowest moral and spiritual stagnation—everyone who dared to oppose his opinions. . . . It was not to be wondered at that the proposals which Marx supported in the meeting were never adopted; that those whose feelings he had hurt by his behavior were inclined to vote for everything to which he objected; and that not only did he win no new followers, but he repelled many who might have supported him.

It was clear that nothing could be expected from any further forward march of the democratic forces. In August, when the Prussian king decided to call off the war against Denmark, Marx was reduced to making as much capital out of the Danish war as possible, by condemning a cease-fire as a betrayal of democracy because the only countries that had been against the war on Denmark from the beginning had been Russia, England, and Prussia, the three most counter-revolutionary powers in Europe. Marx called for a "German" war against Denmark on behalf of progress and democracy, incidentally denouncing the Danes— indeed all Scandinavians—as barbarians in the most extravagant language.

The end of the war against Denmark, which the Prussian king was now bent on, heralded a general reaction throughout Germany. Marx's *New Rhine Gazette* was allowed to continue, perhaps because it provided a convincing pretext that some action against the extremist democrats was still necessary. The paper was finally stopped, not by the authorities, but by the insolvency of the backers. Marx himself had to be very circumspect: his gesture, on his arrival in Brussels three years before, of formally renouncing Prussian citizenship, which at the time had seemed rather cagey, now rebounded against him. As a non-Prussian he could always be expelled by a simple police decree.

Marx was allowed, however, to carry on the newspaper as a personal venture. He invested in it the remnants of the money his mother had given him a few months previously and managed to drum up more in Vienna and from Polish sympathizers. He also hoped that Engels would get some money out of his father, but Engels balked.

Marx found himself bellowing battle-cries in a practically total vacuum. Reaction was on the march everywhere. The "counter-revolution" was striking one effective blow after another, the Habsburgs were back in northern Italy and Prague, and Vienna was safe under the thumb of their troops. In Paris, too, where just before the bloody attempt at a coup d'état in June, 1848, three-quarters of the electorate had voted for democracy, now, at an election held in December, 1848, nine-tenths voted for two

representatives of what seemed to be a longed-for stability
—Louis Napoleon or General Cavaignac, the general who
had suppressed the 40,000 rebels in June. Napoleon won
by an immense majority. Thus he became the perfectly
legitimate president of the Second French Republic. In
December, also, the King of Prussia put an end once and
for all to the parliamentary forms he had been compelled
to treat indulgently; he announced that the Prussian National Assembly was dissolved and that a new constitution,
devised by himself, was in force.

In the midst of this, Marx remained resolutely optimistic. He kept writing articles, hectic in tone, about the extravagant developments he persisted in thinking imminent
—the "revolutionary terror" that was soon to break out,
the "mailed fist of the people," wars and upheavals. On
the first day of 1849 he predicted a "new uprising of the
French working-class—and world war."

None of these predictions materialized. There were only
tiny flare-ups here and there in Germany. There was a
little outbreak in the kingdom of Saxony, whose most important aftermath was the elimination of Bakunin as a
political force for many years. He was caught, handed over
to the Austrian police, then to the Czarist police, and in
the end spent twelve years in jail. In Prussia there was a
slight spark in the Rhineland itself, Marx's birthplace—
some excited students, workers, and artisans and shopkeepers took over Engels's home town, Barmen, for a few days.
The incident inspired one of Marx's most extravagant and
grotesque summons to battle—a demand that the Rhineland take on the Prussian army! The episode lasted no
more than a few days. The Prussian army suppressed the
movement with absurd ease, and—most important of all
—Marx was expelled from Prussia in May, 1849.

This was to prove fateful for him in two ways: first of

all, it made it impossible for him to realize his dream of
effective action in his own country, since renouncing his
citizenship, which he had thought so shrewd a few years
before, now meant that he had no recourse at all to the
government's action.

In a larger sense, moreover, it was to separate him from
the field of politics for the rest of his life, by hampering
his personal activities and thus emphasising the bookworm
qualities he had already demonstrated to such a formidable extent. Though he later visited Prussia, he was never
to carry on any revolutionary activities there, because he
could always be deported. As it was to turn out, ironically,
this consequence of a maneuver he had thought so clever
at the time was to handicap him precisely against his rivals
for influence in the socialist field. He was never again to
agitate personally in Germany or to lead the life of an organizer, that is, to work in the arena of practical politics
in his own country and in his own language.

And he had shown great abilities as a practical leader,
abilities all the more remarkable because so many of his
personal qualities made it hard for him to work with people. His masterful temperament, his rhetorical suppleness,
and his powers of tactical improvisation had controlled
men in spite of his dogmatism in the face of evidence that
refused to conform with his "scientific" predictions and his
grotesquely over-optimistic miscalculation of events.

From now on, because of a silly and altogether meaningless blunder made as a young man, he was never to become
the leader of a socialist party.

At the moment he was still optimistic—he held firmly
to his extravagant predictions of an imminent disaster for
the bourgeoisie despite its apparent triumph. He printed
the last number of the *New Rhine Gazette* in red and
threatened the contemptible "terrorists" of the King and

the bourgeoisie with his own terrorism once he came into his kingdom. It was on this note that he left Prussia. After a hopeful stop-over in Bavaria and Baden, where an insurrectionary flicker or two seemed possible, he made his way to Paris.

Marx now had three children; his beloved wife was expecting a fourth. The political terrain looked absolutely hopeless. Throughout Europe the dust had settled on the abortive attempts to forcibly install democracy. By the summer of 1849, the whole continent gave the appearance of reactionary stability.

Marx's only sustained attempt at practical political agitation had turned out to be a total failure, largely because it was based on a theoretical estimation of what was possible, and even more because he lacked the human flair to sense the immense difference between his theories and the specific political aspirations of flesh-and-blood people. His ingenuity in devising purely abstract rhetorical and intellectual maneuvers had finally proved irrelevant to the concrete political moods of the moment—his talents in the abstract were nullified by his alienation from the concrete. His shortcomings, allied with the deflation due to events, outweighed his positive abilities as a leader.

This was made all the more obvious by the plain fact that the European economy had not been seriously damaged. Marx's practical activities had all been based on the broad predictions extracted from his general philosophical and historical "science." He had forecast an economic collapse in the wake of the stock market crash of 1847, which in its turn he took to be the sure harbinger of the radicalization of society that was to engender great advances in the direction of socialism.

The contrary had happened. Not only had the democratic revolution failed to lead inevitably to the proletarian revolution, but it had collapsed in its own terms. The *de facto* differences between the bourgeoisie and the working-class that were supposed to be generalized and radicalized into a raging hatred of class against class had come to nothing at all. Most workers and bourgeois had drawn closer in the joint struggle against absolutism and were in favor of nationalism, a concept whose emotional power was always alien and almost incomprehensible to Marx.

In short, every single prediction Marx had extracted from his general theory had been contradicted by the actual course of events. Yet Marx was not in the least discouraged. On the contrary, he was sure his errors called for nothing more than a slight rearrangement of the time schedule, after which the grand procession of foreordained history would go marching on. He was sustained by faith in his own system.

But during his few months in Paris he was under the watchful eye of Louis Napoleon's police, who finally, after seeing him move in circles that were still suspect, asked Marx to leave Paris for Brittany. When told by the poet Freiligrath that the climate there was bad, Marx felt indignant at this "thinly disguised attempt at murder" through "banishment to the Pontine marshes" of Brittany.

He decided to leave France altogether and make his way to the one great capital that had not been touched in the slightest by the turbulence on the continent. In London, he thought, he would stay for a few weeks, at the most a few months, before a new upheaval, which he was certain was inevitable, broke out and settled things in Europe once and for all. He wrote asking Engels to join him. They would start a German paper and confidently wait for a decisive turn in continental politics.

It was a decision that transformed Marx's life.

The transformation was in a way imperceptible, not least of all to Marx. His optimism kept him thinking that he was simply on the verge of a return to great events, and since in his recent political activities he had been a writer and thinker, too, there seemed no reason not to go on playing the same roles.

Yet it was his London exile that was to make Marx preponderantly a scholar; as a man of action he was to be frustrated. Though in exile he continued to agitate to some extent and struggle to create political organizations, he was to do so with singular aloofness and only fitfully, without leaving London. The general impression that just after his thirties Marx abandoned the life of action for that of the intellect, while quite misleading, is founded on his enforced isolation in exile, and on the fact that his scholarship was ultimately responsible for the immense influence he was to acquire, largely after his death, in the development of the modern socialist movement.

For all practical purposes Marx was to be in a state of hermetic isolation. Though he was moving to a most dynamic and rapidly changing society, which was at the very crest of the phenomenal ascension that was making it a world power, and working out processes that were to provide him with the material for his major work, he was never able personally to experience the remarkable social transformation of England. With the ending of his brief career as a political agitator on the Continent, he was to become incorrigibly bookish in exile. His temperament, his foreign appearance, his inadequate command of English—at least at first—obliged him to study the life around him by a sort of remote control.

He had taken himself for granted as a man of action not only because of his philosophical identification of "theory and practice," but because of his commanding tempera-

ment. Now he was to be insulated from serious political
action and compelled to exercise his influence, in ways
that were still unforeseeable, through the creations of his
mind.

And all because of his youthful folly in "defying" the
Prussian government! For as things were to turn out, it
was only his loss of citizenship that kept him chained in
exile and prevented his return home when liberalism once
again blossomed on the Continent and he could easily have
played a role in the politics of his own country.

Marx's departure from the Continent was the watershed
of his life.

CHAPTER VI

The Watershed: Exile and Decline

Marx arrived in London in the summer of 1849, thirty-one years old. It was to be his home for the rest of his life.

In the aftermath of the 1848 democratic debacle a flood of foreign refugees poured into London from every country on the Continent. Almost all impoverished, they represented a large variety of political species and subspecies of socialists and democrats, faiths that sometimes coincided and often did not. They all thought of themselves as *émigrés,* a word that was to become increasingly popular through the decades. They were all somewhat chilled by the reception they were given in England.

The characteristic insularity of the English had not been remotely modified by the recent turbulence on the Continent. The political and philosophical issues that had been churning up the continental intelligentsia had scarcely aroused any echoes in England, gripped by the phlegmatic self-assurance of a middle class in full ascension. Foreigners, including revolutionaries, were not disturbed at all as long as they behaved themselves; on the other hand, there was scarcely any intellectual give-and-take. It was clear to the revolutionaries, many of them from an effervescent milieu devoted to agitation of all kinds, that their activities were looked on by their English hosts with nothing more than indulgent amusement or indifference. Those Englishmen who showed some interest in them accentuated, if possible, their homesickness. The unquestioning acceptance of the social order, the unchallenged stability of British institutions had a most deflating effect on all the exiles except those of the most unyielding resolution. While the tolerant indulgence of English society created a sort of decompression chamber after the recent exhausting events on the Continent, it also emphasized their remoteness from any milieu in which the exiles, many of them men of great energy, could once again play some sort of role.

It embittered many. Marx, rigid in character and never particularly sentimental, was to be plagued also by constant poverty. At first he could not even speak English, and was instantly reduced to a very narrow circle—his family, Engels, and an odd German friend or two. Naturally thorny and imperious outside his family circle, he found the idea of becoming an effective public personality in his London exile impossible. As the years wore on, moreover, his natural snobbishness, jealousy, and detestation of all rivals within his self-chosen milieu increased to the point of making it difficult for him to enjoy normal social intercourse.

He grew to dislike English society intensely. While usually polite—or barely—to English "bourgeois," he loathed all socialists who were not directly under the sway of his own formulations. With Engels he did not need any other help, but the seclusion in which he lived drastically restricted any contact with his immediate surroundings. He was, after all, practically penniless in a country he had only the shallowest acquaintance with. Nor at this time did he have the glamour of romantic revolutionaries like Garibaldi, who became social lions.

On his arrival in 1849, his situation was not yet hopeless. He received some more money from his mother, through the sale of some property in Trier. More particularly, some friends who had stayed on in Germany during the years of political decline, content to take advantage of the new stability, did their best for him.

One of these friends, Ferdinand Lassalle, some seven years younger than Marx, had been celebrated as a socialist orator during the 1848 upsurge and had conceived an admiration for Marx. Like Marx, Lassalle was of Jewish origin. While very young, he had become the lawyer for a Countess Hatzfeld who was suing her husband for divorce. For some reason this aristocratic divorce case came to symbolize the split between liberalism and conservatism. It lasted for years and made Lassalle very famous. He was remarkably energetic, magnetic, and talented. He undertook to collect some money for those of his fellow-revolutionaries who had been exiled; Marx lived on his generosity for the first few months in London.

But he began to be subjected to terrible strains. His home life became increasingly painful. Jenny had a second son, their fourth child; the infant was sickly. The German newspaper Marx had hoped to launch dwindled away to a monthly review, which had to be supported out of Marx's pocket. His influence among the members of the Communist League, very great as recently as the spring of 1848, had also dwindled. Marx became obsessed by petty organizational intrigues in which he was not very successful.

By the next year the Marxes' financial breathing-spell was over. All their sources of income dried up at once. Lassalle, Jenny's mother, and Freiligrath in Cologne could no longer help. Marx was in the humiliating position of owing money to tradespeople in Chelsea, where the Marxes, with four children and their servant Helen, had a little flat of three rooms, and to the landlord as well. They were turned out of the flat; Jenny, whose brother, ironically, had meanwhile become the Prussian Minister of the Interior, describes the wretched scene:

Two bailiffs came into the house and took possession of all belongings—bedding, clothes, everything, even the baby's cradle and the little girls' toys, so that the children wept bitterly. The bailiffs threatened to take everything away in two hours. If this had happened, I should have had to lie on the floor, with my freezing children beside me, and with my aching breasts.

As all the tradespeople lined up to present their bills, the Marxes were not allowed to leave until they had taken everything they possessed to a pawnbroker in the neighborhood. When everything was settled, they had nothing left.

They finally moved to Soho, the famous London quarter that at the time was an appalling slum. They found two furnished rooms for all seven people, a real hole, where the sickly infant, in convulsions and screaming at the top of its lungs, was to die in its first year of life. In addition, Jenny was about to give birth once again, the fifth child after a marriage that had lasted seven years.

Marx's problems with the tiny German groups in London were insoluble. After a series of complicated entanglements with former adherents and present rivals, he lost control of all groups completely; by the autumn of 1850 he had little power. He had always set immense store by organizational attachments, and he struggled as hard as he could, but in the present political climate, poisoned for him by the obvious fact that his predictions had not been fulfilled, he was in too weak a position to impose his authority even on a small *émigré* organization.

It is true that he never admitted that his predictions had not been fulfilled. In the *German Review* that finally appeared, the recent events in France were analyzed once

again: Marx succeeded in explaining them in a way that
at least made them dovetail with his long-range analysis
of history and his sweeping specific predictions. His article
was to be reprinted many years afterward as *The Class
Struggles in France;* Engels thought it of particular significance.

This form of interpretation, which hostile critics have
found easy to describe as apologetics, was to constitute a
permanent literary genre in the later Marxist movement.
It was only one aspect of a systematic defense of his intellectual position that Marx was obliged to work out on
the spot in order to counter the accusations of his rivals,
who made the obvious point that harping on his "science"
was futile in view of its manifest failures in application. In
the course of his many-sided self-defense, Marx was to
evolve a theory that was to have some important repercussions—the theory of the Permanent Revolution.

To explain the defeats and fiascoes of the recent period
against the background of his general theory and defend,
particularly, his frequent statement that the "proletarian
revolution" was imminent—in fact "immediately" imminent—Marx had to generalize his theory to include all
activity against the established order, until all the "more
or less propertied classes" were dislodged from power and
"the proletariat has achieved the conquest of state power."
This formulation, because of its very generality, could not
be pinned down to any specific collision. By definition it
could be extended indefinitely and has been ever since.

Under the distressing pressure of the 1848 fiasco, accordingly, Marx changed his political approach on two points
that were to become of some consequence for posterity.

The first was a weakness he developed for a funda-
mentally non-Hegelian idea, one that had been advocated
by both the wandering German socialist tailor Weitling

and the French putschist Blanqui. They felt that a successful revolution could be carried out by a tiny spearhead of
trained revolutionaries. This small group of people would
then be supported by the massive advance of the proletariat as a whole, since the bulk of the people could
hardly be expected either to govern themselves or understand what the whole process was about. It was this inter-
lude that Marx meant specifically by the phrase "permanent revolution"—a form of "elitism" that has always ap-
pealed to adventurous spirits. Marx decided that this
elite was not meant to be clandestine, as Blanqui himself
had thought, nor headed by a single person, as Bakunin
sometimes seemed to suggest, but was to be a corps of dedicated individuals, much as the French revolutionist Babeuf
had conceived it in 1796.

It was perhaps this particular doctrine that was to have
the most far-reaching consequences for posterity, for it provided a theoretical justification for an analysis made by
Leon Trotsky in 1905 and accepted by Lenin in 1917. In
fact, it became the political model for the Russian Revolution of 1917.

Marx himself, curiously enough, lost faith in this idea,
doubtless because of the disappointments of 1848. He was
discouraged by the power of a regular army and the hopelessness of an unself-conscious proletariat. Hence he returned to the view that it was essential for the proletariat
to become imbued with a self-consciousness that would
enable it to understand and hence to perform its historic
task.

This somewhat revised program led to a second change
in his political attitude. He was still bound to believe that
a bourgeois revolution was essential as a transition to communism, but the bourgeoisie seemed to him so strong
now, in Germany and France, that it would be too dan-

gerous for a still feeble proletariat to enter into an alliance with it. The proletariat was too weak, in short, even to think of running a country clandestinely or in a masked form. Marx turned to the idea that the proletariat had to keep itself free of any debilitating alliances with stronger powers, retain and fortify its purity, and ultimately act independently.

This view is the intellectual background for the massive development of European socialist parties that were to busy themselves with the gradual extension of their electoral power and with putting systematic pressure on employers and governments through trade-unions, etc.

Thus two basic theses in Marx's general position, because they were emphasized differently in different sociopolitical contexts and had different aims, branched out into two different kinds of political movement.

As indicated above, Marx's basic ideas, broadly put, were that the socialist order was inevitable and also that a revolution had to be made. The logical contradiction inherent in the juxtaposition of these two statements was accommodated in socio-historical fact by a change in emphasis. The placidity of classical European Marxist parties was thus a development, intellectually quite defensible, of an aspect of Marx's analysis of the 1848 fiasco, while the boldness of the Bolshevik initiative in Russia in 1917 was an equally justifiable variant of the other, "elitist," view developed by Marx before the enthusiasm of the initial upsurge of 1848 had been eroded by disaster.

Marx's immediate situation in London was very difficult; not only were the catastrophes of 1848 uppermost in the minds of the *émigrés,* but the biggest and most aggressive contemporary English movement of the working-class—Chartism—had been completely overestimated by Engels and others. This movement, a beacon to Conti-

nental socialists who saw it as the independent expression
of the most advanced proletariat in the world, had been
shattered by events in England. By 1850 the economic
crisis that had begun in 1847 was finished, to be followed
by the same boom that bolstered all the continental regimes against the democratic upsurge. Chartism in England expired completely.

Moreover, Marx's isolation by 1850, after the loss of the
Communist League to his rivals and even his enemies, was
due, after all, to a lack of faith in his mesmerizing powers
as a "scientist." That faith was not based on Marx's person
—it was not the "cult of personality" that was to develop
generations later in the Soviet Union. It was based on
Marx's scientific authority, which was doubtless what had
been damaged most seriously by his organizational squabbles. His erudition, his polemical powers, and his total
self-assurance had convinced both followers and onlookers
that he really had discovered the key to some source of insight; the failures of his predictions were thus quite disil-
lusioning. Anyone who predicts specific events with "astro-
nomic certainty" has, after all, a real problem if the predictions fail to come off.

Now everyone's faith in him was shattered. It is true
that many of the verbal battles in this small *émigré* group
were somewhat academic, since its members believed that
the revolution was imminent, but Marx's personal prestige
was seriously hurt. The urgency to restore it arose precisely from the belief that another revolution was around
the corner. When it arrived, Marx, of course with Engels's
support, wanted to be assured of a guiding position.

The way to do this was clear—he must restore his prestige by supplying the scientific proof that carpers and dissidents as well as his own supporters (including Engels) had
been demanding for so long. He must demonstrate that the

attractively but sketchily written *Communist Manifesto* was based on incontrovertible evidence.

Though he had lately been referring to himself as an economist, he had written nothing on economics that could be considered substantial. His arrestingly novel formulation of a new approach to economics as well as to world history had not yet come out in book form. Most of his writings consisted of polemics—with a certain admixture of philosophy and history—but they were still polemics, revolving around all-inclusive, shattering generalizations. Engels's insistence was perfectly rational. It was indispensable to have a book that would contain, in a compendious and convincing form, the whole factual background underlying Marx's ferocious polemical onslaughts on all rival thinkers, writers, and political agitators.

Marx now had to sink himself, from the autumn of 1850 on, as he put it to Engels, in the "economic crap" again. Since his research into economics in Paris six years before, there had been an exhilarating period of action and potential action, in which a new world had seemed just around the corner. Now the new world had failed to appear. He was utterly dejected at the thought of returning to a bookworm's life, but he had no choice. He had broken the contract with the German publisher long ago, and had persuaded Annenkov and other friends that for years a book had been lying around in his trunk that no publisher had the courage to print. Now he finally had to produce it, if only because there was nothing else to do. The title he had once thought of for the book that had been commissioned by the German publisher was *Critique of Politics and Economics*; he decided to change it to *Critique of Political Economy*.

Meanwhile, to make financial ends meet, it was agreed that Engels must go back into the family business. Some

six years previously he had abandoned what he called
"filthy commerce," but he was not wholly estranged from
his family. His sister, writing on behalf of the family, suggested that he work in the firm at least until his "party had
a reasonable chance of success." He accepted at once,
because it was necessary to feed the Marxes, and even
put up with joining his father's branch in Manchester as a
lowly clerk.

In addition, to help promote their affairs still more ef-
ficiently, it was decided that Engels would become a military specialist. With his unusual capacity for grasping the
essentials of a subject quickly, it would be easy for him to
become enough of an expert to cope with some of their opponents in the *émigré* German colony, who based their
prestige on actual military experience. It was also obvious
that in the imminent revolution there would be an indispensable military position of command that clearly
ought to be occupied by a professional revolutionary Marx
could depend on.

Thus the immediate duties were shared out between
the two partners. Marx was to provide the scientific framework for the theory that had so far been enunciated only
in a sketchy, fragmentary, and polemical form, while
Engels was to earn the money for them all to live and in
addition digest the military expertise they would need for
the great events they expected.

In the autumn of 1850, armed with a reader's ticket,
Marx began his vigil in the celebrated Reading Room of
the British Museum. It was to be a long drawn-out ordeal.

Marx went there daily, generally staying from nine in
the morning till it closed at seven at night. He would then
work on at home, smoking without a stop. By now he
found the soothing qualities of tabocco indispensable, although it was to have a permanent effect on his health.

At first he was optimistic, as he sat in the Reading Room boning up on economics. But it bored him more and more. After some eight months, he wrote Engels hopefully assuring him that in another five weeks he would be through with the whole "economic crap" in the library and could begin working on it at home. Whether or not he was sincere, his optimism proved groundless—it was to be many years before he wrote so much as a page.

His health began to deteriorate. While still in his forties, his hair turned gray. He suffered from more and more crippling ailments and developed monstrous outbreaks of boils and carbuncles that were to plague him from now on in bouts of scarcely endurable virulence. A remark of his, that the bourgeoisie was going to pay dearly for every one of his carbuncles, was to become famous. He started to be afflicted by headaches, piles, rheumatism, liver trouble—a whole catalogue of ordeals that thrust Job into the shadow.

All this was attended by one family tragedy after another. The death of the sickly fourth child was followed by the birth of a fifth, a little girl who also died in her first year. Jenny had a sixth child, another girl, whose health remained uncertain for years, and a seventh child, who was stillborn. Jenny's health also began declining, and she hovered near death. Then there took place the most poignant of Marx's family tragedies—Edgar, a sickly child who was more gifted and even more ardently loved than the others, died at the age of nine. Marx's letter to Engels was a wholly human outcry of grief:

The house is desolate and orphaned since the death of the beloved child who was its life and soul. I cannot attempt to describe how we all miss him. I have had all kinds of bad luck, but now, for the first time, I know what real unhappiness is. Amid all the misery of these days, the thought of you and your friendship has kept me going—and the hope that you and I may still find it possible to do something worth doing in the world.

A confidential report on the family was sent to the Prussian Minister of the Interior, Jenny's brother Otto, who made a point of keeping himself abreast of their situation on behalf of the Prussian government and because of his own concern. It conveys a touching picture:

One of the rooms serves as a living room, and behind it is the bedroom. In the whole apartment there is not one sound piece of furniture, everything is broken, shabby, and ragged, and there is the greatest muddle everywhere. In the middle of the living room there is a big table covered with oilcloth. On it are piled his manuscripts, books, and papers; the children's toys; his wife's sewing; chipped tea-cups; dirty spoons, knives, and forks; lamps, an inkwell, glasses, claypipes, tobacco ash; in a word, it is the most indescribable muddle—and all on the one table. When one goes into the room, one's eyes are so blinded by coal and tobacco smoke that it is like walking around in a cave until one becomes accustomed to it and objects begin to loom up through the fog. Everything is so dirty, and the whole place is so full of dust, that sitting down is a dangerous business. One of the chairs has only three legs; and the children are playing at cooking on another one which happens to be whole, and which they offer to the guest; so if you sit down it is at the risk of ruining your trousers.

For years Marx was in the grip of almost total destitution. He received a sort of commission from an American newspaper, *The New York Tribune,* edited by Horace Greeley, a paper with Fourierist tendencies. He got the job through Freiligrath, but since he could not spare the time or the energy to write the articles, it was Engels who obligingly did so for him. For the first year, beginning in 1852, Engels wrote them all; later on he wrote the majority. In 1855 Lassalle helped get Marx a job as correspondent for a progressive German paper, but that lasted only a year.

Engels kept helping, but as he had agreed to a clerkship, his own resources did not go very far. He would enclose odd banknotes in his constant letters to Marx, a pound or two or three. At one point in 1852 Marx could not even leave the house—his clothes were in hock. He could not eat meat—they owed the butcher too much money. When their fifth child died in her first year, they could not pay for the funeral. Jenny had to rush off to a nearby French refugee, from whom she borrowed a couple of pounds. Here is a characteristic letter from 1852:

My wife is sick, little Jenny is sick, and Lenchen Demuth has some kind of inflammation of the nerves. I cannot call the doctor because I have no money for medicine. For eight or ten days now I have fed my family on bread and potatoes, and it is doubtful whether I can get any today. I cannot write the article for New York because I have no money to buy the newspapers which I need. Last week I borrowed a few shillings from some workers. For me that was the worst of all, but I had to do it if I was not to starve.

The grotesqueness of Marx's position in London is highlighted in an anecdote that was treasured in the family: Mrs. Marx told it later to H. M. Hyndman, one of Marx's few English admirers:

On one occasion Marx himself, being in great need, went out to pawn some household silver. He was not particularly well dressed, and his knowledge of English was not so good as it became later. The silver, unfortunately, as it turned out, bore the crest of the Duke of Argyll's family, the Campbells,

with which house Mrs. Marx was directly connected. Marx
arrived at the Bank of the Three Balls and produced his spoons
and forks. Saturday night, foreign Jew, dress untidy, hair and
beard roughly combed, handsome silver, noble crest—evidently
a very suspicious transaction indeed. So thought the pawnbroker to whom Marx applied. He therefore detained Marx,
on some pretext, while he sent for the police. The policeman
took the same view as the pawnbroker and also took poor
Marx to the police station. There again appearances were
strongly against him. "Saturday night, foreign Jew, handsome
silver, noble crest, etc.": the case was already decided before
the investigation began. In vain Marx . . . expostulated. His
explanations were futile, his expostulations useless. To whom
could he refer as to his respectability? Whence had he this
handsome silver he was so anxious to get rid of? Why did he
wait until dark to pledge the plate? There was nobody he
could call in at the time. His truthful statement as to the origin
of the spoons and forks was received with laughing incredulity.
The number of the house where they lodged was not considered sufficient.

So Marx received the unpleasant hospitality of a police
cell, while his anxious family mourned his disappearance, and
awaited in trepidation the husband and father who did not
come and the cash that they so badly needed. So Saturday night
passed. So Sunday. Not until Monday was the founder of
Scientific Socialism able to show conclusively, by the evidence
of quite "respectable" friends resident in London, that he
was not a thief and a burglar, and that the Campbell-crested
silver was honestly his property.

There was a breathing-spell in 1855, when some family
connections of Jenny's, including her mother, bequeathed
her some money. It enabled the Marxes to leave their
Soho rat-trap and move to a pleasant part of north London, near the endless stretches of the charming park on
Hampstead Heath. But it was no more than a breathing-

spell; by 1857 they were again living in extreme poverty.

Despite all his afflictions, Marx's morale was not affected. His relations with his family were a complete
antithesis to his prickly attitude toward others. The mutual devotion of himself and Jenny, his love for children,
and a sort of natural gaiety kept him emotionally stable at
home while he tilted intellectually against the windmills
of his time.

His natural dignity enabled him to keep up appearances. The confidential report to his brother-in-law, for
instance, after describing the utter squalor of his surroundings, comments: "But none of this embarrasses
Marx or his wife. You are received in the friendliest way
and cordially offered pipes, tobacco, and anything else at
hand. An intelligent and interesting conversation soon
springs up that makes up for all the domestic shortcomings; it makes the discomfort bearable. . . ."

His daughter Eleanor gives a moving picture of Marx
at home:

. . . To those who knew Karl Marx no legend is funnier than
the common one which pictures him a morose, bitter, unbend-
ing, unapproachable man, a sort of Jupiter Tonans, ever
hurling thunder, never known to smile, sitting aloof and
alone on Olympus. This picture of the cheeriest, gayest soul
that ever breathed, of a man brimming over with humor and
good-humor, whose hearty laugh was infectious and irresistible,
of the kindliest, gentlest, most sympathetic of companions, is
a standing wonder—and amusement—to those who knew him.

In his home life, as in his intercourse with friends, and even
with mere acquaintances, I think one might say that Karl
Marx's main characteristics were his unbounded good-humor
and his unlimited sympathy. His kindness and patience were
really sublime. A less sweet-tempered man would have often
been driven frantic by the constant interruptions, the continual

demands made upon him by all sorts of people. That a refugee of the Commune—a most unmitigated old bore, by the way —who had kept Marx three mortal hours, when at last told that time was pressing and much work still had to be done, should reply *"Mon cher Marx, je vous excuse"* is characteristic of Marx's courtesy and kindness.

But it was in his intercourse with children that Marx was perhaps most charming. Surely never did children have a more delightful playfellow. My earliest recollection of him is when I was about three years old, and "Mohr" ["the Moor"] was carrying me on his shoulder round our small garden in Grafton Terrace, and putting convolvulus flowers in my brown curls. Mohr was admittedly a splendid horse. In earlier days —I cannot remember them, but have heard tell of them—my sisters and little brother—whose death just after my own birth was a lifelong grief to my parents—would "harness" Mohr to chairs which they "mounted," and that he had to pull. . . . Personally—perhaps because I had no sisters of my own age— I preferred Mohr as a riding-horse. Seated on his shoulders, holding tight by his great mane of hair, then black, with but a hint of grey, I have had magnificent rides round our little garden, and over the fields—now built over—that surrounded our house in Grafton Terrace.

But if Mohr was an excellent horse, he had a still higher qualification. He was a unique, an unrivaled story-teller. I have heard my aunts say that as a little boy he was a terrible tyrant to his sisters, whom he would "drive" down the Markus- berg at Trier full speed, as his horses, and worse, would in- sist on their eating the "cakes" he made with dirty dough and dirtier hands. But they stood the "driving" and ate the "cakes" without a murmur, for the sake of the stories Karl would tell them as a reward for their virtue. And so many and many a year later Marx told stories to his children. To my sisters—I was then too small—he told tales as they went for walks, and these tales were measured by miles not chapters. "Tell us another mile," was the cry of the two girls. For my part, of the many wonderful tales Mohr told me, the most wonderful, the most delightful one, was "Hans Röckle." It went on for months and months; it was a whole series of stories. The pity no one was there to write down these tales so full of poetry, of wit, of humor! Hans Röckle himself was a Hoffmann-like magician, who kept a toyshop, and who was always "hard up." His shop was full of the most wonderful things—of wooden men and women, giants and dwarfs, kings and queens, workmen and masters, animals and birds as numerous as Noah got into the Ark, tables and chairs, carriages, boxes of all sorts and sizes. And though he was a magician, Hans could never meet his obligations either to the devil or the butcher, and was therefore—much against the grain—constantly obliged to sell his toys to the devil. These then went through wonderful adventures—always ending in a return to Hans Röckle's shop. Some of these adventures were as grim, as terrible, as any of Hoffmann's; some were comic; all were told with inexhaustible verve, wit, and humor.

And Mohr would also read to his children. Thus to me, as to my sisters before me, he read the whole of Homer, the whole *Niebelungen Lied, Gudrun, Don Quixote,* the *Arabian Nights,* etc. As to Shakespeare he was the Bible of our house, seldom out of our hands or mouths. By the time I was six I knew scene upon scene of Shakespeare by heart.

On my sixth birthday Mohr presented me with my first novel—the immortal *Peter Simple.* This was followed by a whole course of Marryat and Cooper. And my father actually read every one of the tales as I read them, and gravely discussed them with his little girl. And when that little girl, fired by Marryat's tales of the sea, declared she would become a "Post-Captain" (whatever that may be) and consulted her father as to whether it would not be possible for her "to dress up as a boy" and "run away to join a man-of-war" he assured her he thought it might very well be done, only they must say nothing about it to anyone until all plans were well matured. Before these plans could be matured, however, the Scott mania had set in, and the little girl heard to her horror that she herself partly belonged to the detested clan of Campbell. Then came plots for rousing the Highlands, and for reviving "the forty-five." I should add that Scott was an author to whom Marx again and again returned, whom he admired and knew as well as he did Balzac and Fielding. And while he talked about these and many other books, he would, all unconscious though she was of it, show his little girl where to look for all that was finest and best in the works, teach her—though she never thought she was being taught, to that she would have objected—to try and think, to try and understand for herself.

And in the same way this "bitter" and "embittered" man would talk "politics" and "religion" with the little girl. How well I remember, when I was perhaps some five or six years old, feeling certain religious qualms and (we had been to a Roman Catholic Church to hear the beautiful music) confiding them, of course, to Mohr, and how he quietly made everything clear and straight, so that from that hour to this no doubt could ever cross my mind again. And how I remember his telling me the story—I do not think it could ever have been so told before or since—of the carpenter whom the rich men killed, and many and many a time saying, "After all, we can forgive Christianity much, because it taught us the worship of the child."

And Marx could himself have said "suffer little children to come unto me" for wherever he went there children somehow would turn up also. If he sat on the Heath at Hampstead —a large open space in the north of London, near our old home—if he rested on a seat in one of the parks, a flock of children would soon be gathered round him on the most friendly and intimate terms with the big man with the long hair and beard, and the good brown eyes. Perfectly strange children would thus come about him, would stop him in the street. . . . Once, I remember a small schoolboy of about ten, quite unceremoniously stopping the dreaded "chief of the International" in Maitland Park and asking him to "swop knives." After a little necessary explanation that "swop" was schoolboy for "exchange," the two knives were produced and compared. The boy's had only one blade; the man's had two, but these were undeniably blunt. After much discussion a bargain was struck, and the knives exchanged, the terrible "chief of the International" adding a penny in consideration of the bluntness of his blades.

One word as to the name "Mohr." At home we all had nicknames. (Readers of *Capital* will know what a hand at giving them Marx was.) "Mohr" was the regular, almost official, name by which Marx was called, not only by us, but by all the more intimate friends. But he was also our "Challey" (originally I presume a corruption of Charley!) and "Old Nick." My mother was always our "Mohme." Our dear old friend Helen Demuth—the life-long friend of my parents—became after passing through a series of names—our "Nym." Engels, after 1870, became our "General." A very intimate friend— Lina Schöler our "Old Mole." My sister Jenny was "Qui Qui, Emperor of China" and "Di." My sister Laura (Madame Lafargue) "the Hottentot" and "Kakadou." I was "Tussy"—a name that has remained—and "Quo Quo, Successor to the Emperor of China," and for a long time the "Getwerg Alberich" (from the *Niebelungen Lied*.)

The same impression is conveyed in a reminiscence of his son-in-law, Paul Lafargue, a middle-class Cuban, apparently of creole blood:

To get to know and love the heart that beat within the breast of Marx the scholar you had to see him when he had closed his books and notebooks and was surrounded by his family, or again on Sunday evenings in the society of his friends. He then proved the pleasantest of company, full of wit and humor, with a laugh that came straight from the heart. His black eyes under the arches of his bushy brows sparkled with pleasure and malice whenever he heard a witty saying or a pertinent repartee.

He was a loving, gentle, and indulgent father. "Children should educate their parents," he used to say. There was never even a trace of the bossy parents in his relations with his daughters, whose love for him was extraordinary. He never gave them an order, but asked them to do what he wished as a favor or made them feel that they should not do what he wanted to forbid them. And yet a father could seldom have had more docile children than he. His daughters considered him as their friend and treated him as a companion; they did not call him "father," but "Moor"—a nickname that he owed to his dark complexion and jet-black hair and beard. The members of the Communist League, on the other hand, called him "Father Marx" before 1848, when he was not even thirty years of age. . . .

On Sundays his daughters would not allow him to work, he belonged to them for the whole day. If the weather was fine, the whole family would go for a walk in the country. On their way they would stop at a modest inn for bread and cheese and ginger beer. When his daughters were small, he would make the long walk seem shorter to them by telling them endless fantastic tales which he made up as he went, developing and tensening the complications according to the distance they had to go, so that the little ones forgot their weariness listening.

Marx was always a prodigious reader, with a remarkable memory. Reading, as well as walking, was his chief pleasure, to the exclusion, apparently, of music and painting. He loved poetry, and was particularly fond of Shakespeare, who in the Marx household was endlessly recited, acted out, and discussed. He is supposed to have read Aeschylus faithfully once a year. He thought both poets the greatest dramatic geniuses ever born. On first coming to England, with only a reading knowledge of English, he set about methodically listing and memorizing all Shakespeare's idioms. When he learned Russian toward the end of his life, he did the same with Pushkin and

Gogol. His taste in German literature was conventional and catholic; he kept re-reading old favorites. For distraction he read light novels, especially the older Dumas and Walter Scott. He loved Cervantes and Balzac—especially Balzac because of his obsessive concentration on the dissection of bourgeois society.

He knew the works of Heine and Goethe intimately; in his conversation he quoted them all the time. Dante and Robert Burns were also special favorites.

He was, of course, a polyglot: he could read numerous European languages and write in three—German, French, and English.

He had a remarkable respect for mathematics, though he was mediocre in it as a boy. He did not think a science was really developed until it could make use of mathematics. In view of his sweeping historical generalizations, this judgment has, perhaps, an endearing quality.

In middle age Marx made a very different physical impression from the description of him in his youth. According to his son-in-law, Lafargue, he was "of powerful build, more than average height, broad-shouldered, deep-chested, and had well proportioned limbs. . . . Had he practised gymnastics in his youth he would have become a very strong man. The only physical exercise he ever pursued regularly was walking: he could ramble or climb hills for hours, chatting and smoking, and not feel at all tired. One can say that he even worked walking in his room, only sitting down for short periods to write what he had thought out while walking."

Lafargue also remarks on Marx's relative short-leggedness, to which Marx's biographer Mehring adds that, like Goethe, he belonged to the class of what the Germans call "sitting giants"—people who look big only when seated.

Despite Marx's morale and an essential emotional balance—as opposed to his unyielding intellectual monism—there was a contrast between his hopes and actual way of life that makes the impression of a classical comedy —or tragedy. This contrast oppressed Marx all the more because he was not remotely a bohemian at this time, and he found his way of life excruciating.

He had a painful combination of pride and sensitivity that, combined with his vast fund of personal energy, often sent him into convulsions of rage against real and fancied adversaries. His feuds with individuals were endless, envenomed by a pervasive paranoia. He saw plots against him in every corner.

His correspondence during his lengthy London exile is filled with a sort of obsessive concentration on the activities of various enemies or rivals of his in the emigration, which he and Engels came to detest wholeheartedly, though it is hard to avoid the impression that in their loathing there was a strong percentage of sour grapes.

Marx kept working on his opus, constantly prodded on by Engels and also by Liebknecht and Lassalle in Germany, but it was constantly interrupted, partly because Marx felt bored with the whole subject, partly because he got caught up in the journalistic or polemical exigencies of the moment.

He had a brief moment of glory, in which his polemical energies were fully deployed, when the King of Prussia, irritated by the escape of a political prisoner who was aided by the exiled German democrat, Carl Schurz, decided on a public trial to incriminate the plotters against the regime. The best his agents could come up with was a mass of material implicating the Communist League in London, or rather the two Communist Leagues in London. The trial gave Marx a chance to explain away at great length some of the things he had written that could clearly be interpreted as incitements to violence and to demonstrate the falsity of other evidence.

But the glory was over quickly. During the first phase of his London exile most of his time was spent in futile and destructive sniping and countersniping at various members of the emigration. His suspiciousness and vindictiveness against individuals grew sometimes to fantastic dimensions. Acquaintances and friendships were sacrificed. His old friendship with Freiligrath, who had helped him so often, was ruptured when Freiligrath and a poet whom Marx detested were invited to speak at a celebration in honor of Schiller. As Freiligrath, despite Marx's wishes, insisted on giving his speech, Marx turned permanently against him, from then on referring to him in the most disagreeable language.

He also turned on Lassalle, who, though not politically active at the moment, was in Germany and in the midst of a brilliant career. Lassalle had been a comrade of Marx's in the movement triggered by the upheavals of 1848, and had served a prison sentence of six months. By the age of thirty he had become famous throughout Europe as the victor in Countess Hatzfeld's divorce suit, which had dragged on for ten years of the liveliest legal tussles and had gone through some thirty-six trials. Lassalle had not only become a celebrity, but he also got a share of the Countess's considerable annual income, and decided to install himself in Berlin.

Lassalle's personal qualities were considerable. A marvelous talker and very attractive physically, his unorthodox views made him socially "interesting," especially since he had spent some time for them in jail. His career was in

some ways a parallel to Disraeli's, though Lassalle was
openly a Jew and was wholeheartedly on the radical side
of politics.

Marx had never had any reason to complain about
Lassalle, who had obeyed his instructions in political matters and looked up to him. He was convinced by Marx's
political views, and their relationship was not marred by
any personal friction—Lassalle had always helped Marx
financially and found him work. But all this was now
ruined. Some groundless and capricious rumors reached
Marx's ears in 1856 through a traveling salesman. These
unfounded rumors—supposedly views held by the Düs-
seldorf "workers" about Lassalle's private feelings and
ambitions—kindled Marx's suspicions of him. From then
on he and Engels spent an enormous amount of time discussing Lassalle's activities.

The strange thing about their relationship to Lassalle
was that the main target of their vituperation, which was
extravagant, seemed to be Lassalle's origins. Expressions
like "Yid," "kike," "Ikey the Yid," "the greasy Jew from
Breslau," "Baron Ikey," "Jacob Weasel," and "Ephraim
Clever" filled pages of the letters that passed between
Marx and Engels. Whenever Engels expressed himself in
anti-Semitic terms, as he did quite often, Marx leaned
over backward keeping up with him. Marx was particularly irritated by Lassalle's finishing a big book on Greek
philosophy while engaged in a brilliant social and political
career.

The course of European politics also hampered Marx's
serious writing. French politics, which enabled Louis
Napoleon to install himself as Emperor Napoleon III, inspired Marx to write a long article that was to become
famous later as the *Eighteenth Brumaire of Louis Bonaparte.* But for the time being Marx's reputation was so

low that he could get it published only by a small German printer in New York City.

Balkan affairs, too, were in turmoil once again in the 1850's. Marx immersed himself in a study of eastern European and Balkan politics. In 1853, Palmerston, a Cabinet minister, later Prime Minister and one of the most celebrated of British statesmen, came out in favor of calming down the Russian government, and Marx, who was in favor of a war against Russia, attacked him vigorously in the articles he was currently writing for *The New York Tribune*. These articles brought him the acquaintance of one David Urquhart, an eccentric newspaperman. It was Urquhart's conviction that Palmerston was actually an agent of the Czar, which explained his policy of appeasement. Though Marx considered Urquhart a "harmless monomaniac," this particular argument suited him very well. He seems to have believed it; in any case he praised Urquhart, an obvious crank, as an eminent adversary of Palmerston's, and wrote anti-Palmerston articles for Urquhart's paper. He contributed at least fifteen articles to the campaign against Palmerston, all rather pointless, since the Crimean War finally broke out anyhow, and Palmerston became Prime Minister.

Marx also immersed himself in constant polemics and analyses of the immediate situation at other points of friction in the complex entanglements of continental politics, especially the conflict between the Habsburg empire, Germany, Italy, and so on—an endless field!

His interest in European politics was, to be sure, not that of a journalist—he was an observer scrutinizing the sky for signs of the imminent revolution. He and Engels kept postponing the outbreak of the revolution from one year to the next—or rather from one crisis or pseudo-crisis to another. The crises were most promising, of course, if they contained an economic element, in view of Marx's belief in the primacy of the economic factor.

Until October, 1857, however, there was no serious economic crisis. The boom, without a precedent, had lasted a whole decade. Marx and Engels's idea that the periods between depressions had to become shorter and shorter obviously needed revision. Nevertheless both were elated at the prospects in 1857. In a letter to Engels (December 8, 1857) Marx wrote: "I'm working like a madman, day and night, assembling my economic researches so that I can at least have the outlines clear before the deluge comes."

But there was a disappointment once again—a favorable upswing in world trade took place before the year was over. The same thing was to be repeated year after year.

These constantly failing predictions demonstrated the basic difficulty in Marx's whole scientific approach: if someone simply guesses wrong no real harm is done. Reaction to the error amounts to not much more than saying that people make mistakes. But Marx's and Engels's claims, based on their "science," were constantly being presented, both to each other and to their readers, as the results of an infallible scientific *method*.

This method was grounded theoretically in the inevitable compulsions of the economic process, but since economic crises were rare, while political crises, upheavals, or frictions were common, Marx would often expect the fulfillment of his hopes from the development of purely political skirmishes. He expected, for instance, a revolution to follow hard on the heels of Louis Napoleon's seizure of power, which was a mere political maneuver, from Marx's own long-range point of view. The scientific theory predicted the outbreak of a revolution only in countries where the forces of production were mature, but Marx, to back up his optimism, did not hesitate to claim that Russia, though economically very backward, had also become a likely arena for a revolution.

Marx and Engels were, in short, guessing in much the manner of the man in the street, except that their guesswork was the product of enormous pent-up passions. They had a vested interest, of an emotional kind, in their guesswork at the very moment that they claimed it was the product of methodological prescience. This curious combination of passionate optimism—based on a longing for a catastrophe that would herald the new order—plus the extravagance of their mock-scientific certainty, made the predictions of Marx and Engels diverge far more wildly from what happened than the guesswork of the merest novice.

There was one hopeful aspect in this series of false prophecies: Marx was at least working hard on his book —"before the deluge comes." It is true that Engels had so far seen nothing of the manuscript; in their close relationship this was very strange. But a publisher was interested—this time through "Baron Ikey," who was quite unaware of what Marx and Engels were saying about him in their private correspondence.

Marx signed a contract for his forthcoming book—of which nothing yet had been written—in March, 1858, through Lassalle's good offices. He received more than the usual advance. The publisher had agreed to start publishing the "several volumes" of the book, as Marx said, section by section, sight unseen. The first section was promised in a couple of months.

Marx's small circle was elated. Everyone was persuaded that the book would shatter all other economic theories and at last provide the great proof of what had been serving all this time as the groundwork of Marx's polemical thrusts. Wilhelm Liebknecht, a young German philologist and member of this small circle, was particularly enthusiastic about the forthcoming work.

But it was not until February, 1859, that Marx finally succeeded in sending in the first part of the first volume, consisting of two chapters. Now the publisher delayed a little, claiming that he had had to wait so long that his printer had no free presses. Marx was deeply suspicious. He suspected conspiracy once again and this time blamed it on Lassalle's malicious envy. Marx regarded the whole delay as a "trick" of the "little Jew."

But in June, 1859, the first part of the *Critique of Political Economy* finally came out—to cause a general let-down. Those of his circle, including Engels, who had been expecting some revelation about the imminent collapse of the whole bourgeois economic system found no such thing in this book of Marx's, which was supposedly on economics but was actually a philosophical exposition of the "labor theory of value."

The idea that labor was involved in the value of commodities is a very old one. It can be found in the very origins of all economic discussion and was a cardinal element in the writing of the English economist Ricardo, whom Marx had begun studying years before.

Marx's contribution in the *Critique* was that the value —not the price, which he could not explain by this theory —of any given commodity was a function exclusively of the amount of labor incorporated in it. By labor, in its turn, Marx meant manual labor. He disregarded intellectual labor completely and the labor embodied in the machines that performed various essential functions in the manufacture of commodities. For Marx, in this work, any object was bound to have value that contained what he called "congealed labor-time," while the value of all objects could be determined by the amount of "labor-time" they contained.

This was the entire point of the book. The fact that it did not pretend to explain the pricing mechanism made it a purely abstract statement of a philosophical position— i.e., the "meaning" of value. It was of no use as an explanation of the actual economic process, since it is obvious that the *price* of any commodity is not a function *only* of the amount of manual labor that has gone into it, as Marx was claiming.

As a philosophical theory it was not only irrelevant to the functioning of the economic system but obviously, from everyday observation, in actual contradiction to universal and well-known phenomena. It is well-known that rare objects have a value given to them by their rarity, just as it is evident that a subjective factor—desirability, or demand, in later economic theory—is also a component of price.

Everyone knows, for instance, that a newly discovered diamond mine is immensely valuable although not one minute's labor has been expended. It is equally true that some things steadily rise in price, regardless of the expenditure of labor on them—an ancient, vintage motorcar with an audience of enthusiasts costs much more than it did when the laborers finished it at the factory.

This is all perfectly obvious, as it must have been to Marx too. His theory was a mere philosophical formulation—or rather a manipulation of intellectual categories. As far as meeting the expectations of his few followers, who had been eagerly looking forward to a concrete, practical demonstration of some reason why the current system was bound to collapse, the disappointment was monumental.

Liebknecht, Marx's most enthusiastic follower at the time, was deeply depressed. He had never, Marx wrote Engels, "been so disappointed in any book." Not only were Marx's immediate friends and followers, a tiny handful, disappointed, but the book itself did not arouse a ripple of interest. Marx was bitterly hurt. In a way that was becoming more and more characteristic, he blamed it on Lassalle, who he assumed had been busy organizing a conspiracy to stifle the book. Marx begged Engels to stop "Lassalle's plan to destroy" him. For his part Lassalle excused Marx to the German publisher, who was a little bewildered by Marx's complaints; Lassalle said the whole thing was nothing but the understandable quirk of a great man's temperament.

The main problem was the remainder of the book. The impatient publisher kept harassing him for further sections of the manuscript but months and years went by. Marx found it impossible to finish the work. He was bogged down in the economic quagmire, the "crap," as he still called it. By the beginning of 1861, two years after he had sent in the first two chapters of the Critique, he had lost patience with the publisher, and told Lassalle he was through with him—unless a big house could be interested in putting out the remainder of his work he refused to publish anything at all. Lassalle, surprisingly, found a really big publisher and wrote Marx that the whole thing was settled—the new publisher would publish the rest of the book. Marx was so vexed that he did not even answer this letter. In fact, the remainder of the book was never published, though later on the two chapters that had already appeared were incorporated in his magnum opus, Capital.

He had made his major appearance on the international scene as an independent thinker, with doctrines of his own, some seventeen years previously. Ever since then his torrent of polemical writings had had his novel scientific theory as their groundwork. He had started work substantiating his assertions twice, once sixteen years before and then five years after that. He had signed two contracts for the book of demonstration, the second of them three years before, and all he had written was two chapters, of merely philosophical interest.

He had been keeping up a running commentary on European politics, including English politics, and suffering heart-breaking privations. Bored by the drudgery of research in economics, he was still optimistic about the development of upheavals on the continent, and it was this that sustained him. The labor he expended on everything else was essentially a way of marking time until real things happened.

By 1860 Marx was at the lowest point in his career. When he lost control of the little colony of German socialists in London following the 1848 debacle, he became, from the public point of view, an obscure journalist and scholarly writer. No one knew much about him after the casual interest in communism as a systematic doctrine had declined in the wake of the Prussian treason trials of 1851 in Cologne, the last time Marx played a public role. Since then there had been a general resurgence of industry and trade and a concomitant euphoria concerning the spread of liberal ideas, the possibility of peaceful progress, and, of course, science.

Marx, though only forty-two in 1860, seemed prematurely old, with his gray hair and his afflictions. To many people he was already a figure bypassed by history.

But only a half-generation later his position was radically altered. While he remained relatively unknown in England, he finally achieved celebrity on the continent.

He became the legend that to a certain extent he has remained to this day—a heroic figure to his partisans, an evil genius to his enemies, the prophet of a new order and the devil of the old. By the mid-seventies he was regarded by enemies as the dogmatic and fanatical dictator of a subversive and wicked political movement designed to undermine all morality and society, and hence the mastermind of all subversion in general. On the opposite side he was regarded as a fountain of wisdom on theoretical questions and the architect of a movement of righteousness aimed at the installation of a secular kingdom of heaven.

CHAPTER VII

A Return to Practice:
A Consummation of Theory

By the beginning of the 1860's Europe seemed immersed in a new tide of liberalism. In 1861 the serfs were freed in Russia, the same year that the American Civil War broke out, which led to the emancipation of the Negro slaves. Even in Prussia a liberal parliament was returned in spite of the franchise based on an element of social privilege. Marx regarded all liberalism as another aspect of bourgeois power and was bound to consider himself outside the various liberal trends on the continent. The American Civil War, which made him optimistic as usual about the possibility of a revolutionary outbreak, put an end to his small income from *The New York Tribune,* which had no room now for European comment.

In the new liberal climate of Prussia, Lassalle was encouraged to go ahead with the establishment of a big newspaper for the "party" to which both he and Marx theoretically belonged. This upset Marx for a simple personal reason—his envy of Lassalle convinced him that this was just another career opened up to Baron Ikey's talents, while he himself remained stranded in exile. Lassalle's optimistic letter was followed by a general amnesty in Prussia accompanying the accession of a new monarch, Wilhelm. Marx was at last free to go back to Prussia, and he did so at once.

It was twenty-five years since he had lived in Berlin.

His hair almost gray, his figure massive, he was a staid middle-aged man, with followers. Lassalle met him at the station and put him up at his own house. Marx was to spend a month in the Prussian capital. He was delighted by everything he saw, because, as usual, he saw all about him the signs of imminent collapse: "Everything reeks of decay; people of every class are sure a catastrophe is bound to take place. . . . In army circles there is a general conviction that if it ever comes to fighting Prussia will be beaten from the outset."

Lassalle's evident activity and fame made a disagreeable impression on Marx. Lassalle seemed to be as enthusiastic about him as before, but Marx remained suspicious. Lassalle took it for granted that Marx would be the editor-in-chief of a new "party" newspaper, but Marx found it odd that he wanted to be co-editor, and though Lassalle accepted Marx's insistence on Engels as a third editor, he wanted to have the same influence as Marx and Engels jointly, in order not to be consistently outvoted.

Marx wrote Engels how vexing this was but complained that Lassalle's very devotion made it difficult to indicate to him that Marx wanted him only in a subordinate position. The main hitch at the moment was that Marx, while no longer under an edict of deportation, was still not a Prussian citizen and could be expelled at any moment if his activities warranted it. This was obviously of capital importance for the editor of a radical paper. Lassalle offered to help him in getting his status as a citizen restored. But it was to prove impossible—Marx was to pay again for his piece of youthful braggadoccio in surrendering his citizenship at the age of twenty-seven.

Marx left for London, once again discouraged. It seemed clear to him that there was no chance for him to play a personal role in his own country and that Lassalle would be the leader on Marx's own stamping-ground, in complete charge of any socialist movement that might develop. On his way back he stopped off at Trier, to see his mother again after twenty years of absence, or at any rate, as he said, to get more money out of her.

His failure to write a magnum opus oppressed him more and more. While he had been bogged down in factional squabbles, ephemeral journalism, and the drudgery of research in London, Lassalle had been an active figure on an active scene. Marx decided that the need for his masterpiece was more urgent than ever. In June, 1861, he started again on the work he was supposed to have begun a number of times already. He resumed his work at the point in his *Critique* where he had stopped a couple of years before, outlined three whole volumes, and flung himself with renewed energies into the composition of *Capital*. It was, as he conceived it now, not merely a thesis of academic interest, but a lever in another struggle for power that was again around the corner, and in which his paramount rival now seemed to be Lassalle.

This time a manuscript began growing, in the midst of financial troubles that were more and more burdensome, vexatious, and almost crippling.

Meanwhile Lassalle, in Berlin, was hurriedly organizing a party that was to have the most fateful consequences for Germany and the world. In the spring of 1862, while Marx was still absorbed in *Capital*, Lassalle began a new political career by haranguing the workers in a Berlin suburb on the "concept of the working-class." He gave a lively, simplified paraphrase of the *Communist Manifesto* that was reprinted as a pamphlet. It gained a remarkable popularity. Though it paid full credit to his efforts, Marx was vexed by its "vulgarization" of the *Manifesto,* and even more by the unmistakable symptoms of Lassalle's new career. Lassalle was working to found a powerful German working-class party. It would be largely imbued with Marx's ideas but also the handiwork of Lassalle's organizational and oratorical abilities.

Lassalle came to London in the summer of 1862 for the World Exhibition, an unprecedented international occasion. Marx naturally returned his hospitality but only with the greatest difficulty—he had to pawn everything in order to be able to show Lassalle any hospitality at all. His material embarrassment was heightened by his reserve about Lassalle's discussion of the prospects of the German party.

Lassalle was completely puzzled: what objection could Marx find to the formation of a big German workers' party, based on Marx's own ideas?

But Marx, irritated by Lassalle's role in the party, kept throwing up barriers to all Lassalle's tactical proposals. In any case, by the time Lassalle left, Marx hated him as never before. He came to the strange conclusion that Lassalle was not merely a Jew, but a "Jewish nigger." "It is perfectly obvious," he wrote Engels, "from the shape of his head and the way his hair grows that he is descended from the Negroes who joined Moses [sic] on the exodus from Egypt, unless maybe his mother or his grandmother had relations with a nigger."

The ridiculous charge was typical of Marx's frustration, envy, and malice toward Lassalle, who had, curiously enough, only just come to realize how much Marx loathed him. Lassalle did not turn on Marx. He seems to have retained his own somewhat twitchy respect for him; he took the view that the trouble with Marx in the field of practical politics was that his ideas were too "abstract."

Marx was still deep at work on *Capital*. He was writing the draft at a breakneck pace. By the summer of 1862 a sizable first volume, of the projected three, was finished. Marx became preoccupied in building it up to as massive a size as possible—since years before Engels had advised him that the length of the book would itself be an invaluable aid in promoting its influence. "Add to the number of pages by sheer force; fill them with quotations, etc. . . . The main thing is that when you make your debut it should be with a really fat volume." That had been written in November, 1851, and was still true. Marx wrote in June, 1862: "I am stretching this volume out, since these swine in Germany assess the value of a book according to its cubic content."

By the end of 1862 the whole of the first volume of *Capital* was now finished. The final draft had been readied in only a year and a half. The problem for the moment was the lack of a publisher. Meanwhile Marx plunged ahead into the second and third volumes, accumulating vast amounts of material.

In 1863, Engels suffered a personal tragedy. His longstanding relationship with Mary Burns, who was his common-law wife, was brought to an end by her death. Engels was shattered with grief. Marx, who had been a friend of Mary Burns for the best part of twenty years, wrote Engels a note of condolence, but he was so preoccupied with his own financial problems that the condolence sounded shockingly thin. "Dear Engels: The news of Mary's death surprised as well as crushed me. She was so good and witty, and she was so devoted to you." This perfunctory acknowledgement was then followed by a conventional complaint about Marx's habitual money worries.

This chilled his relationship with Engels for the first time. Engels actually revolted. He sent a curt note back, saying he had no money. This in its turn astounded Marx to such a degree that, very unusually, he felt it necessary to apologize, and did so. Engels relented at once. It was the only note of bitterness that ever arose between them.

There is, of course, a somewhat complicated background to this personal incident. Jenny Marx had steadfastly refused, for purely "bourgeois" reasons, to receive Mary Burns. Also, at the beginning of the 1860's, Marx's own family life was disturbed by what was at least a physical love affair between himself and the devoted family servant, Helen Demuth. This affair produced, in fact, a son whose existence was to be an embarrassment to Marx's straitlaced followers. The son, Frederick Demuth, was never told who his father was, nor did Marx ever do anything for him. Perhaps Jenny's intense jealousy, as well as her respectability, made it impossible for Marx ever to acknowledge his son; he may not have wished to, since he seems to have had no affection for him. Despite Frederick's striking resemblance to Marx, it was given out that the boy was a bastard of Engels's!

As far as posterity is concerned, to be sure, these intimate upheavals were always subordinate to politics.

In the spring of 1863, Lassalle embarked on a major campaign. It was one of the most thrilling political actions ever undertaken in Germany. He went from one city to another preaching the most intransigent form of class warfare that had ever been heard of by masses of people in Germany before. He developed an unprecedented magnetism and became a popular idol. He was followed by literally thousands of people in different cities, his oratorical powers were displayed as never before, and he also developed an astonishing ability to captivate his audiences. Through his singular combination of qualities— scholar, writer, speaker, actor, hero, tactician, prophet, and opportunist—he managed to launch the first socialist working-class party.

Marx and Engels both took the view that this campaign of Lassalle's was somehow his own personal enterprise, that he had used "their" ideas in order to promote his career. Marx especially disregarded the obvious fact that Lassalle was in most respects a mere exponent of Marx's radical social views, and therefore his successful campaign could only rebound to the benefit of the socialist cause. Lassalle's political brilliance was particularly galling to Marx by contrast with his own writing and research, which were bogged down in insurmountable financial difficulties.

His financial problem was driven home to him with redoubled force by the death of his mother, since for years he had been counting on his share of the "fortune." The entire sum came to £12; his mother, whom he had accused of "rascalities," had obviously not been able to give him his "share."

He was bitterly disappointed. He and his family were still sunk in the deepest poverty, though the preceding year had been an improvement over others—he had received some £370 from Engels. Many people in England lived on less. But there was no getting around his failure to keep up with the demands of his family. On top of that he was suddenly felled by a violent outbreak of boils on a visit to his Dutch relative Philips. For a long time he had been suffering from them; now, as 1864 began, boils, abscesses and carbuncles would plague him steadily. He was in pain, ran a fever, and was unable to do anything, sleep or eat. He could not go to London and had to stay on in Holland for two months. When he arrived in London, after a temporary remission, he was laid low again. He could scarcely work at all and dragged himself about, acutely uncomfortable in any position.

Lassalle was now one of the most famous men in Germany. His reputation almost rivaled that of Bismarck, the new Prime Minister, who on taking office had abruptly started a war against Denmark as part of his plans for the unification of Germany. The liberals and democrats were more perplexed by Bismarck's war than they had been over their own version of the same war in 1848. In progressive eyes the very fact that the war was waged by Bismarck and not at their instigation made it suspect. Lassalle's name was growing by leaps and bounds among the workers, while to the liberals he was becoming a tremendous threat —May 1864 saw the first anniversary of the founding of the immensely successful Workers' Association. Lassalle had made a name for himself in scholarship, too, by publishing a scientific attack on the evils of capitalism. He was also involved in a dozen lawsuits, his speeches were being published in numerous pamphlets, and songs about him were being sung everywhere.

But in the middle of 1864 Marx finally received some good news. He was bequeathed some money—a substantial sum, more than £800—from an old follower. Lassalle was killed in a senseless and unexpected duel over a woman, which to Marx meant that the leadership of the German workers' party was now free. Most important of all, he became involved, in the most casual way possible, with the event that was to be the cornerstone of his political revival.

This event took place in 1864, with the establishment of the International Workingmen's Association—the "International," as Marx was always to refer to it later—whose role in the development of modern socialism was fundamental.

The chain of events leading up to it was seemingly casual, almost haphazard.

In the summer of 1862, when a delegation of French workers had visited the World Exhibition, links had been established between them and some English trade-unionists. The next year these links were reinforced as a reflection of the sympathy felt in many circles for some Polish rebels who had been forced into exile in the wake of an unsuccessful uprising that year.

Marx was asked by some young Frenchmen for the name of a German worker who could speak enough English to make a short speech on behalf of the Poles. It was proposed to give the whole affair a flavor of international solidarity.

Marx gave the Frenchmen the name of a former member of the Communist League, a tailor with whom he was friendly. He sat in on the meeting himself to see what it was likely to turn into. It was, after all, a meeting held on the initiative of bona fide workers' organizations, and might provide a beacon of hope in the generally gloomy field of his political activities.

The first meeting also touched on some practical questions—wages, strike-breaking, etc.—and another meeting was called by the leaders to discuss these practical questions in greater detail. This time it was attended by various kinds of systematic dissidents, who were more than willing to generalize the solution of specific practical questions involving workers into a massive onslaught on the economic system as such.

The meeting was held under the chairmanship of Edward Beesly, a London University professor of ancient history who had come under the influence of some French socialists. At the meeting it was decided to set up an international federation of working-men—a novel idea— that would work not for the reform of the current economic system but for its destruction via methods that would ultimately bring about the elimination of private property.

The meeting was thus an inherently radical enterprise and also one that was dependent on the support of bona fide working-class organizations with aims that could be linked to Marx's own.

Such an organization was of course highly welcome, even though the somewhat innocent, limited working-men and trade union leaders who envisaged the international organization meant by it a loose association in which each country would retain its independence, whereas Marx had always envisaged a strongly centralized organization tightly run by a dominant executive.

Marx was well enough aware of his personal shortcomings as a politician to take pains not to tread on anyone's toes; he determined to be modest and diffident. As things turned out, it was a simple matter to take the suggestions made at the General Council—all put forward by political amateurs—and offer simply to smooth them out, coordinate them, and edit them generally. For this his experience as a writer was of course invaluable.

He was appointed by the German artisans in London as their deputy on the executive committee set up by the meeting. By the time the constitution was voted on by the whole gathering, it was Marx, with his manifest intellectual superiority, energy, and will-power, who had taken complete charge. He was dissatisfied with the platitudinous nature of the draft of the statutes, which had been the assignment of the French and Italian delegates, and he did one of his own, as well as an Inaugural Address.

He tightened up the composition of the constitution to make it a clear-cut, unsentimental, rather belligerent document binding the members to help each other in improving their conditions and promote the general subversion of the existing order through overt political activity. Members were also supposed to enter democratic parliaments, which was now the accepted procedure of Lassalle's followers in the German countries.

Marx's Inaugural Address is rhetorically very effective. It is written with the same verve and concentration that characterized the prose of the *Communist Manifesto* itself. It starts out by proclaiming:

. . . that the emancipation of the working class must be conquered by the working class themselves . . . that the economic subjection of the man of labor to the monopolizer of the means of labor . . . lies at the bottom of servitude in all its forms of social misery, mental degradation, and political dependence. That the economic emancipation of the working class is therefore the great end to which every political movement ought to be subordinated as a means. That all efforts aiming at this great end have hitherto failed from want of solidarity between the manifold divisions of labor in each country, and from the absence of a fraternal bond of union between the working classes of different countries . . . for these means the undersigned . . . have taken the steps necessary for founding the International Working Men's Association.

After surveying the socio-economic situation of the working-class since 1848, it makes much of the contrast between the growing prosperity of the propertied classes and the depression of the workers. The fiasco of 1848 is acknowledged, but the lesson is drawn that it has led to the unification of the workers in various countries. The evolution of international solidarity is said to have helped limit the length of the working day, a victory for the first time over the unbridled laissez-faire of the capitalists. The workers are beginning to realize that they must not be misled by their capitalist exploiters into being exploited through national or religious prejudices, thus losing sight of their authentic self-interest. Regardless of the outcome of wars waged for nationalist or dynastic reasons, the workers are bound to lose. They must remember that their numbers could be decisive, though only if united, organized, and made self-conscious. Politics must be entered into and not refrained from as recommended by the followers of Proudhon and Bakunin. The achievement of essential social justice depends on transforming the current economic system, which, despite minor reforms, is bound to work toward the debasement and enslavement of the working-class.

Then the Address reiterated Marx's old idea—one class, because of its fundamental situation in society, was the only one with an authentic interest in stopping the downward movement of the economic process. It was the class with no possessions, the class that by its very nature had no links, of interest or feeling, with the traditional order of injustice and misery, the class that had been brought into being by the machinery that enslaved it. The address ended like the *Manifesto* itself: "Workers of all countries, unite!"

Marx was careful to soft-pedal socialism, since European workingmen, as well as workers in the world at large, did not hold uniform views. Thus his Inaugural Address, while couched in the boldest of terms, bypassed the actual mention of socialism. Two phrases were even inserted in it about "duty and right" and "truth, morality, and justice," even though Marx said they were placed in such a way that they could "do no harm."

With the passage of the new constitution, Marx, after a period of obscurity that had lasted some fifteen years, was once again catapulted into a life of action. He had assured himself of a material weapon in his political ambition—the acquisition of power over the proletariat, the "material arm of philosophy," as he had once put it, at around the same time that his great work seemed on the threshold of completion.

In spite of a renewed attack of his now practically chronic ill-health he felt inspired to perform the immense labor required by his manipulation of the International and by the completion of his great work. By the end of 1864, he had finished the first draft of the second volume of *Capital* and was well away on the assembly of materials for the third. By the spring of 1865, Marx was at last able to answer affirmatively and with legitimate hopefulness the questions about the book that Engels had been asking him for so many years. His work in the International also gave him great pleasure; the amount of time he spent on it was well worth the effort.

The new organization was supposed to establish close relations between workers of different countries and trades, assemble and distribute relevant data, discuss mutual interests, coordinate activities, and so on. Though somewhat elastic in form in terms of its constitution, the organization became almost entirely Marx's mouthpiece. He dominated the whole thing through the force of his personality; he was once again in his element, especially since he had no rivals.

The most enthusiastic members of the International in the beginning were the French and English trades-union people, but as they were not very interested in theory, all general questions were left in the hands of the General Council—i.e., Marx. As long as this practical state endured and the members of the First International Workingmen's Association were still enthralled by the horizons of prosperity and authority they saw shimmering before them, Marx could exercise his gifts unhindered by any serious rival.

Bakunin had turned up again in Europe after his twelve years in jail and Siberia, but though he had been in London since his release, he and Marx, because of mutual dislike and Marx's ancient slander of Bakunin as a Czarist "agent," had not seen much of each other. It was unfortunate that the slander had been republished on Bakunin's arrival in London by Marx's associate, the "monomaniac" Urquhart—Bakunin naturally assumed that Marx was behind it.

Yet the launching of the International was a major event, after all, and it was necessary to sound Bakunin out. To Marx's surprise, Bakunin proved amiable about the whole enterprise and about Marx personally.

Bakunin's personal prestige was still enormous, but there was no tactic or doctrine associated with it. Hence his following was not organized. Like other followers of Proudhon, his disciples joined the International, but since they were in principle against the overt political action the International was advocating, they were in a somewhat contradictory position that hampered their efforts.

The sudden death of Lassalle had removed Marx's chief rival in Germany. This had raised Marx's hopes, somewhat illogically, for he was clearly unable to go back to Prussia. Within the International the authority Lassalle had wielded over his own party prevented the German section from ever giving London—that is, Marx—their whole-hearted support.

The International was to play a certain role in a question that was being discussed all over Europe—the question of the general franchise. In one country after another, pressure was being brought to bear to accept the vote as a political means for setting up a government. The International was active in this agitation and, in fact, after functioning for no more than seven months, it could claim credit for having exercised some influence over politics.

But perhaps the main point of the new organization, for Marx personally, was the primacy of his own role. As he wrote Engels in March, 1868, he was "the head of the whole works." He was moreover, the head quite secretly —the official leaders had to be British, so Marx took pains to keep in the background. He did it so successfully that many members did not even know he was there.

In his personal life things were not going as well. Marx found himself in financial straits again. The legacy he had received in May, 1864, was exhausted less than a year later, and he turned, in vain, to his relative in Holland. Once more Engels had to support him. But as business was good, appeals to Engels would bring in substantial sums instead of the odd pound-notes he used to send in letters.

In addition Marx was plagued by a tremendous outbreak of his boils. At the beginning of 1866 he was laid low by an attack that was more serious than ever.

On the other hand, the work on his magnum opus was proceeding apace—the rough preliminary draft of all three volumes of *Capital* was finished by the end of 1865. Marx could take a breathing spell. When his boils broke out again, after *Capital* was finished, he went off to the seashore for a well-earned rest.

While he was there, the map of Europe was changed.

Bismarck had finally succeeded in arranging the unification of Germany under Prussian hegemony in the space of several weeks. In the spring of 1866, only four years after taking the helm in Prussia, Bismarck was in a position to ensure Prussian control of Germany by ousting Austria altogether and crushing some smaller German states allied with it. The Prussian troops defeated the Austrian army

at the celebrated victory of Königgrätz—in only eight
hours the armed forces of the ancient Habsburg empire
were annihilated.

Prussia is generally agreed to have been the most brilliant war-machine in Europe at this time, perhaps one of
the most impressive military entities in history.

Some five years before, on his visit to Berlin, Marx had
been wrong about Prussian efficiency. Engels assured him
in April, 1866, that now, too, Prussia was bound to be
routed. By the end of May he was absolutely certain that
since the Prussian army was "incapable of carrying on a
war of attack . . ." there was "no doubt that (it) will be
crushed to a jelly instantaneously by the furious Austrians."

Engels was well-known in the Manchester newspaper
world. He was universally regarded as a first-class military
expert ever since he had studied to equip himself for his
role in the imminent proletarian revolution. He was given
a column in the *Manchester Guardian* to discuss the war
from a military point of view. His five articles on the
Prussian simpletons were all printed. Unfortunately, his
demonstration that the Prussian army had failed to grasp
the "higher laws of warfare" made its appearance the same
day the battle of Königgrätz took place.

The revolution was also in the bag, like the defeat of
the Prussian army. Marx and Engels were agreed on this.
A point that preoccupied Marx was the bloody consequences—in December he wrote Engels that "a good
many heads will have to roll."

When these predictions failed to materialize, both Marx
and Engels went on prophesying the nature of the peace
settlement. They were both persuaded that the Austrian
empire would be absolutely dismembered by the three
"hyenas," Russia, France, and Prussia. This also came to
nothing—no territory was taken from Austria at all.

What was impressive in this display of deduction from Marx's and Engels's cast-iron certainties was not merely that they were wrong on the positive prognosis, but that they also failed to take into account what actually happened.

With the consolidation of a new German empire under Prussia, including, for the time being, some three-quarters of the German states, Germany began its phenomenal growth as a world power. German self-esteem—that is, nationalism—began to grow in the wake of Bismarck's sensational victories, as did German industry and trade. On top of that, Bismarck—a "donkey" and an "ox" to Marx —confounded the German liberals by granting universal and equal franchise to the empire he had just formed. The development in Germany had shown Bismarck that a liberal regime would not necessarily be at loggerheads with the masses of the people—why shouldn't they vote? Marx's hopeful predictions of disaster, ostensibly grounded in scientific calculations but really prompted by personal despair, were still being consistently contradicted by facts.

The International was not giving him much satisfaction in the spring of 1866 either. The English were cooling off toward Marx's personal role, while the French—largely socialists, but unlike Marx, anarchistic, anti-state socialists —were called by him "ignorant, vain, presumptuous, chattering, dogmatic, and arrogant."

The whole of *Capital* was not yet finished, but the first volume was. A publisher had offered to print it in the early spring of 1865, but had wanted the manuscript for all three volumes first. Two years later Marx was impatient. He felt that the first volume, ready for the printer, had to be published alone, as the other two were still in the form of drafts. The project was of such importance that he personally took the manuscript of the first volume to the publisher in Hamburg and persuaded him to go ahead.

It was a momentous decision; it gave Marx the first money he had earned in years—some £60—an advance on the thousand copies that were supposed to be printed. *Capital* was finally assured of a public, ironically enough a public that enjoyed the prosperous economy of a bourgeois state its author was intent on overturning. Just as in England he had been allowed by the bourgeois regime to carry on his researches into the means of destroying it, so in Germany his major work, intended as a substantiation of his claims of total destruction for the whole property system, was printed without the slightest hindrance.

He went back to London, to await the arrival of the proofs that meant so much to him. He sent each section to Engels for his comments. The proof-sheets, corrected by him with some suggestions from Engels, were sent back in August, 1867, to the publisher in Hamburg. It was a day he had been dreaming about for many years now—precisely twenty-three, in fact, ever since he had first had his insight into the nature of bourgeois economy. He had the triumphant feeling of a man who has completed a major task in his life. He had found and was submitting to the world the proofs of a scientific theory that would shatter all traditional economic views and put the whole science on a new foundation. He felt, perhaps, like Darwin or Copernicus.

The book that was to have such momentous consequences for the world saw the light on September 2, 1867. It was the first volume of the projected three, the only one to be completed by Marx himself and to have any general impact; the other two volumes, prepared from Marx's drafts after his death by Engels, were to remain objects of special study.

But though *Capital* was to exercise the most si..g fascination over many, its appearance caused no stir at first.

Marx was determined that the silence with which his first book on economics, the *Critique of Political Economy*, had been received would not befall *Capital*. He and Engels took great pains to have as many reviews appear in the appropriate places as possible. As Marx put it, the thing was to make a stir about the book, and it seemed clever to Engels to have reviews appear attacking it. Engels, accordingly, wrote some reviews from different standpoints, including the bourgeois standpoint, but it was difficult to get their somewhat talentless subordinates to write anything readable on the subject. After two months had gone by without a single review appearing, Engels himself, with his unusual energy and fluency, wrote a great many rather vociferous reviews both for and against the book, and some of these were published.

Capital is an immense work—almost nine hundred pages long—and it contains such an accumulation of philosophical analysis, data, and statistics, that its description of the process of capitalist accumulation is difficult to wade through.

On the other hand, it is far from being a mere exposition of facts. It has a broad philosophical theme that makes it in some ways far more readable than might be expected.

Marx begins by demonstrating the curious subtlety in the very conception of a "commodity," arising as it does out of the "use-value" embodied in a certain object. He then goes on to demonstrate the transformation of money into capital: if one value is exchanged for another, equal, value, the ability of a man with money to buy commodities at one value and sell them at another value and in so doing receive more value than he had given—that is, profit by the transaction—becomes a puzzle.

The puzzle is solved by the existence of a special type of commodity—labor-power. This labor-power is embodied in a certain commodity, while the person originating the labor-power—i.e., the laborer—requires in his turn a certain quantity of food, clothing, and so on for himself and his family in order to maintain this labor-power. The value of his labor-power is represented by the labor-time required for the production of the laborer's requirements and those of his family. But this value, which is in the form of wages, is in fact much less than the value that the purchaser of this labor-power is in his turn able to get out of it. The surplus-labor, then, of the worker, beyond the labor-time needed to replace the value represented by his wages, is the source of surplus-value.

Surplus-value, Marx explains, is the origin of the constant accumulation of capital that characterizes the bourgeois economy. This extra segment of the worker's labor is allocated generally among all those members of society who do no work themselves. It is the foundation of our whole society.

Unpaid labor has, of course, always existed, since time immemorial; it is the essence of any society based on social inequality. Wage-labor, as it exists in modern society, is simply the current historical form of unpaid labor. Modern capitalism began with the establishment of the modern world trade market, dating from the sixteenth century.

The primary accumulation required to begin it was based on the people's mass deprivation of land, food, and their own means of production. It was this deprivation that reduced them to the status of having nothing to sell beyond their own labor-time. Wage-labor has brought about a further differentiation of the present system from previous systems by increasing the voracity of capital for the consumption of surplus-labor. In older societies, where the use-value of a commodity had greater importance than its exchange-value, there was still such a thing as surplus-labor, but its application was limited. But where the exchange value of a commodity exceeds the importance of its use-value, a situation is created in which the appetite of capital for further surplus-labor becomes insatiable.

Marx's theory of wages (divided into time-wages and piece-wages) describes them not as a timeless economic relationship but as an historic social category. It is the relation of surplus-value and wages that makes the capitalist mode of production go on reproducing the capitalist's capital and the worker's poverty. Society is divided into the capitalist class, which owns everything—all the sources of food, all the raw materials, and all the means of production—and into the working-class, the great bulk of humanity, which must sell its labor-power to the capitalist to go on existing and reproducing itself. Capital does not reproduce itself as a constant; it steadily keeps increasing its relative volume.

The description of "primary accumulation" is based on an excursion into history—moving, because of the details—in which Marx describes the struggle in England between the capitalist class and the nascent working class. The effect of large-scale industry in giving rise to misery greater than ever known before is given a dynamic conclusion because of the way Marx demonstrates that while society is constantly being churned up by more and more advanced machinery, it is also, by that very process, being prepared for a higher stage of social life.

Such—very broadly—is the series of basic definitions on which *Capital* is built up.

Marx regarded this book as a treatise in economics, but it is a singular mixture of many elements—theory, history, sociology, and a form of propaganda. Its basic difference from other treatments of economic subjects is its historicism—Marx tried to show the capitalist mode of production as an historically conditioned, not timeless, category. Thus in his first volume he tried to create what he regarded as fundamental theorems in economics as an historical science and simultaneously describe the nature of the new capitalist order that had arisen during the preceding generations.

Yet though it was Marx's contention, and has remained the contention of many who are not even his disciples, that the book was an objective "scientific" work, its principal conclusions are now, at least, manifestly illusory.

The theme that makes the book relatively easy to read is simple: it is the old theme, familiar even before the *Communist Manifesto,* that the capitalist system in its very nature, because of the very laws of its being, is bound to lead to progressively increasing misery. This had always been Marx's contention; the system was the motor that was to bring about the transition from the old order to the new. *Capital* is simply an attempt to demonstrate the ultimate causes of the phenomenon Marx has always made so much of—why this increasing misery *must* take place, i.e., its mechanism. All his studies in economics, all his accumulation of data, were designed to clarify the hidden mechanism whereby most people are bound to get poorer and poorer.

This proposition in the past had been accompanied by another proposition: the complementary reason capitalism had to collapse was that the forces of production had matured to the point of the celebrated explosion, the bursting asunder of the outmoded stage of society. *Capital* scarcely mentions this familiar old contention, and then merely as a rhetorical flourish. *Capital* is based on the other fundamental contention that misery must go on increasing constantly.

Marx maintains that he has proved, in *Capital*, that the condition of the working-class worsens inevitably as capital accumulates—the polarization of society between the constantly increasing wealth of a constantly decreasing number of capitalists is paralleled by the constantly increasing misery of a constantly increasing number of laborers.

For Marx this leads, naturally, to a revolt of the masses against their increasing "misery, agony of toil, slavery, ignorance, brutality, and mental degradation." In short, the theory of the necessarily increasing misery of the constantly growing bulk of society, radically polarized in the process, gave a comprehensible, and for many people plausible, explanation of why the capitalist system had to give way to a succeeding social order, in which the former oppressed masses could, by freeing themselves, create a new society.

Logically, if it could be shown that the condition of the working-class can improve, perhaps precisely because of an increase in the technological efficiency of the system itself, which might result—and historically has resulted—in the cheapening of commodities, there would be no reason for the capitalist system to expire at all. Hence the point about increasing misery is fundamental both in *Capital* and in the general socio-politico-economic structure of Marxism as a whole.

The whole burden of *Capital*, in fact, is an amplification of the theme of increasing misery that Marx had mentioned in different, casual writings before. The *Com-*

munist Manifesto, for instance, is satisfied with a mere mention or two: "ever-decreasing wages" and "ever-increasing burden of toil." It is of course illuminating that even before he wrote the *Manifesto,* Marx had the same general historical scheme in his mind. It is also revealing that this scheme had been in his mind ever since he had had his insight into the motor of social change during his first stay in Paris and had worked it out in greater detail during his conversations with Engels in Brussels. It is a reminder that *Capital* was designed to provide the proof of the basic contentions that had been demanded for so long by Engels—and by common sense.

Hence, *Capital* is merely a way of supporting with data an idea Marx had formed prior to the accumulation of any data. It articulates his early references to this idea on the basis of a number of points, of which a sampling should be adequate.

The working day, Marx says, keeps on lengthening, while wages go on dropping. The unemployed grow in number. The pace for those who go on working becomes more and more severe. Capital equipment in the shape of factories and machines deteriorates, as does the quality of food itself, so that the health of the workers is bound to suffer—their lives get shorter and shorter.

These points are sometimes given illustrations, often very moving ones, for Marx couched the most depressing accounts of human degradation in a very flat, dry style in thoroughgoing contrast with the lush ferocity of his polemical sections. Practically half the book is documented with quotations from all sorts of sources for the picture of human misery past and present.

It should perhaps be noted that the copiousness of detail in these descriptions of misery is quite irrelevant. The point is not, after all, that people have been miserable for a long time, but that their misery has been *increasing* and in the present epoch must necessarily increase because of the nature of the system itself. The descriptions of misery do not establish a trend of any kind, but quite the contrary, since Marx took many descriptions from sources published as long as a century before. If they prove anything, they prove the exact opposite. Marx incorporated in his book a good deal of the work done by Engels more than twenty years previously, in his *Condition of the Working-Class in England*. In other words, precisely at a time when English capitalism was being transformed at a breakneck tempo, Marx was obliged to buttress his major work with data that were outmoded.

Aside from that, it is a fact that all the points Marx makes so much of were contradicted by data well-known to Marx himself, as they were to even the most superficial students of social affairs.

Perhaps the answer is that Marx, while apparently engaged in the study of data, statistics, and so on, is in reality articulating what for him is a series of *logical* deductions. He is taking for granted some premises, from which he then extracts conclusions in a logical or pseudo-logical manner, but since the premises are arbitrary, the conclusions naturally fall outside experience, too. It is, however, their rigor that has proved attractive for many people— the semblance of "scientific certainty" that Marx and all his followers have considered to imbue the whole of his work.

Here is a celebrated passage from Chapter 22 of *Capital* (Volume I):

While there is a progressive diminution in the number of capitalist magnates, there is of course a corresponding increase in the mass of poverty, enslavement, degeneration, and

exploitation, but at the same time there is a steady inten-
sification of the role of the working class—a class which grows
ever more numerous, and is disciplined, unified, and organized
by the very mechanism of the capitalist method of production
which has flourished with it and under it. The centralization
of the means of production and the socialization of labor
reach a point where they prove incompatible with their
capitalist husk. This bursts asunder. The knell of private property sounds. The expropriators are expropriated.

"The expropriators are expropriated"—the very form of
this statement, its timeless present, shows that it is in reality
a logical statement. It is there because of some preceding
stage in a logical series. The "expropriation of the expropriators" never took place in history in these terms,
even if various "expropriators" had their property con-
fiscated. It is not taking place in the present, and if it
occurs in the future it will also be a manifest contingency,
not a law of nature. Yet Marx puts it as a law; it has, in
fact, the timelessness of a law in logic.

His sweeping assertion that capitalism must give rise
to increasing misery is based on a purely logical chain of
definitions, as indicated above: all capitalist values in
bourgeois economy are exclusively the product of the
working time of manual laborers; profit consists of the
unpaid work-hours of manual laborers; profit tends to decrease with the introduction of every new machine, since
with each new machine the capitalist must reduce the
number of his laborers and thus also reduce the source of
his profit. Hence, the final stage in this process is reached
when the capitalist is forced to get more and more unpaid labor-time from his laborers, which is the ultimate
reason for the squeeze he has to put them in and for the
increasing misery of their lives.

This is a perfectly logical progression—but it is obviously unrealistic, not to mention that it flies in the face of well-known facts. The item about the machinery decreasing profits is perhaps most revealing of all, since it completely fails to explain one of the cardinal aspects of the whole growth of the system to begin with—the extensive application of technology. According to the logic of *Capital,* it is quite impossible to explain how any capitalist could be so foolish as to spend money on machines that are bound to *decrease* his profit. So it is clear that this stage in his exposition is forced upon Marx by the mere logic of his argument and is anti-historical—in a word, false.

One of the oddities in Marx's argument is his awareness of this point. He actually says (p. 335: Kerr translation) that the law that machinery destroys profits seems "clearly to contradict all experience" and that there is an enigmatic "contradiction" in the conduct of capitalists who on the one hand are doing their level best to maximize their profits while on the other hand they keep installing more and more machines that destroy their profits. After noting this piece of experience, Marx then goes on with his general exposition as though nothing had happened!

Marx was always enthralled by abstract ideas. Even when engulfing empirical data, his mind arranged those data in a logical structure. He claimed to have put Hegel "on his feet" by basing his conclusions on the real experience behind such data, yet it is clear that they had meaning for Marx only insofar as they constituted a purely logical process. It is true, after all, that there are workers and capitalists, proletarians and bourgeois: that is why statements about them sound convincing. But Marx was not referring to *real* workers or bourgeois at all, that is, to ordinary human beings performing certain socio-economic functions. He actually meant the *Idea* of the Bourgeoisie, the *Idea* of the Proletariat, and so on—mere links in a logical chain. Historically this has, of course, been and still is quite misleading.

This use, or abuse of logic was, ironically enough, one of the factors in the spread of his influence. Marx's mind, powerful enough to apply what he called the "force of abstraction"—his method of fitting real data into the Procrustean bed of his logic—to the world at large and to extract from the experience a coherently organized scheme has impressed many people aside from his own followers.

Only logic can explain the structure of this remarkable book, which is intended to demonstrate the working-out of an inevitable law in the very bowels of reality. An all-powerful, unswervingly rigid capitalist class is forced to compensate for the steady dwindling of its profits from the exploitation of manpower by increasing the degree of exploitation, and hence the misery, of a growing segment of society. The misery increases relentlessly. Because of this, the revolution inevitably takes place, coming to fruition from the "seeds of destruction carried within the system itself."

The whole process, in short, despite its deceptively realistic, empirical underpinnings, is utterly logical, that is, unhistorical and unrealistic. The *logic* is Hegel's; it is simply another way of saying that the negation of capitalism is achieved through the socialism it is bound to engender.

Aside from its unreality, the shortcoming of the systematic exposition attempted by Marx is precisely this logical quality. If it were restricted to a historical analysis of real phenomena, or even to an analysis and philosophical definition of economic categories, it might or might not have a certain value. But it is really committed to a global explanation that conditions and is conditioned by its parts.

The whole thing makes up an indivisible entity, a *system* —a logical structure. It would snap altogether if one of its links were broken, since it depends on its acceptance as a *whole*. Doubtless this explains the fanaticism that has always raged around the subject.

This shortcoming of the system was also its strong point, for instead of discussing the pros and cons of capitalism as opposed to some other, ideal system, whose qualities were undemonstrable because it was not yet in existence, Marx's dogmatic temperament pitched on the one quality of his system that has given it an endless appeal to many intellectuals and others. Its inevitability lent an immense self-assurance, indeed a mystical faith, to those who wanted something firm to cling to. His analysis of vast forces inevitably tending to bring about massive changes in an ideal direction gave a devotional intensity to the zeal for world-reform on the part of countless youthful idealists. By claiming that capitalism must "fall" not because it had faults, or was in general undesirable, but because its fall was part of the very fabric of reality, Marx's partisans had the satisfaction first of battling for the good and second of knowing that their battle would be successful.

In view of Marx's intellectual vivacity there has always been a question of sincerity involved in any discussion of whether or not he believed in his own theories. The factual defects in his intellectual constructions are glaringly obvious, after all—must he not have realized them himself?

The discussion may be pointless, for one of Marx's primary traits of character was the utter identification of his thought with logic. He was the kind of intellectual whose intellect is expressed through abstract rationalism. His ability to make endless, rigorously demonstrated deductions from either nothing at all or from tiny and essentially ambiguous pieces of evidence was part of the very fiber of his mind. His prose, generally tortuous and obscure when dealing with abstractions and mordant when arrangements of fact can be constrained within logical structures, is proof that he was often quite unconscious that he lacked a sense of proportion. His love of logic for logic's sake completely obliterated his common sense; he piled obscurities on obscurities.

In economics he always remained a peculiarly partisan student, the sort of fanatical theoretician who looks to a given field simply for confirmation of theories formed elsewhere. He was not actually interested in economics as such; the economics he forced himself to study was exceptionally boring. He studied it only insofar as it could give him the proof of something else he was interested in —and that was, of course, politics and history on the grandest scale.

Marx not only thought *Capital* his major work; he even thought his "own recent scientific discovery marks indeed an epoch in the history of the development of the human race" (p. 85). This remarkable statement indicates the importance he ascribed to it and also shows the extent to which his own self-esteem had become bound up with the structure of his thought. In his youthful productions he might have been expressing himself with the verve natural to his tempestuous mind; perhaps his remarks about the necessary evolution of history need not have been taken so seriously. In *Capital,* on the other hand, all his energies were poured into something he did consider a treatise on economic science—hence his lopsided discussion of impersonal, empirically ascertained data seems particularly pernicious.

One must acknowledge that the main element in its acceptance, from the very beginning, was faith. There is no denying that the book became, rather quickly, an icon of devotion. And the faith was generated, curiously enough, by precisely the basic element whose essence he sought to clarify and explain through economics—his labor theory of value.

For whether or not this theory is accepted, even tentatively, as an abstract definition of value, whether it is considered an ideal tendency toward which real prices may move, or a vital element in human attitudes toward value, or whether it is simply a metaphysical explanation that need have no relationship at all to actual prices—as indeed it has not—what was effective about the theory was that it seemed to give a factual substantiation of a deeply implanted human instinct.

The idea is, put as simply as possible, that some people are not receiving their due. The whole notion has exercised an irresistible tug on workers and their leaders. Its axis was the assertion that there was only one class in society that was not getting its just desserts, and that was their own.

It was, and always has been, quite out of the question for untrained people even to begin to thread their way through the labyrinth of Marx's "demonstrations." What remained after all his analysis and description was the simple idea that workers were being done out of something that they were inherently entitled to, and that this was being channeled away from them simply because of the historically conditioned, and hence altogether *changeable*, structure of society. That structure put into the hands of non-workers all the means of production—natural resources, machinery, means of communication, credit, and so on—and thus the workers were condemned to go on working for those who, because they owned these vital instruments, could impose their will on all mankind.

The argument was made all the more forceful through

the parallel demonstration by Marx that this state of
affairs was kept deliberately obscure by what amounted to
a general conspiracy of the intelligentsia to keep the world
organized—by deception, lies, myths, and propaganda—to
favor the exploiting classes. For in addition to their control over the means of production, the possessing classes
also owned whole groups of people. They had an army, in
fact, of paid hacks, ideologists, propagandists, apologists,
etc., providing a whole network of ramified apologias for
the system that has everyone blinded. By using all the resources of art, they keep the system decked out with charm
and glamour. In this way the losers in the system do not
notice what is happening. The arts thus heighten the
morale of those who benefit by the system and also soothe
their moral sense, while at the same time they contrive to
gull the masses into thinking this monstrous system is at
bottom delectable.

Thus Marx's formula had a built-in psychic motor—the
longing for justice on earth; the conviction that the nature
of the world confirmed one's desires; and indignation at
the actual social hierarchy, blind and selfish, that blocked
the road of righteous progress embedded in nature.

The publication of the book was a decisive moment in
Marx's life. *Capital* was his greatest contribution to a
cause he regarded as the liberation of mankind. He had
wanted to dedicate the book to Darwin, who he thought
had succeeded in doing for the natural sciences what he
considered himself to be doing for the history of man.
Darwin hastened to evade the honor, saying in his cour-
teous way that he unfortunately knew nothing about economics but wished Marx well in what he assumed they
were both striving for—the increase of knowledge.

The book was to establish an altogether new reputation
for Marx. His previous books had been disregarded even

in German-speaking areas, but *Capital* was to be reviewed and argued about everywhere in Europe. During the following decade, after an initial period of silence, it was translated into French, English, Russian, and Italian. The first translation, curiously enough, was into Russian—the book became a must for generations of Russian intellectuals.

Yet all this still lay in the future. The actual publication of *Capital* was followed by a sort of void in Marx's own life.

His financial problems were solved a year after *Capital* was published. Engels's business in Manchester had been doing so well that Engels was able, at last, to retire from the drudgery of the "commerce" he had been steeped in for eighteen years. He was bought out by his partner and took advantage of the negotiation to settle a fixed income on Marx for life, as well as provision for illness and all emergencies. All Marx's debts were also to be paid. The sum fixed on as an annual income for him was very respectable for the time—£350.

Engels was finally able to move to the capital, to be at Marx's side. In place of Mary Burns he took along with him her sister Lizzy.

Thus, scarcely more than a year after Marx finished *Capital,* he was a retired gentleman in London, living in respectable circumstances that enabled him to do as he pleased. This was the first time in his adult life that he had had a dependable income. Ever since his days in Paris he had been in a state of constant worry and uncertainty, now over with for good.

The immediate effect was a slackening of his activities. Though the draft of the second two volumes of *Capital* had been ready since the beginning of 1865 and he had promised the publisher to complete them in autumn 1867 and spring 1868 respectively, the reception of the first volume was a disappointment.

During the first year the total sales amounted to no more than two hundred copies of the edition of one thousand. This was so discouraging that no English publisher would take a chance on it, and Marx had been looking forward to an English edition especially. He explained the total silence that had greeted *Capital,* just as it had the *Critique* before it, as the result of a plot, but he nevertheless felt terribly disappointed. Even before being given a secure income by Engels, he had stopped working on the two last volumes of *Capital.* With his present economic security he gave up the whole project. Nor could he explain this by his health, which was much better.

He also abandoned his attempts to play a leading role in the German party. Some four years before, after the death of Lassalle, he had made an effort to suggest in a systematic way that Lassalle had been an agent of Bismarck's. He had conceived this as an attempt to get a foothold, even from afar, in the party still standing in Lassalle's shadow. But this story, based on a malicious exaggeration of some peculiar suspicions he had felt after hearing of an interview between Lassalle and Bismarck, had had no effect, and he was reduced to depending on a rival workers' party that was being built up by his admirer Wilhelm Liebknecht, the former philologist. But even Liebknecht had begun wavering in his fidelity to Marx's ideas, and Marx had turned sour on Liebknecht too.

The International remained the source of his only hopes. It had been growing steadily in the four years of its existence. Though the English unions represented the most solid part of the membership, with some 25,000 people, the International was by now quite widespread—it even had a few sections as far away as America. It had also taken on a certain importance in the public imagination and was blamed for the strikes that were becoming fairly commonplace in Europe. The role played by the International was exaggerated by its enemies, but the exaggeration itself increased its importance. It was, in short, being talked about—something indispensable for any public organization.

Marx thought it vital to consolidate his position in the International and swing it over to his own views. He had to contend with the "stupidity" of the English, and especially with their lack of a "spirit of generalization and the revolutionary passion." All they wanted was higher wages and shorter working hours, while the "babbling French" wanted a peaceful, "mutualistic" transition to socialism. Even the Germans, whom Marx had despised for so long, now seemed to him magnificent—"with heads on their shoulders, they are capable of generalizing."

Marx did not like attending congresses, which he thought so much tinsel; he preferred a backstage role. He finally maneuvered a more or less socialistic resolution through the Brussels Congress of 1868. The word socialism was not used, but the idea of the resolution—that all agricultural land, mines, and railroads belong to "society"—was in its essence socialistic, overriding English opposition, and for that matter state-socialistic, overriding French views.

In the autumn of 1868, however, some disquieting news came. An organization recently founded in Switzerland— The "International Alliance of Socialist Democracy"— wanted to join the International.

Bakunin had started this and was its head. Though some four years before, during his last talk with him, Marx had been pleasantly surprised by Bakunin's affability, the actual

prospect of having such a glamorous figure, with his oratorical gifts, in the same organization as himself was alarm-
ing.

From Marx's organizational and political point of view,
Bakunin was all the more dangerous since—though Bakunin himself was not much of a theoretician—his non-
Marxist socialism had struck roots in many places, especially in Italy and Spain. There was for the first time a
fairly serious Bakunist movement, which seemed about to
infiltrate the International too.

Bakunin's position, now as before, was based on a dislike of the state. Essentially an anarchist, he wanted to destroy all forms of central compulsion. Hence he wanted the
state simply pulverized altogether and replaced by some
form of local, non-general authority "from below."

Marx had of course always preached the "ultimate"
disappearance of the state. Since he defined the state as
the instrument of the class oppression of the proletariat, his
theory that all classes would end after the proletariat had
been successful in conducting society into socialism implied that there would be no longer be any need for the
state. Thus, from a polemical point of view, he could quite
convincingly maintain that he too wanted the same goal
as those numerous members of the proletarian movement
who were violently opposed to the state as such, that he
was entirely on their side, and that there was no conflict,
since he too believed that the state would "wither away."
The phrase summing up this process is: "The State is not
abolished, it withers away. The government of persons is
replaced by the administration of things."

It was true that before this happened the State must
be made more powerful than ever. *Later* it would wither
away, to be replaced by "administration."

This whole view depends, of course, on defining the word state in a highly specialized way, as meaning only those functions of a state that can be interpreted as holding down the lower classes. All other functions were simply lumped together as "administration."

It was a purely semantic distinction, and it could not deflect Bakunin's attention away from what he regarded as the essentially pernicious role of the state structure as such, regardless of what it was called.

Organizationally, too, Marx was bound to be extremely hostile to Bakunin's new grouping, which had international claims of its own and branches in a number of countries. Marx flung all his energies into counteracting Bakunin's organizational efforts, maneuvering against him behind the scenes, in correspondence, and through his various instruments in the International.

A somewhat ironic twist was given to all this after the appearance of *Capital*, which Bakunin, quite unknown to Marx, greatly admired and undertook to translate into Russian. Bakunin always regarded Marx, whose character he loathed, as a valuable person for the international working-class movement, despite his statist ideas. Though his own project of translation came to nothing, he always spoke of *Capital* with respect.

In 1870 Bismarck's enterprise of German unification was completed for him by the frivolity of Napoleon III, who declared war on Prussia, in the summer of 1870, and enabled Bismarck, now representing a wholly new German nationalist euphoria that engulfed even the south German states, to destroy the French power in the biggest war in two generations.

In only six weeks the Prussians wiped out two French armies, the second with Napoleon at the head. The empire was finished with his capture. A republic was quickly set up in Paris but soon left as the Germans approached, while the city readied itself for a siege.

Marx and Engels were both very enthusiastic about the war and the prospect of Prussian victory. Engels sounded like a conventional German patriot, though he based his own enthusiasm on the "progressiveness" of this particular war, with its destruction of Bonapartism. Marx agreed, but since Liebknecht had proclaimed neutrality as the right policy for the working-class, he had to resort to diplomacy. Liebknecht, whose attitude Marx approved of, was nevertheless condemned by many of his comrades, and also, more importantly perhaps, by Engels, who disagreed completely—unusual for him. Hence, Marx's own published statement was very vague and gave no guidance at all as to how workers should react to the war.

But the International's attitude was quite overshadowed by the war itself.

Bakunin feared above all the emergence of a strong, centralized Germany. For him the victory of the Prussian army meant not only the defeat of France but of all prospects for liberty. He produced a characteristic explosion of energy—he slipped into Lyon just as the first German troops were reaching Paris, and after haranguing some crowds, exhorted them to form communes that would turn the war into "an elemental, mighty, passionately energetic, anarchistic, destructive, unrestrained uprising of the popular masses of the people over the whole territory of France." He was arrested and released the same day. A little later he was back in Switzerland, penniless, his legs swollen with gout, and his weak heart weakened further. He felt that all Europe was about to succumb to German despotism, with the workers especially in the hands of a robot, Marxist socialism.

Paris was under siege and in the grip of famine. Some longed for peace; others, including the leftists, both bourgeois and socialist, were clamoring for a continuation of the war. There was no means to carry on the war against the overwhelming power of Prussia at the moment. Despair raised the accusation of national betrayal that has been a constant motif in French as perhaps in all politics.

Carrying on the war was all the more difficult because outside the city in Versailles, only half a year after the beginning of the war, Bismarck's life-work—the unification of the German Empire—was consummated. William of Prussia was proclaimed Kaiser.

Now Bismarck, a remarkably moderate politician, did his best to ease the transition to peace. Paris surrendered, only ten days after the proclamation of the German Empire, and even as the Prussians, taking great pains not to offend anyone, moved in convoys of food to the starving population, elections were held with no German interference. Unrestricted agitation was carried on both for and against the continuation of the war. The elections gave the peace party a two-thirds majority, and the new National Assembly sent delegates to Bismarck for the peace terms: five billion francs and the surrender of Alsace-Lorraine. These terms in their turn were accepted by a huge majority. In the midst of general gloom France swallowed its defeat.

But less than three weeks after the peace terms had been accepted, there was a revolt in Paris, and a commune was established. It seemed to have been launched by the National Guard, a volunteer unit with radical sympathies. In March 1871, when the government tried to disarm the National Guard, it refused to surrender its arms, proclaimed the autonomy of Paris, and elected a revolutionary committee as the French government. Regular troops were moved to Versailles, and a slow and painful campaign followed, recognized by both sides as an overt war between "classes."

The Commune had nothing to do with the International. In doctrine it was not, in fact, socialist at all but a mixed bag of individuals, largely followers of Blanqui, Proudhon, and Bakunin, with a great many intellectuals—writers, soldiers, painters, scholars, and many liberal foreign exiles. There was also a large percentage of ordinary enthusiasts, inflamed by the prospect of putting an end to all despots, priests, and Prussians. The only common view on social organization was a detestation of any centralized government. The old state was abolished, and the people-in-arms were summoned to self-government.

The commune in Lyon had been, apparently, an exclusively working-class enterprise, which Marx had been against, perhaps because of Bakunin's connection with it. The Paris Commune, with its huge admixture of moderate bourgeois and amorphous leftist forces, was now heartily endorsed by him.

This was odd because in spite of the actual composition of the Commune representatives, there was no trace of socialism in any of its pronouncements—for that matter no workers' demands were ever even mentioned. As Marx himself was to write a decade later, "the majority of the Paris Commune was in no sense socialist, nor could it be."

Yet Marx was eager to claim the moral and intellectual credit for the Commune in Paris. He did not state that the International had actually launched it, but called it its "child intellectually." Marx was in any case bound to be linked with the fortunes of the Commune, both by his own initiative, through his letters to the members of the International, and conversely, because of the propaganda value his name gave the enemies of the Commune in France.

As the opponents of the Commune throughout France found it convenient to have a scapegoat that could be branded as foreign, the role of the International was inflated beyond all proportions. In spite of the utter confusion in the minds of the Commune leaders, the complete absence of doctrine, and the presence of an element of infantile irresponsibility, they were accused of being the heirs of the notorious massacre of June, 1848, and also the dupes of the foreign conspiracy called the International, run behind the scenes by the sinister Dr. Marx.

This propaganda made Marx world-famous. It identified him in the minds of people all over the world with an active uprising that was quickly stigmatized as the source of endless atrocities and as a failure to boot.

It was impossible to defend his behavior in the General Council of the International, because the General Council, in agreement with conventional opinion throughout Europe, felt that the Commune represented a simple and unusually stupid crime against a democratically elected government.

The Commune lasted only a short while. A month later troops from Versailles began to drag themselves toward Paris. With the greatest difficulty they reached the suburbs by the beginning of May. An incredible slaughter, impossible to assess, followed for another four weeks. The bloodshed was deplorable, but there was one crime that only the Commune leaders committed: just as the battle was about to end the Commune executed—futilely—some "hostages" they had taken from among various prominent individuals in Paris, including the Archbishop of Paris.

This aroused horror everywhere. Even to socialists like

Louis Blanc the Communards seemed like criminal mad-
men, irresponsibly destroying for the sake of destruction.
Almost the whole of the press in Europe reacted with
revulsion, though occasionally a liberal paper might say
something about extenuating factors.

The International as a whole vacillated. The English
members were uncompromisingly opposed to the whole
enterprise, and Marx had a difficult problem. He solved
it with characteristic boldness.

A couple of days after the destruction of the Commune,
he read a speech to the General Council in which he defended it in an absolutely systematic way. In spite of its
failure to establish a doctrine of any kind or even to do
anything toward the realization of any particular principle,
he maintained that the Commune represented a lofty ideal,
while the members of the Versailles government were
criminal elements of class corruption.

Marx hailed the Commune as the first manifestation in
history of a working-class initiative, the first out-and-out
battle that from then on would be the watershed between
the friends of the working-class and its enemies. He also
claimed that the Commune in and for itself represented an
ideal stage in the progression from capitalism to socialism,
a transitional social form the workers had to pass through
in order to undo the bourgeois state and free themselves.
He retracted, as he had done before, a basic argument of
the *Communist Manifesto,* in which he had insisted not
on dismantling the state but on seizing it in order to
destroy the enemy.

Marx did not approve of the measures of the Commune.
It was not radical enough for him. He thought it, moreover, a first-class blunder, because it was too idealistic.
He considered that it was utopian of its leaders to pro-
claim immediate social and economic equality in a void

—that is, out of the given historical context. Moreover, his enemies, Blanquists and Proudhonists, had been the predominant factor.

Yet his permanent belief in the value of a violent working-class insurrection made him put a halo over the real Commune. He called the slain Communards martyrs in the cause of socialism and assigned them a central role in the formation of the new faith. He created the paramount legend of socialism. His arguments, despite their purely tactical significance at the time he made them, were to be quoted by followers as a justification of any upsurge of heroism, however abortive, as better than a mere accurate analysis of history.

The furore caused in the ranks of the International, and in the socialist movement in general, by Marx's sponsorship of the Commune now became complicated by the endless web of intrigue he had devised against his old enemy Bakunin. The Englishmen resigned from the General Council of the International, and the mood of schism spread. Marx was hemmed in by a growing tide of hostility, both to himself and to the methods by which he had been fighting Bakunin, which consisted chiefly of spreading slanders new and old.

Marx decided to close down his connection with the International in a fitting way. Since he could no longer control it, and since, on the other hand, it was vital to keep it from falling into the hands of his Bakuninist opponents, he decided to scuttle the whole operation and at the same time destroy Bakunin once and for all.

For the first time he and Engels attended a congress, which was to be the last one held by the International, at The Hague in 1872. The International, which only three years before had looked as though it had a future, was sunk in depression. There was a mood of dissolution everywhere. The Italians had also left; other major groups were vacillating.

After the usual turmoil of speeches, reports, and discussions, this time very halfhearted, Engels threw a bombshell. He proposed that the headquarters of the International be transferred—to New York!

There was an immense amount of confusion over this curious proposal, but Marx and Engels retained enough influence to get it passed, especially as it was the only way out of the imbroglio created by the general disaffection, plus the poisonous atmosphere due to Marx's campaign against Bakunin.

By concocting, almost out of nothing, a slander about Bakunin's having cheated a publisher out of 300 rubles, Marx managed to get Bakunin expelled from the International. He went back to London, delighted that in the very hour of his losing control of the International he had nevertheless managed to liquidate it by moving it beyond any conceivable orbit of effectiveness and also by undoing his old rival.

This latter victory was, to be sure, only half a victory: Marx's success in voting Bakunin out of the International needed support, since rumors about his skulduggery had begun to fly about. Marx sat down and wrote a pamphlet, amounting to a hundred and sixty pages, simply to prove that Bakunin was not only a petty swindler, Czarist agent, etc., but one of the most degenerate men who had ever lived. An admirer of Marx, Otto Rühle, has described it as follows: "A malicious pamphlet, in which almost every line is a distortion, almost every allegation an injustice, almost every argument a falsification, and almost every word an untruth."

Nevertheless it hastened Bakunin's exit from the scene. Broken in health, quite impoverished, he sent a Swiss newspaper a letter attesting to his retirement and was never heard of again.

The International, too, was finished. The decision to move it to New York had destroyed it completely, though it lingered on for some months. Bakuninists and others tried to save something from the debris, but the organization simply expired. A year after The Hague Congress, members were invited by the New York office to attend another meeting in Geneva. Almost no one turned up—the International was dead.

CHAPTER VIII

Epilogue: Last Days

At the age of fifty-four, Marx, now quite aged, faced a tranquil life. He had outlived Bakunin and Lassalle, he had published *Capital,* and he had a comfortable income.

Yet he had seemingly little to do. The International had been his last major enterprise. From the time of its collapse on, his life was strangely empty.

His ideas were not unacceptable. On the contrary, there were now two workers' parties in Germany that were Marxist, one of them avowedly so, but though Liebknecht corresponded with Marx, neither he nor any other leaders paid attention to his advice. In England the working-class movement was thoroughly non-socialist, so there was no occasion for Marx to give it advice. In France the socialist tendency was non-Marxist; there, too, his advice was unwanted.

Marx's peak of vexation was reached in 1875 when both German parties, which had originally split because of his aversion to Lassalle, reunited. Marx and Engels learned of it from the newspapers.

The two parties had formed the united Social-Democratic Party, but neither Marx nor Engels was asked to draft the program, to cooperate in drafting it, even to approve it.

The reunification of the two parties was the subject of the last major document that they wrote together, *A Critique of the Gotha Program.* Liebknecht read it without having any idea of what to do about it. It took him a month to reply, to the effect that the program could no longer be changed. This meant something quite simple —even in the German party, which Marx and Engels regarded as their child, they could no longer play the role of consultants.

The article on the Gotha program did not even appear in print for another fifteen years, long after Marx's death. It is of some interest that the document, which had absolutely no effect on the event that inspired it, was to become the source of a whole new theoretical application of what had meanwhile become "Marxism." A formula, pregnant with consequences, had found its way into Marx's published writings—the "dictatorship of the proletariat."

Marx had made much of this in conversation and in letters, to be sure, but he had never yet used it in print, and this ephemeral reference, occurring as part of a couple of transitional sentences, was to justify the seizure of power in Russia and to serve as the cornerstone in the establishment of a new society.

By 1875, with the *de facto* severance of any real relations between himself and the German working-class movement, Marx felt definitely out of the world of affairs. He was once again in a sort of backwater, still an exile in England, and he had no activity besides his scholarship.

But in this he was also somehow inhibited. The manuscripts of the last two volumes of *Capital* remained stubbornly unattractive to him. There can be no doubt that one of the chief reasons, despite what he actually said, was that his predictions, which had always failed to materialize, had now proved so wide of the mark that they had become a source of malaise and in any case of inner frustration. The pride he had taken in his discovery of the labor theory of value was now vitiated, largely by the fact that his thinking had suddenly wound up in a self-contradiction. In the third volume he arrived at a different theory of value, though by the same method of logical development. Capitalism showed no signs of behaving as he had predicted. Misery was not increasing. There were many more well-to-do people, and the condition of the workers was far better than it had been. His strategy, based on that analysis, had also proved wrong an endless number of times.

He had even contradicted one of his major ideas, that socialism must be introduced by violence. In 1872, in a speech made at The Hague Congress where the International ended, he had made a fleeting reference to the possibility of a peaceful attainment of workers' objectives "in England, America, and even Holland." He had said this too, though only once. Now that Marxism had become a science and was gradually being studied by young people in Europe, students of his ideas would ask for explanations. This was a source of endless irritation; it led to his celebrated outburst of cynicism—"all I know is that I am not a Marxist."

The German Social-Democratic Party was to have varied fortunes, but it was beyond his control. No Marxist Party could be founded in France or England. Russia was still far off. In any case, Marx himself could influence none of these events.

His principal English admirer, H. M. Hyndman, the founder of the Social Democratic Federation, was an agreeable, lively journalistic writer. An amateur who admired distinguished figures, and fleetingly attached himself to Marx, he has left a description of him at this time:

The first impression of Marx as I saw him was that of a powerful, shaggy, untamed old man, ready, not to say eager,

to enter into conflict, and rather suspicious himself of immediate attack; yet his greeting of us was cordial. . . . When
speaking with fierce indignation of the policy of the Liberal
Party, especially in regard to Ireland, the old warrior's brows
wrinkled, his small deep-sunk eyes lighted up his heavy brows,
the broad, strong nose and face were obviously moved by passion, and he poured out a stream of vigorous denunciation
which displayed alike the heat of his temperament, and the
marvelous command he possessed over our language. The
contrast between his manner and utterance when thus deeply
stirred by anger, and his attitude when giving his views on the
economic events of the period, was very marked. He turned
from the role of prophet and violent denunciator to that of
the calm philosopher without any apparent effort, and I felt
that many a long year might pass before I ceased to be a
student in the presence of a master.

I had been surprised in reading the *Capital* and still more
when perusing his smaller works, such as his pronouncement
on the Commune of Paris and his "XVIIIth Brumaire," how
he combined the ablest and coolest examination of economic
causes and social effects with the most bitter hatred of classes
and even of individual men such as Napoleon III, and M.
Thiers, who, according to his own theories, were little more
than flies upon the wheels of the great Juggernaut car of
capitalist development. Marx, of course, was a Jew, and to
me it seemed that he combined in his own person and nature,
with his commanding forehead and great overhanging brow,
his fierce glittering eyes, broad sensitive nose and mobile
mouth, all surrounded by a setting of untrimmed hair and
beard, the righteous fury of the great seers of his race, with
the cold analytical powers of Spinoza and the Jewish doctors.
It was an extraordinary combination of qualities, the like of
which I have known in no other man.

But the friendship lasted only until Hyndman published
a short, readable account of Marxism in English, in which
for some curious reason he failed to mention Marx's name

at all, on the theory that as a foreigner he would not go down well in England!

Marx's discouragement with his own ideas was somewhat obscured by an unusual increase in his reading. Always enormous, it now increased to the point where there could hardly be any question of his doing serious work. As he read more and more, he wrote less and less. He even began to learn new languages—including Turkish!

His family, while still a great comfort to him, had gradually grown smaller. His three daughters had all left, one by one. The oldest, Jenny, married a French journalist; Laura, the wife of Paul Lafargue, drifted into a life of such torments, partly through Lafargue's eccentricities, that she was to commit suicide; Eleonore was living with an Englishman, Dr. Aveling—a "perverted character" and "criminal" according to Engels—without marrying him. She, also, was to commit suicide. Always a devoted father, Marx was naturally distressed by his daughters' unhappiness.

His health began to deteriorate again. Soon he was in a state of decline. In 1881, when Marx was sixty-three and Jenny sixty-seven, she developed cancer. As she lay painfully dying, he had to stay in the next room, the victim of a combined attack of pleurisy and pneumonia. Jenny died in 1881. As Engels said, now "the Moor died too."

Marx lived on another two years. He was sent off in search of the sun to the Mediterranean, which had a typically wet and disagreeable winter. Shortly after coming back to London, he got word that his eldest daughter had suddenly died. It was a blow he never recovered from. On March 14, 1883, with an abscessed lung, still tended by the faithful Helen Demuth, he died, quite peacefully, in his sleep.

Only eight people were at his funeral. His two sons-in-law came over from Paris, and Liebknecht came from Germany. At the burial site in Highgate Cemetery, London, Engels's speech was devoted to his unique achievements: "The greatest living thinker has ceased to think. . . ."

His death was scarcely noticed. The report printed by the London *Times* came, oddly enough, from its Paris correspondent, who had been reading the French socialist press. It was only afterward that his fame was to grow, not through the cult of his personality, as with so many popular heroes, but through the steady infiltration of his ideas into the minds of millions.

Capital was to become the cornerstone of the Marxist edifice. Moreover, its influence later proved to be strong enough to make Marx's ideas the principal tendency in the maelstrom of currents that had been contending with each other, somewhat shapelessly, in the international socialist movement. It was "Marxism," rounded off and systematized by Engels and largely based on *Capital*, that became, in fact, a sort of Pole Star for the socialist movement. Other varieties of socialism were obliged to orient themselves by it and to define themselves in terms of their attitudes toward it.

Capital's initial period of obscurity was followed by a period, not yet ended, when it became an icon of worship for countless numbers of people who could hardly be expected even to begin to read it. It also became a symbol of evil for enemies of Marxism and of socialism in general. Together with other constituents of the Marxist "system," *Capital* has given rise to a host of exegetes. As an actual book, it has long since been almost obliterated beneath the endless numbers of books that make up its commentaries. Among Marx's followers, it is quite simply an emblem of faith.

It is doubtless because *Capital* seems the most "scientific" of Marx's writings that its role is paramount in the Marxist system. If Marxism is to be thought of as a religion—an approach that has always had a certain vogue—it must be recalled that its attraction is bound up with its claims to rationality in general and to scientific validity in particular.

It can scarcely be denied that Marxism has the structure of a messianically conceived religion. It has a doctrine of Final Things brought about *in a certain way* via a Savior. Its absence of a specific ritual may be thought of as made up for by the emphasis on Good Works—devotion to the Cause.

It is, of course, a secular faith. In the retreat that religion in general has been engaged in ever since the Enlightenment and the phenomenally rapid ascension of the scientific point of view, all those longings still rooted in the hearts of millions could be satisfied only by something in the guise of science.

Faced by the rationalistic and materialistic tendencies of the epoch, no faith would have been possible without the underpinnings of science. The mere preaching of human betterment would have been relatively futile; a mere analysis of society would have interested only a handful of specialists.

But a sermon preached by a prophet dressed like a scientist, a claim scientific in form but crystallizing the passions of millions, created a devoted following, secure, indeed fanatical in the assurance that its cause was part of the fabric of the universe and *in the nature of things* must be triumphant.

Indeed, Marxism may be thought of as the first great modern religion; it has assimilated history, science, technology, and—of course!—atheism.

Marxism must be considered the most successful branch of classical German idealist philosophy or, for that matter, of philosophy in general. It created a sort of conversion mechanism that transformed the socialism launched by the French Revolution into the Soviet and the Chinese states. Thus it spanned continents and changed the world.

And it is surely here, in Marx's influence, that we encounter the most striking contradiction of his theories.

Marx's cardinal thesis, doubtless, was that ideas do not determine the course of history, but are themselves the product of other, objective historical forces. Yet it was precisely the faith generated by his own ideas that made them decisive in the shaping of events.

Hence the very fact that Marx, despite the palpable shortcomings of specific intellectual constructions, became one of the most influential men ever born really validates the proposition that the irrational is the wellspring of our conduct.

It is faith, after all, that moves mountains.

SUGGESTED READING

There is a vast body of literature on Marx and Marxism. In this bibliography I mention only a few recent works that I think of interest to the general reader.

Aron, Raymond. *The Opium of the Intellectuals*. London, Secker & Warburg Ltd., 1957.

Berlin, Isaiah. *Karl Marx: His Life and Environment*, Third Edition. (Galaxy Books), Oxford University Press, 1963.

Eastman, Max. *Marxism, Is it Science?*. New York, W.W. Norton and Company Inc., 1940.

Fromm, Erich. *Marx's Concept of Man*. New York, Frederick Ungar Publishing Company, Inc., 1961.

Hook, Sidney. *From Hegel to Marx*. (Ann Arbor Books), Ann Arbor, University of Michican Press, 1962.

Hook, Sidney. *Toward an Understanding of Karl Marx*. New York, The John Day Company, Inc., 1933.

Lichtheim, George. *Marxism: A Historical and Critical Study*. London, Routledge & Kegan Paul, 1961.

Marcuse, Herbert. *Reason and Revolution*. London, Routledge & Kegan Paul, 1955.

Mehring, Franz. *Karl Marx: The Story of His Life*. New York, Covici Friede, 1935.

Popper, Karl. *The Open Society and its Enemies*. London, Routledge & Kegan Paul, 1949.

Schwarzschild, Leopold. *Karl Marx: The Red Prussian*. (Universal Library), New York, Grosset & Dunlap, Inc., 1958.

Wilson, Edmund. *To the Finland Station*. (Anchor), New York, Doubleday & Company, Inc., 1953.

SOURCES OF QUOTATIONS

Quotations from Marx's and Engels's letters and writings are based on the *Marx-Engels Werke* (Collected Works) published under the auspices of the Soviet Institute of Marxism-Leninism. *Capital* is quoted in the C. H. Kerr & Company (Chicago) edition.

Reminiscences of Marx are taken from the following works:

Pavel Vasilevich Annenkov. *Literaturnye Vospominaniya* (St. Petersburg, 1909).

Mikhail Bakunin. *Sobranie Sochinenii*, Y. M. Steklov, ed. (Moscow, 1935).

Erich Fromm. *Marx's Concept of Man* (New York, Frederick Ungar Publishing Company, Inc., 1962). Quoted from Paul Lafargue and Eleanor Marx-Aveling.

Karl Heinzen. *Erlebtes* (Boston, published by the author, 1864).

H. M. Hyndman. *The Record of an Adventurous Life* (New York, The Macmillan Company, 1911).

Carl Schurz. *Reminisences* (New York, McClure Company, 1907-8).

HIGHLIGHTS IN THE LIFE OF
KARL MARX

1817   Hirschel Levi, son of the Rabbi of Trier, joins the Christian Church and changes his name to Heinrich Marx.

1818   Karl Marx is born to Heinrich Marx and his wife, the former Henrietta Pressburger, a Dutch Jewess.

1824   All seven Marx children are baptized.

1825   Karl's mother, also of rabbinical lineage, follows her husband and children into the Lutheran Church.

1835   Karl enters the University of Bonn where he plays the classical role of scapegrace student, squandering money, being arrested for drunkeness, even fighting a duel.

1836   Karl enters the University of Berlin.

1838   Karl steeps himself in Hegel's philosophy.

1841   A month before his twenty-third birthday Karl obtains a Ph.D. degree—by mail—from the University of Jena.

1842   Marx becomes associated with the *Rhine Gazette* and shortly thereafter its editor.

1843   A self-styled martyr as a result of the official suppression of the *Gazette,* Marx becomes interested in socialism.
       About to leave Germany for Paris, Karl marries his childhood sweetheart, Jenny von Westphalen.

1844   The *German-French Yearbooks* are published by Arnold Ruge and Karl Marx.
       An edict of expulsion from Prussia is issued against Marx as a result of his advocating armed revolution on behalf of socialist theory.
       Marx meets Friedrich Engels.

1845   Expelled from France because of a diplomatic incident in
       which he was not directly involved, Marx arrives in Belgium
       with his wife and family.
       There founds the first Communist Party. He renounces Prus-
       sian citizenship.

1848   The *Communist Manifesto* is drafted by Marx and Engels.
       In the political upheaval in Europe during 1848 both men
       play an active role.

1849   The *New Rhine Gazette* is begun and soon discontinued.
       Prussia issues a decree of expulsion against Marx in the after-
       math of the reaction following the turbulence of 1848.
       Marx moves with his family to London to permanent exile.

1850   Marx loses control of the Communist League that he had
       dominated.

1859   The first part of *Critique of Political Economy* is published.

1864   Marx is involved in the establishtment of the International
       Workingmen's Association (the International).

1867   The first volume of *Capital* (completed in 1862) is published.
       Vols. II and III were published posthumously by Engels.

1870   The Franco-Prussian War ends with the unification of Ger-
       many under Bismarck.

1871   Marx claims moral and intellectual credit for the Paris Com-
       mune established after the peace treaty with Germany ends
       the Franco-Prussian War

1872   Marx presides over the dissolution of the International.

1875   Marx and Engels are ignored by the reunified Social-Dem-
       ocratic party, originally split by the rivalry of Marx and Las-
       salle. Marx's role in world affairs is finished.

1881   The death of Jenny Marx.

1883   Marx dies, attended by Helen Demuth.

INDEX

Absolute Idea, Hegel's 31–34, 84, 85
absolutism of monarchs, 14–15
abstractions, 96, 101
  Marx's preoccupation with, 8, 39, 46, 83, 85, 92
  Marxian, 105
Annenkov, Paul
  description of Marx by, 134
  money borrowed from, by Marx, 135
armed revolution, Marx's belief in, 77, 86
atheism, *Rhine Gazette*'s downfall due to, 52–53, 65

Bakunin, Mikhail, 68, 98, 159, 210, 231
  attack on, by Marx, 153
  description of, 97
  expulsion of, from the International, 240
  hostility of Marx toward, 231–233, 236
  Marx described by, 97–98
  meeting of Marx and, 97
  revival of slander concerning, 210
Bauer, Bruno, 47, 58, 61, 126
  Marx's early association with, 41, 46

Marx's reply to article on Jews by, 75
Strauss's book attacked by, 36–38
violent attack on, by Marx, 102–103, 105
Beesly, Edward, 205
Belgium
  Marx expelled from, 142
  Marx family move to, 110–111
Berlin, University of, Karl's years as a student in, 12, 16–44
Bismarck
  Germany unified under, 211, 213, 233, 235
  Lassalle an agent of, 230
Blanc, Louis, 98, 143
  radical journalist, 55
  socialist party founded by, 127
Blanqui, 144, 147, 148, 154, 170
Bonaparte, Eighteenth Brumaire of Louis, 188
Bonn, University of
  Karl's attendance at, 12–15
bourgeoisie, 76, 116, 117, 141, 151, 155, 175
  English, 99, 166
  French, 155
  German, 149
Burns, Lizzy, 229
Burns, Mary, 125

common-law wife of Engels, 99
death of, 201

Cabet, Etienne, radical writer,
54–55
Capital, 194, 199, 200, 215, 247–
248
Bakunin's admiration of, 233
draft of third volume finished,
211
outline of contents of and
quote from, 214–230
publishing problems concerning, 213
translations of, 229
capitalism, 57
Cavaignac, General, 154, 159
Chartism, 171–172
Chartists, 77, 125
Civil War, American, 197
class conflict, 79–80
Cologne, Marx's activity in, 148–
150
Cologne Gazette, 46, 53, 58
Commune, Paris
establishment of, following
Franco-Prussian War, 235–
239
communism, 71
Hess-Engels promotion of, 104
origin of word, 51–52
communists, German, Engel's report on, 103–104
Communist League, 139, 140,
167, 172, 186, 205
Communist Manifesto, 140–143,
173, 207, 218, 219–220
Engels's part in formulating,
139, 142

explained to French by Marx,
147
Lassalle's paraphrase of, 199
Communist Party
Kriege expelled from 131–132
Marx's control over, 131
members of the original, 127–
128
Weitling expelled from, 131–
132
Correspondence Committee,
Communistic, 128
Proudhon's reaction to, 129
Critique of Political Economy,
122, 173, 192–194
work resumed on, 199
*Critique of Politics and Eco-
nomics, The,* 105

Danish War, 157–158
democracy, 73, 74, 151
demonstrations in European
cities, 142, 146
Demuth, Helen, 111, 135, 167,
246
Marx's affair with, 202
mother of Marx's illegitimate
son, 87
Demuth, Frederick, son of Karl
Marx and Helen Demuth,
202
depression, economic (1847), 137–
138
periods between, 190
destruction, seeds of, 71, 113, 114
dialectic, Hegelian, 33, 113, 117
dialectical method, Marx's, 136
dictator, proletarian, Marx characterized as, 134
Disraeli, 5

economics
  Marx's discovery concerning, 106–109, 112, 123
  Marx's study of, 92–93
emigrés, in London, 165, 171–172
Engels, Friedrich, 49, 74, 85, 98
  attack on Bauer by, 102
  attitude of, toward Hess, 50
  characterization of, 99, 100
  harmonizing views of Marx and, 99–100
  influence of Hess on, 49, 70, 71
  meeting of Marx and, 100, 101
  reaction of, to Hess, 50, 71
  report by, on socialism, in Germany, 103
  teamwork between Marx and, 100–101
  work of, incorporated in Marx's Capital, 221
England, Marx's first trip to, 125–126
European politics, democratic current in, 14–15
European Triarchy, The (Hess), 55

Feuerbach, Ludwig, 83
  materialism of, 83–85
Fourier, Charles, 53, 54, 55, 57, 82
  phalanx theory of, 50
France
  Marx expelled from, 110
  Marx invited to, 143
"Freemen," The, 57
  Marx's break with, 61
Freiligrath, Ferdinand, 162, 167,

  Marx aided by, 176
  Marx's break with, 187
French republic, 143, 159
French Revolution, far-reaching effects of, 1, 4, 13, 15, 28, 50, 79, 90, 143
  Marx's fascination with problems of, 91–92

Gans, Eduard, 19, 39
General Gazette, 60
German-French Yearbooks, 73–74
  demise of, 86–87
German Ideology, The, 107, 108, 122, 126–127, 130–131
German Workers, Club of, organized by Marx, 145
Germany, Marx's opinion of, 92–93, 150–151, 152, 154

Hegelianism
  Marx's break with, 76
  Marx's interest in, 66, 85–86
  Marx's involvement with, 22–44
Heine, Heinrich, 5, 11, 74, 110
Heinzen, Carl
  Karl Marx described by, 61–62
Herder, ———, 28–29
Herwegh (poet), organization of German Legion proposed by, 144–145
Herzen, ———, 66
Hess, Moses, 49, 70, 74, 77
  comparison of, with Marx, 72
  ideas of, on poverty and property, 55
  Marx described by, 49
  Marx's opinion of, 49–50

member of the original Communist Party, 128
resignation of, from Communist Party, 132
history, Marx's concept of, 93–94, 96, 112, 114
Holy Family, The, 103, 107
Engels's reaction to, 103
humanitarianism, 90
Hyndman, H. M., description of Marx by, 244–245

Inaugural Address, Marx's, at International founding, 206, 207–208
inevitability, idea of, 71, 76, 78, 81, 83, 86, 91
infiltration technique, 149
International, The, 213, 230, 234, 242
Bakunin expelled from, 240
end of the, 241
idea of the, 128
Marx's domination of, 209, 211
official attitude of, toward Paris Commune, 236–239
International Alliance of Social Democracy, 231
International Workingmen's Association, 204, 206, 209–210

Jena, University of, Karl's mail-order Ph.D. degree from, 44
Jews, essay by Marx on, 74–76
Journey to Icaria, A (Cabet), 55
Jung, Georg, 47, 49, 52, 104

Königgrätz, 212
Köppen, ————, 41–42, 43, 47, 58

Kriege, Marx's attack on, 131–132

labor theory of value, 192–193, 243
Lafargue, Paul
description of Karl Marx by, 183–184
Marx's daughter, the wife of, 246
Lamartine, French poet, 143
Lassalle, Ferdinand, 72
an agent of Bismarck, 230
death of, 204, 210
German political campaign by, 202
Marx aided by, 167, 177, 191, 194, 198
Marx's antipathy toward, 187–188, 191, 192
Marx's envy of, 197–198, 200
Marx's rival, 199
"Law of Motion," 109, 122, 136
League of the Just, 95, 125, 128, 139
Leibnitz, Gottfried Wilhelm, 24, 30
Lenin, 170
Levi, Hirschel, 4
See also Marx, Heinrich.
liberalism, political and economic nineteenth-century, 13–15, 19
Liebknecht, Wilhelm, 192, 194, 242
attitude of, toward war on Prussia, 233
Marx turned against, 230
Life of Jesus (Strauss), uproar caused by, 36–38
London exile, Marx's, 162–196

Louis Napoleon, 159, 162
Luddites, 57, 77

Manchester Guardian, Engels's
column in, 212
Marx, Eleanor (daughter of Karl)
description of Karl Marx by,
179–183
Marx, Heinrich (father of Karl),
2–7, 8, 9, 20, 21
concern of, for Karl's character, 23
death of, 23
See also Levi, Hirschel.
Marx, Henrietta (mother of
Karl), 2–3, 6, 48
death of, 203
Karl's attitude toward, 6, 22
money to Karl from, 40
See also Pressburger, Henrietta.
Marx, Jenny (wife of Karl), 87,
91, 105–106, 108, 111, 135,
161, 167, 246
death of, 246
family poverty described by,
168
health of, 175
See also Westphalen, Jenny
von.
Marx, Karl
absorption of, in philosophy,
42
attitude of, toward Paris Commune, 236–239
attitude of, toward religion, 5,
46
birth of, 1, 2
characterizations of, 7, 8, 9–10,
19, 100, 133, 166, 186

childhood of, 6
children of, 101, 111, 135, 161,
167, 168, 175
comparison of, with Hess, 72
death of, 246
descriptions of:
by Annenkov, 134
by Bakunin, 97–98
by daughter Eleanor, 179–
183
by Heinzen, 61–62
by Hyndman, 244–245
by Lafargue, 183–184, 185
by Schurz, 157
destitute condition of, 176
duel fought by, 13
as an economist, 131
editorship of *Rhine Gazette,*
for, 59–65
engagement of, 16, 43, 48
family background of, 2–6
financial assistance for, by:
Engels, 100, 111
Hess, 111
Jung, 88
financial problems of, 87, 88,
135, 166, 167–168, 176–179,
203, 211
first book by, 103
first published articles by, 47,
58
funeral of, 247
health of, 135, 174–175, 203,
209, 211
inability of, to earn a living,
43, 48, 135
idle periods of, 40, 47–48
income of, from mother, 40, 48
influence of, *vii–viii*
journalistic career of, 46

lack of interest in family shown by, 67
legal studies of, 15, 16, 19, 42
legend of, 195–196
marriage of, 69
martyred by suppression of *Rhine Gazette*, 65, 103
money bequeathed to, 204
personal qualities of, 160
Ph.D. obtained by, from University of Jena, 44
philosophical interests of, 42, 52
poetic ambitions of, 10, 11, 19–21, 39, 40
political activity of, 19, 128, 133, 150, 160, 163–164
Prussian citizenship renounced by, 125, 160
reading habits of, 10, 39, 41, 42–43, 91, 184–185
rhetorical ability of, 41, 155, 156
school years of, 6–7, 12
sincerity of, in question, 225
teaching career considered by, 40, 42, 43–46
writing habits of, 15, 19, 40, 48
youthful extravagance of, 13, 21, 22
See also Communist Party; Hegelianism; Marxist socialism
Marx, Laura (daughter of Karl), 246
Marx, Sophie (sister of Karl), 10, 11, 48
Marxism, 24, 78, 117, 118, 120, 123, 124, 132, 137, 244, 249
cornerstone of, 79

Marxist movement, 126–127
Marxist socialism, four principles of, 76–83
Marx's views, effect of, 120
Mehring, Franz, biographer of Marx, 103
description of Marx by, 185
polemical style of Marx's writing described by, 103
quoted on *German Ideology*, 130–131
monarchs, nineteenth-century attitude toward, 14–15
"Moor, the," nickname of Karl Marx, 7–8
"Motion, Law of," 109, 122, 136
Marx's and Engels's agreement on, 112

Napoleon, lingering shadow of, 1, 3–4, 18, 28
New Rhine Gazette, 148, 150–160

Oppenheim, Dagobert, 47, 49, 52
Organization of Labor, The (Blanc), 55
Owen, Robert, 55, 57, 77
social system devised by, 51, 53, 54
words "communism" and "socialism" coined by, 52

Palmerston, British statesman, Marx's attack on, 189
Paris
armed rebellion in, 154–155
commune established after revolt in, 235–239
Marx asked to leave, 162

Marx's years in, 73–110
political exiles in, 89–90
phalanxes, Fourier's idea of, 50
Philosophy of Misery, The, 136–137
polemics, 101, 135–136, 173, 189
Marxian, 52, 63, 103, 124
poverty, ideas concerning, 54, 55, 56
predictions, false, 77, 81, 111, 115, 159, 160, 161, 162, 168, 172, 190, 191, 212, 243
Pressburger, Henrietta, 6
See also Marx, Henrietta.
Professors' Club, 39–41, 43, 44, 53, 57, 61
proletariat, the, 57, 94, 95, 96, 134–135
dictatorship of the, 144, 243
in France, 144
German, 151
role of, in class war, 79, 80, 81, 171
proof, Marx's disregard of need for, 120–121
property
ideas concerning, 55, 71, 72, 76, 81, 114
Proudhon, Pierre-Joseph, 77, 82
Karl's reading of works by, 60
Marx's attack on, 136–137
meeting of Marx and, 96–97
radical view of, concerning property, 54
reaction of, to Communistic Correspondence Committee, 129
Prussia, 1, 2, 4, 5, 12, 18–19, 23, 34, 58, 62–63, 64, 65, 67, 86

Marx barred from, 87, 159
Marx's return to, 197
publishing problems, 191–192, 194

rationalism, 24–29
reality vs. rationality, 31–32
revolution, industrial, 14, 56, 90
in France, 90
revolution, predicted, 130, 135, 138, 154, 156, 169, 172, 174, 189
Rhine Gazette, 46, 52–53, 57, 58
financial aid for Marx from one-time stockholders of, 88
Marx's association with, 47, 48, 59
suppression of, 63–65
Ruge, Arnold, 42, 47, 48, 58, 59, 110
attack on, in print, by Marx, 102, 105
attitude of, toward socialism, 74
Marx's editorial venture with, 67–68, 69, 72–73, 74
split between Marx and, 87–88
Russia
Marx's attitude toward, 63–64
war against, favored by Marx, 152–153, 189
Rutenberg, Dr., 61

Saint-Simon, Duke of, 55, 57, 77, 82
socialistic system devised by, 50–51, 53, 54
Schurz, Carl, 186
description of Marx by, 157
science and socialism, 80–82

scientism, 83, 86
secret societies, 14, 15
socialism, 71, 114–115, 136, 137
    Hess's version of, 70, 72
    in Germany, Engels's report
        on, 103–104
    Marxist, 80, 81, 82–83
    Marx's beginning interest in,
        50, 60, 65–66, 72, 73, 74, 76
    Marx's serious study of, 91
    origin of the word, 51–52
    science and, 80–82
    system of, devised by Saint-
        Simon, 50–51
socialist ideas, beginning of, 53–
    54
socialist movement
    Marx's personal biography in-
        tegrated with, 111
    relation of Marxism, to, 78, 79
socialists, French, 79, 82, 147–148
socialist working-class party, first,
    launched by Lassalle, 202
social system, Robert Owen's, 51
Stirner, Max, 42
Strauss, David Friedrich, 36–38

theological hoax, repercussions
    of, 45–46, 48–49
theories, Marx's:
    of "historical materialism," 63
    of Permanent Revolution, 169
    of social irreconcilability, 80
theory, joint, of Marx and En-
    gels, 112–123
treason trial, Prussian, 186–187,
    195
Tribune, The New York
    Marx's connection with, 176,
        189, 197

Trier, birthplace of Karl Marx,
    1–2
Trotsky, Leon, 170

Urquhart, David, 189, 210
    value, labor theory of, 192

Weitling, Wilhelm, 95, 97, 125,
    169
    attitude of Marx toward, 126
    expelled from Communist
        Party, 131–132
    member of the original Com-
        munist Party, 128
Westphalen, Edgar von, 69
    member of the original Com-
        munist Party, 128
Westphalen, Jenny von, 10, 11,
    13, 16, 19, 20, 22
    characterization of, 69, 70
    engagement of, to Karl Marx,
        16, 48, 68–69
    marriage of, to Karl Marx, 69
    See also Marx, Jenny.
Westphalen, Ludwig von, 7, 10,
    11
    death of, 48
Westphalen, Otto von, 69, 176
Weydemeyer, Joseph, 130
    efforts by, to have German
        Ideology published, 130
workers
    Marx's attitude toward, 94, 96,
        125–126
    poverty of, 56–57
Workers' Association, 204
"Workers' Club," 156
Workers' Guard, 144
working-class, 81
    help for the, 54, 55
    See also proletariat.